Dickens and Religion

The importance of understanding Dickens's religion to obtain a full appreciation of his achievement has long been admitted; but this is the first critical study of the interaction between Dickens's religious beliefs and his creative imagination throughout his career.

The novelist's religious beliefs are a pervasive and deeply felt presence in his works even if they are not always clearly thought out or expressed. Too discreet and humane to be as explicit, or as dull, as most of the professedly religious novelists of his time, Dickens nevertheless suggests in his own way a liberal Protestant belief, shot through with Romantic, transcendental yearnings, which undoubtedly appealed to a very wide range of readers. Dickens's religion is shown to be that of a great popular writer, who created a unique kind of fiction, and a unique relationship with his readers, by the absorption and transformation of less respectable contemporary forms, from fairy-tale and German romance to tract and print.

Professor Walder's thoroughly researched and lively book provides students of Dickens and the Victorian period with an original perspective on the novelist's methods and attitudes. He offers a judicious and informed exploration of Dickens's obsessive themes, from the 'fall' of innocence in *Pickwick Papers*, to the search for a religious 'answer' in *Little Dorrit*. Each chapter focuses upon the striking congruences revealed between individual novels, or groups of novels, and particular religious themes. The views expressed in Dickens's lesser fiction and non-fiction are drawn on throughout, as are those in the influential contemporary press

Dennis Walder is Professor of Literature at the Open University and chaired the university's Nineteenth Century Novel course. He has published widely on 19th and 20th century literature, including the best-selling *Literature in the Modern World*.

Dickens and Religion

Dennis Walder

Routledge
Taylor & Francis Group

LONDON AND NEW YORK

First published 1981 by George, Allen & Unwin (Publishers) Ltd
40 Museum Street, London, WC1A 1LU, UK

First published in paperback 2007 by Routledge

2 Park Square, Milton Park, Abingdon, Oxon, OX14 4RN

Simultaneously published in the USA and Canada
by Routledge
270 Madison Ave, New York NY 10016

Routledge is an imprint of the Taylor & Francis Group

Transferred to Digital Printing 2007

Typeset in 10 on 11 point Plantin by V & M Graphics Ltd,
Aylesbury, Bucks

British Library Cataloguing in Publication Data
A catalogue record for this book is available from the British Library

Library of Congress Cataloging in Publication Data
Walder, Dennis.
        Dickens and religion
Bibliography: p.
Includes index
    1.   Dickens, Charles, 1812-1870 – Religion and ethics
    2.   2. Religion in literature. I. Title
PR4592.R4W3   823'.8   81-10983
ISBN: 0-04-800006-X (hbk)   AACR2
ISBN: 0-415-42526-3 (pbk)
ISBN: 978-0-415-42526-1 (pbk)

Publisher's Note
The publisher has gone to great lengths to ensure the quality of this reprint
but points out that some imperfections in the original may be apparent

Contents

List of Illustrations

Acknowledgements are due to the British Library for permission to reproduce all the illustrations in this book.

For Mary

Preface

Anyone threatening to add to the daunting outflow of material continuing to gush, apparently inexhaustibly, from the well of Dickens studies, must have good reason for doing so. But it is now nearly twenty years since Dickens's religion was identified in the pages of *The Dickensian* (by Professor K. J. Fielding in 1963) as 'the greatest gap (that might be filled) in our knowledge about Dickens'. Despite a growing number of voices on both sides of the Atlantic repeating this claim – sometimes, indeed, responding to it – nobody has come near filling the gap. I hasten to add that it is not my purpose here, even supposing it were possible, entirely to fill this gap myself. Rather, I have attempted to further our knowledge, understanding and appreciation of Dickens and his achievement by scrutinising different aspects of his religion as these emerge at different stages of his career. His fundamental outlook as a liberal Protestant with radical, Romantic leanings is expressed in remarkably different ways at different times, variously reflecting personal impulse as well as prevailing currents of belief. It is less Dickens's actual beliefs than the nature and timing of their appearance in his novels that I find of greatest interest and significance.

The novelist told Mrs Dickens in 1853 that 'the intense pursuit of any idea that takes complete possession of me, is one of the qualities that makes me different – sometimes for good; sometimes I dare say for evil – from other men' (Dexter, 1935). Dickens's genius typically expressed itself through single, large, dominating conceptions, embodied successively in works published at different periods of his life. My approach has been to analyse his fiction from the earliest writings onwards, concentrating at each stage upon striking congruences between individual novels, or groups of novels, and particular religious themes. At the same time, to provide a controlling perspective, I have drawn throughout on the religious views expressed in his other writings (usually more explicit, and less profound, than his fiction), and have related his works to the *relevant* contemporary context of belief – a context often most sharply evident in religious periodicals, which, as Maurice Quinlan pointed out some time ago, were 'next to the Bible in authority' (1941, p. 185). In my view it is in *Little Dorrit* that Dickens makes his most serious attempt to find a religious 'answer' to life's painful mysteries. For this reason, and because Dickens's later works ask for a level of attention that simply cannot be given to them all on the same scale, I have chosen to give particular attention to it.

I owe a debt to many other scholars and critics in the field, but I should like to single out the supervisor of the doctoral research from which this book has grown, Professor K. J. Fielding of the University of Edinburgh, for particular thanks. I should also like here to acknowledge the financial support of the University of Edinburgh, which elected me to the Aytoun Fellowship in English Literature for two years. Much of my work was done in the friendly environment of the National Library of Scotland, an undervalued resource if ever there was one. The enthusiasm and encouragement of Dr Robin Gilmour (now of the University of Aberdeen) made the project seem worthwhile from the start; the energetic conscientiousness with which my friends and colleagues Mr P. N. Furbank and Professor Graham Martin read and commented on draft versions ensured that I might finish it. Naturally I am responsible for remaining errors or deficiencies. Aileen Arnot and Wendy Macey exercised their typing skills speedily and accurately on my behalf. I owe more than I can easily say to the dedicatee.

London, 1980

Note on References and Abbreviations

References to works other than those by Dickens are listed at the end of the book. With the exception of *Oliver Twist, Dombey and Son, Little Dorrit* and *Edwin Drood*, references to Dickens's works are to the New Oxford Illustrated Dickens (1947–58); references to the other four novels are to the Clarendon edition (1966–). For Dickens's letters, speeches and journalism, the following editions have been used and are cited in their abbreviated form:

Dexter *Letters: The Letters of Charles Dickens*, ed. Walter Dexter, 3 vols (London: Nonesuch Press, 1938).

Coutts *Letters: Letters from Charles Dickens to Angela Burdett-Coutts 1841–1865*, ed. Edgar Johnson (London: Cape, 1953).

Pilgrim *Letters: The Letters of Charles Dickens*, ed. Madeline House, Graham Storey and Kathleen Tillotson, Vols 1– (Oxford: Clarendon Press, 1965–).

Fielding *Speeches: The Speeches of Charles Dickens*, ed. K. J. Fielding (Oxford: Clarendon Press, 1960).

MP: Charles Dickens, *Miscellaneous Papers*, ed. B. W. Matz (London: Chapman & Hall, Universal Edition, 1914).

UT & RP: Charles Dickens, *The Uncommercial Traveller and Reprinted Pieces*, New Oxford Illustrated Dickens (London: Oxford University Press, 1958).

Stone, *Uncollected Writings: The Uncollected Writings of Charles Dickens*, ed. and intr. Harry Stone, 2 vols (Bloomington, Ill.: Indiana University Press, 1968; London: Allen Lane, 1969).

References to Dickens's prefaces are to *Collected Papers*, Vol. 19 of the 'Special Authorised' edition of *The Works of Charles Dickens* in 20 vols (London: Cassell, n.d.).

Introduction

> With a deep sense of my great responsibility always upon me when I exercise my art, one of my most constant and most earnest endeavours has been to exhibit in all my good people some faint reflections of the teachings of our great Master, and unostentatiously to lead the reader up to those teachings as the great source of all moral goodness. All my strongest illustrations are derived from the New Testament; all my social abuses are shown as departures from its spirit; all my good people are humble, charitable, faithful, and forgiving. Over and over again, I claim them in express words as disciples of the Founder of our religion; but I must admit that to a man (or woman) they all arise and wash their faces, and do not appear unto men to fast.
> (Dickens, letter to Rev. D. Macrae, repr. in Macrae, 1876, p. 127)

> Beyond the world of what may be called respectable religion lay a sub-culture of popular religion, about which historians at present know very little.
> (Harrison, 1971, p. 131)

I

Most conspicuous among those critics who have recently pointed out the existence of a gap in our knowledge about Dickens has been Angus Wilson. In a collection of essays on the English novel, Wilson remarked (Wilson and Dyson, 1976, p. 55):

> For a very long time now the Christian aspect of Dickens's work has been badly neglected. It is in fact an absolutely essential part of his development as a novelist. He thought of himself as centrally a Christian. Two of the most important foreign writers who were influenced by him, namely Dostoevsky and Tolstoy, both speak of him as 'that great Christian writer'. He is Christian not merely in the formal sense of the word; in profound ways the Christian religion makes sense of his work.

All this is true, although not without qualification. To begin with, it is more helpful to talk about the 'religious' aspect, or aspects, of Dickens's work, than the specifically Christian. The broader term begs fewer questions, and enables one to draw the kind of distinction Wilson himself begins to make here, between 'formal' and other senses of 'Christian'.

Angus Wilson's remarks are not followed by any evidence. This is not to slight him, for it is typical of those who have commented upon the novelist's religion, from whatever standpoint.[1] The most common view has been simply (as Samuel Johnson remarked of Milton's religion in *Lives of the English Poets*) 'we know rather what he was not, than what he was'. In orthodox Christian terms, there is much that is missing, or at best negatively expressed, in Dickens's works. The role of priest and church is minimal, and certain kinds of chapel-going and sermonising are typically represented as ludicrous and reprehensible. The Bible is drawn on more than any other source, but not as a literally inspired text, nor even always with veneration – although it is treated as a guide to those elements in the Christian ethic (largely from the New Testament) which Dickens most admired. Prayer, or other overt manifestation of the religious spirit, is more often shown to be hypocritical and self-seeking than a genuine attempt to communicate with the deity. Dickens shows little sympathy with missionaries, at home or abroad. Puseyism, the workings of the Calvinist conscience and any attempt to indoctrinate anybody (but especially the young) with stern views of man's reprobate nature are all abhorred. Intolerant of intolerance, the novelist is at the same time frequently blind in his prejudice on the subject of Jews and Roman Catholics, as he is on the views of other races.[2] But the weaknesses of Dickens's position have been more than sufficiently remarked; it is the strengths which now need emphasising. And to try and define his religion within the terms of a notional Christian orthodoxy would be to cripple a study of his beliefs from the start.

Sir Arthur Quiller-Couch's advice to Cambridge undergraduates to whom he was lecturing on Dickens was: 'To begin with, we must jettison religion.' For, he argued, what the novelist 'simply disregarded' merited no further comment: the Tractarian movement, the Unitarians, the claims and counter-claims of Wiseman, Newman, Gorham, Colenso, the ideas of Darwin and Huxley; in short, all that was 'agitating men's thoughts at the time' (Quiller-Couch, 1925, pp. 72–3). But which men? In fact, Dickens was aware of what stirred thinkers of his time, particularly radical, unorthodox Christians such as W. J. Fox, Thomas Carlyle, Leigh Hunt and the Unitarians – all at the liberal end of the religious spectrum. More important, he did not write for those who aspired to the subtlety and abstraction of Wiseman, Gorham and the rest, any more than he approved of their interest in theoretical questions. For Dickens and his readers the details of Tract XC, for example, or of Bishop Samuel Wilberforce's clash with T. H. Huxley over evolution, were of far less interest and concern than, say, the fate of *The Dairyman's Daughter* (Richmond, n.d.) a young girl whose premature death was piously recounted by the chaplain to Queen Victoria's father in what became probably the most successful tract ever published. As George Kitson Clark has observed (1966, p. 147):

> Since the religious history of the nineteenth century presents a series of extremely important and extremely interesting intellectual problems it is natural for historians to place these problems in the foreground and to consider most carefully the very remarkable men who became involved in them. But viewed from, so to speak, more nearly the ground level of the ordinary not very intelligent, not very erudite human being the scene changes, the intellectual issues raised – the problems propounded by biblical criticism or the question of the whereabouts of authority in religion or even the challenge of evolution – fade into the background and other equally important problems take their place.

Kitson Clark's words apply as much to literary critics and scholars as they do to historians, if not more. Humphry House observed of Tom Pinch at the organ in *Martin Chuzzlewit*, of Amy Dorrit asleep in church, and of other such moments, that 'A theologian would find little in all this to justify the claim that Dickens was a Christian; a historian could hardly gather from his books that during the years in which they were written the English Church was revolutionised' (House, 1942, pp. 110–11). Of course not. We do not in the first place contemplate such images as theologians or as historians (even if we did we should still need to ask: what kind of theologian? what kind of historian?), but as readers of the novels, trying to grasp their contribution to a total imaginative effect.

Dickens articulates his beliefs by the methods of a novelist, by means of the typical elements of his medium. And his beliefs are rarely explicit, they are embodied in the texture of his work. So it is fruitless to concentrate on the easily abstractable, surface reflections of his views which have generally been accepted as a complete version of them; one must explore the implications of significant moments, images, themes, so as to elicit his deeper thoughts and feelings, and the ways these relate to his readers' experience. A novel is 'an impression, not an argument', wrote Thomas Hardy in the preface to *Tess of the D'Urbervilles*; and to press novels too quickly into explicitness may well reveal intellectual confusion or contradiction, where a closer, more patient and informed reading will reveal the true shape of a writer's attitudes.

Dickens's beliefs are those of a great popular novelist, who created a unique kind of fiction, and a unique relationship with his readers, by the absorption and transformation of less 'respectable' narrative kinds. This is reflected in, for example, the tendency of his good young women to be simplified into icons, 'unreal' but evocative in their appeal to a religious consciousness nurtured on scriptural prints and religious tracts; as it is in his preference for 'mixed' forms such as obtain in the Christmas Books, designed to suggest to an audience familiar with fairy tales, German romances and other forms of 'low' art a sense of the reality of the supernatural. Dickens was less interested in problems of doctrine and theology than in touching the religious consciousness of a vast reading public, the new populations of the great towns. His use of popular forms was a way of doing this, as was his demand (in *Bleak House*, for example) for a 'social gospel'.

Victorian novelists have to be seen in relation to the most important social change of their time, the industrial revolution, in all its many ramifications and implications. But this does not mean that we should concentrate exclusively on the social aspects of their works. It would in any case be foolish to assume that social changes are not themselves part of larger shifts in consciousness. At least we should begin by taking into account what writers and readers of the time felt was important to *them*, before we advance on the basis of what appears to be important to us. Whether Christian or humanist, or some combination of both, nineteenth-century novelists were all concerned to adopt some position in relation to the religious activities and ideas prevalent then; and Dickens was no exception.

II

We all tend to reshape what we study according to our own preconceptions, and no account of Dickens's religion can pretend to be free of bias. If I were asked to define religion – something notoriously difficult to do, given the enormous variety of its historical manifestations, as well as the diversity of ideas and practices in the world today – then I would refer to William James's explanation of it as *'the feelings, acts, and experiences of individual men in their solitude, so far as they apprehend themselves to stand in relation to whatever they may consider the divine'* (James, 1902, p. 31). This sense of religion stands prior to the 'theologies, philosophies, and ecclesiastical organisations' which may grow out of it, although any study of an individual's religion must include this secondary meaning, too. The drawback of this definition is its reliance upon the term 'divine', itself almost as problematic as 'religion'; and James does not quite solve the problem when he goes on to suggest that it is what is seen as 'godlike', the limits of which he defines so as to include Emersonian optimism at one extreme and Buddhist pessimism at the other. But the advantage of his definition is that it begins with one's personal response to what is considered divine – with subjective apprehensions, which is surely where literary imaginings have their source. In the Victorian period, renowned not only for intellectual and theological activity, but also for great institutional developments in religion – in and among churches, between denominations, and beyond, in the missionary movement – there is an inevitable tendency to concentrate on the secondary sense of religion. James's definition (first delivered to an Edinburgh University audience as part of a series of Gifford Lectures at the turn of the century) is historically appropriate: it was Friedrich Schleiermacher (1786–1834), the German Romantic theologian, who first established this subjective conception of religion; and it was taken up by, amongst others, William Ellery Channing (1780–1842), the famous Boston Unitarian, and one of the contemporary religious figures for whom we know Dickens expressed great admiration (for example, in *American Notes*, ch. iii, p. 26).

I should like to think I have not tried to enrol Dickens as a member of any particular camp, religious, non-religious or anti-religious, while identifying as far as possible the area of contemporary belief with which he associated himself, and which he found sympathetic. It has been the besetting flaw of attempts to comment upon his religion to do so from a partisan viewpoint, invoking inappropriate criteria. In his own time Dickens could not have failed to notice the impact of his beliefs – or supposed lack of them – upon committed readers, ecstatically welcomed as he was by liberal Christians, especially in America, and reviled by the more evangelical wing of the faith. As early as 1842 the Boston *Christian Examiner* was praising him for showing what 'Fancy, baptised with a Christian spirit, may achieve' (quoted in House, 1942, p. 112); by the time of his death in 1870 'eulogies, almost idolatrous' could be heard, 'every Unitarian and Universalist pulpit' in Boston sending him 'to heaven immediately' (quoted in Nisbet, 1952, pp. 1–2). Other allegiances led to remarks of a different kind: the High Church *Christian Remembrancer* (vol. 4, December 1842, p. 595) found 'mere pagan sentimentalism' in his pages; the *Dublin Review* (vol. 21, September 1846, p. 188) accused him of 'libel' against the Catholic religion, and concluded after his death that his works were 'as false as any of those of the undisguisedly materialistic writers of the day' ([Hoey?], 1871, p. 318). But it was particularly the evangelicals who found 'the joke', as the Reverend W. Kirkus put it, 'far too personal to be agreeable' (Kirkus, 1863, p. 5). Stiggins, Little Bethel and Chadband were all equally 'objectionable' to them (*Eclectic Review*, n.s., vol. 1, October 1861, p. 459); and death brought no forgiveness, a Noncomformist minister hissing from the pulpit the Sunday after the novelist died that he was a man who 'never ceased to sneer at and vilify religion' (quoted in Watson, 1912, p. 512). In time, all this died down, Dickens's religion becoming more acceptable as Broad Church liberalism of the Dean Stanley stamp advanced: the dean thought Dickens's a 'simple but sufficient faith', he told attenders at the novelist's funeral (Stanley, 1870, p. 10). By 1884 lay-preacher C. H. MacKenzie was inspired to write a book entitled *The Religious Sentiments of Charles Dickens*, the forerunner of a series of naïve anthologies proving Dickens's 'vital religious character', so 'strangely ignored, misunderstood, and actually denied, in places' (MacKenzie, 1884, p. 8: see, for example, Proctor, 1930).

The criteria by which Dickens's religion is judged have swung from being too demanding to being too undemanding; and rarely, if ever, has it been allowed that what he was writing was fiction, not confession. American critics follow their Unitarian forebears in exercising low demands for what may constitute a faith; on this side of the Atlantic, Quiller-Couch's gentlemanly disdain seems to have been accepted as a model, while we continue to inject a little bias of our own: Valentine Cunningham's useful and sympathetic survey of Dissent in Victorian fiction repeats almost verbatim Humphry House's attack on the alleged lack of religious experience reflected in Jo's death in *Bleak House* (Cunningham, 1975, p. 11; House, 1942, pp. 131–2). Neither critic offers any reason for assuming that Dickens himself believed Jo's repetition of the Lord's Prayer would be any more useful than the viaticum of Snagsby's half-crown; nor is any attempt made to appreciate the function of such scenes as part of a 'social gospel'. A more objective perspective might allow readers to respond more fully to Dickens's expression of that union of religious sentiment and humanitarian concern which was central for the Victorian conscience.

III

One way of providing a perspective on Dickens's religion is to examine his life. It has been said that 'in order to know the real Dickens, we should have to live his life, to know the most secret movements of his sensibility' (Maurois, 1934, p. 189). Such an ideal is hardly approachable; perhaps the nearest one can get is to consider what the novelist's close friend and biographer, John Forster, had to say; although on this, as on other subjects, the respectable family friend is not as forthcoming as one would wish. Forster's remarks have to be supplemented from other sources. There is a limit to which this can be done here, since this is not a biography; yet a start can be made. Forster, as far as one can tell, was closer to Dickens's religious position than anyone else who has attempted to write about it.

Forster is noticeably silent on religious influences in Dickens's child hood. The impression this suggests of a lack of interest on the part of the family is borne out by what other evidence we have. The lack of any specifically religious education would simply be another aspect of his parents' general attitude: his father's whimsical response to an inquiry about his education (which Dickens used to repeat with relish) was 'Why, indeed, Sir - ha! ha! - he may be said to have educated himself!' (Forster, 1928, p. 47). It is possible that Mrs Dickens, or some other female in the domestic circle, was less unconcerned. The family was Church of England, and not conspicuously devout, or conversant with doctrine; and Charles was, of course, baptised (at St Mary's, Kingston, in Portsea). His sister Fanny later remarked: 'I was brought up in the Established Church, but I regret to say, without any serious ideas of religion' (Griffin, 1883, p. 177). But she had become 'serious' when she made this confession, having (with her husband, Henry Burnett) joined an evangelical Congregationalist chapel in Manchester at the time. She was bound to be strict in her interpretation of an adequate religious upbringing; and her minister James Griffin's *Memories* also record her saying to her husband, when her father and mother were coming to visit, 'Now, Henry, don't omit family prayer morning and evening during their stay with us. They have never been used to it, but that should not prevent us from continuing our usual habits; it should rather induce us to be firm in maintaining them' (ibid., p. 198).

One suspects that the elder Dickenses might have been a little nonplussed when confronted by their 'converted' daughter and her pious husband. Or had it been forgotten that Mrs Dickens went through a stage of evangelical fervour herself? Was it not his mother who 'dragged' the young Dickens to hear a 'powerful preacher', and who subsequently 'catechised' him closely respecting his 'fifthly, his sixthly, and his seventhly, until I have regarded that reverend person in the light of a most dismal and oppressive Charade'? Dickens used these phrases in the essay 'City of London churches' (*All the Year Round*, 5 May 1860, repr. *UT & RP*, pp. 83–93), usually taken to have a strong autobiographical element. The novelist's young protégé Percy Fitzgerald was the first to suggest, on the basis of this passage, that Dickens's long-lasting antagonism towards religious types such as Stiggins and Chadband, and their female followers, was an 'early religious tyranny' involving his mother (Fitzgerald, 1905, Vol. 1, pp. 59–60). But whose 'female hand' was it that Dickens says caught him and scrubbed him 'as a purification for the Temple', thereafter carrying him off 'highly charged with saponaceous electricity, to be steamed like a potato in the unventilated breath of the powerful Boanerges Boiler and his congregation'? Was it, perhaps, Mary Weller's, the servant who once 'hummed the evening hymn' to him? (Forster, 1928, p. 2). Or was it that of his mother's widowed sister, Mrs Allen, who shared Dickens's upbringing with her? (ibid., p. 6). Or was it, after all, his mother's? We do not, perhaps cannot, know. Nor is it clear where Dickens had this unpleasant early experience, or, indeed, who the minister was. Forster errs in suggesting that

Dickens's first schoolmaster in Chatham was the Baptist minister William Giles (ibid., p. 7): in fact, it was the minister's son of the same name who taught Dickens, an Oxford graduate who seems to have appreciated and responded to the young boy. However, the Reverend Mr Giles did preach at the Providence Baptist chapel, next door to the Dickenses when they were living at 18 St Mary's Place, as well as at the Zion Baptist chapel, also in Chatham, so he *may* have been the model for Boanerges Boiler. But was he?[3]

Care should be exercised in tracing Dickens's later, adult attitudes to what is assumed to have been childhood experience. The novels indicate a lasting aversion to evangelical zeal, just as they do to its female adherents; and this may have been derived from the novelist's childhood. But we cannot be sure. Dickens also records, in 'City of London churches', 'my own village church where, during sermon-time on bright Sundays when the birds are very musical indeed, farmers' boys patter out over the stone pavement, and the clerk steps out from his desk after them, and is distinctly heard in the summer repose to pursue and punch them in the churchyard, and is seen to return with a meditative countenance, making believe that nothing of the sort has happened' (*UT & RP*, p. 87). Hardly an oppressive or demanding institution, it would seem, and perhaps the kind of sleepy, somewhat comic, rural Anglicanism that Dickens always yearned for, since he recreates images of idyllic country churches throughout his works.

There is little evidence of religious affiliation after the Dickens family moved to London from Chatham in 1822, when Dickens was 10. Indeed, 'Sundays', wrote Dickens, 'Fanny and I passed in the prison' (Forster, 1928, p. 27). This was when the family fortunes had sunk to their lowest ebb, with John Dickens in debtor's prison, and his son out at work in a blacking factory, an experience which undoubtedly did leave the deepest impression upon his character. 'I know that, but for the mercy of God, I might easily have been, for any care that was taken of me, a little robber or vagabond' (ibid., p. 28). The religious usage reflects the sense of a Providential guiding hand which Dickens frequently felt as a real force in his life. His warm welcome in Boston in 1842, four years after the death of his beloved sister-in-law Mary Hogarth, suggested 'something of the presence and influence of that spirit which directs my life, and through heavy sorrow has pointed upward with unchanging finger for more than four years past' (ibid., p. 206). The need for some supernatural guiding presence is indicated early on: after his sister received a prize at the Royal Academy of Music, and education and distinction seemed placed permanently out of his reach, 'I prayed when I went to bed that night, to be lifted out of the humiliation and neglect in which I was' (ibid., p. 34).

Like his own fictional images of humiliated and neglected children, from Oliver Twist to Pip, Dickens in fact survived and prospered. He was gifted, and resilient – both traits closely related to his best-known characteristic, his humour. As a child, or youth, he may have felt the force of custom and conscience sufficiently to attend church when he was able, but he could be as careless and as high-spirited as any other boy; indeed, more so. After the recovery of the family fortunes, he went to Wellington House Academy in Camden; and a schoolfellow recorded meeting him 'one Sunday morning shortly after we left', the two of them 'piously' attending the morning service at Seymour Street chapel. 'I am sorry to say', he continued, 'Master Dickens did not attend in the slightest degree to the service, but incited me to laughter by declaring his dinner was ready and the potatoes would be spoiled, and in fact behaved in such a manner that it was lucky for us we were not ejected from the chapel' (ibid., p. 44). It is not surprising that many found Dickens's humour misplaced, especially the more evangelical. His satiric portraits of evangelical (usually Noncomformist) clergymen reflect not only a dislike of their attitudes and a disagreement with their doctrine, but also simply the fact that he found their extreme adherents immensely amusing. The first edition of Forster's *Life* contained a passage from a letter to Dickens's friend Cornelius Felton, liberal-minded professor of Greek at Harvard, whom he met in America in 1842, in which the novelist told of an incident involving him and George Cruikshank with a Noncomformist minister at the funeral of William Hone, indigent publisher. Hone had wanted to see Dickens 'before he went' (ibid., p. 283), and Dickens duly paid him a visit; when Hone died he felt duty-bound to attend the funeral, and in all editions subsequent to the original that was all Forster noted. The full text of the letter may be read in the Pilgrim edition of the *Letters* (Vol. 3, pp. 451–6); and it soon becomes clear why the minister concerned objected strongly (in the *Evangelical Magazine*) to Dickens's version of what happened, and why Forster felt obliged to delete it.

The Reverend Thomas Binney, an eminent Congregationalist divine from Weigh House Chapel, Eastcheap, was in charge of Hone's funeral service. According to Dickens, as soon as those attending were seated, he began by inquiring loudly, 'Mr Cruikshank. Have you seen a paragraph respecting our departed friend, which has gone the round of the morning papers?' Receiving an answer in the affirmative (Cruikshank was the author of the paragraph), the minister continued: 'Then you will agree with me Mr Cruikshank that it is not only an insult to me who am the servant of the Almighty, but an insult to the Almighty whose servant I am.' Asked for an explanation, Binney resumed: 'It is stated ... that when Mr Hone failed in business as a bookseller, he was persuaded by *me* to try the Pulpit, which is false, incorrect, unchristian, in a manner blasphemous, and in all respects contemptible. Let us pray', and he knelt down to begin 'a very miserable jumble of an extemporary prayer'. Dickens observed that he felt very sorry for the family, but that when

Cruikshank whispered that if the man had not been a clergyman, and if it had not been a funeral, he would have 'punched his head', he, Dickens, 'felt as if nothing but convulsions could possibly relieve [him]'.

The manifest absurdity of the minister's language and behaviour could not but amuse, especially when Cruikshank reacted as he did; but when, thirty years later, Dickens's account appeared in the biography, and both Binney and Cruikshank (by then also more 'serious') denied it, Forster had little choice. Dickens may well have elaborated upon what happened for Felton's amusement, unaware that the letter would ever be published; but it is hard not to think that he was also reacting to a strain in contemporary religious life which could be as ridiculous as it was oppressive.[4] There was a 'celebrated sentence' of John Dickens's, uttered to a man who had been 'insisting somewhat obtrusively on dissenting and nonconformist superiorities', which used to delight Dickens: 'The Supreme Being must be an entirely different individual from what I have every reason to believe Him to be, if He would care in the least for the society of your relations' (Forster, 1928, p. 552). This Micawberish father lacked 'seriousness', and bequeathed his lack to his son, whose sharp ear for the comic possibilities of religious inflation is as noticeable as his opposition towards many forms of belief prevalent at the time. Where Dickens was serious was in his conviction that 'neither education nor religion could do anything really useful in social improvement until the way had been paved for their ministrations by cleanliness and decency' (ibid., p. 540), a statement perhaps tailored for its audience of Sanitary Reformers (Fielding *Speeches*, p. 129: 10 May 1851), but which is entirely characteristic in its emphasis upon works rather than faith.

Like Carlyle, whom he first met in 1840, and whose influence upon him (as upon most literate people at the time) was profound, Dickens came to hold the radically Protestant view that nothing interfered more with 'true' religion than the contemporary fetishism of 'Rituals, Liturgies, Creeds, Hierarchies' which obscured the divinely ordained duty to act righteously and serve one's fellow men (*Past and Present*, 1843, quoted in Carlyle, 1872, pp. 196–7). Yet his deeper aspirations involved a more complex set of feelings than this suggests. On 30 September 1844, restless in the foreign surroundings of Genoa and having developed 'the habit of more gravely regarding many things before passed lightly enough' (Forster, 1928, p. 347), he wrote to Forster of a 'curious dream' in which the spirit of Mary Hogarth, draped in blue like a Raphael Madonna, came to him, and he asked it, 'in an agony of entreaty':

What is the True religion? As it paused a moment without replying, I said – Good God, in such an agony of haste, lest it should go away! – 'You think, as I do, that the Form of religion does not so greatly matter, if we try to do good? – or,' I said, observing that it still hesitated, and was moved with the greatest compassion for me, 'perhaps the Roman Catholic is the best? perhaps it makes one think of God oftener, and believe in him more steadily?' 'For *you*,' said the Spirit, full of such heavenly tenderness for me, that I felt as if my heart would break; 'for *you*, it is the best!' Then I awoke, with the tears running down my face . . . (ibid., 348–9)

Dickens's opposition to Roman Catholicism is a familiar fact: of the 1846 Geneva revolution, he said his sympathy was 'all with the radicals. I don't know any subject on which this indomitable people have so good a right to a strong feeling as Catholicity – if not as religion, clearly as a means of social degradation' (ibid., p. 349). His dream does not imply any desire to take up Roman Catholicism; as he said himself, he was doubtless stimulated by his surroundings (convent bells ringing during the night, and a family altar in his bedroom); but, at the same time, it expresses a depth of anxiety and longing which is surprising, and revealing. If he could never accept Mariolatry, he was nevertheless subject to a lifelong yearning for some female image of spirituality, of personal guidance and redemption.

Forster remarked that Dickens's Genoa dream strengthened 'other evidences, of which there are many in his life, of his not having escaped those trying regions of reflection which most men of thought, and all men of genius, have at some time to pass through' (ibid., p. 350). Among such 'evidences' – although Forster in fact offers precious few – we are told that during the 1840's, a time of doubts and uncertainties for Dickens, A. P. Stanley's *Life and Correspondence of Thomas Arnold* (1844) helped him most: 'I respect and reverence his memory', Dickens wrote to Forster, 'beyond all expression. I must have that book. Every sentence that you quote from it is the text-book of my faith' (ibid., p. 350). We do not know if Dickens obtained a copy of this 'text-book'; certainly there are many passages in it which he would have endorsed, attacking the 'Puritans and Evangelicals', for example, for their Old Testament bibliolatry, or affirming his belief that true Christianity was expressed in the spirit of the New Testament; although whether he would also have enthused about Arnold's view that the 'childishness' of Rugby boys was attributable to the 'great number of exciting books of amusement, like Pickwick and Nickleby', seems less likely (Stanley, 1845, Vol. 1, p. 257, Vol. 2, pp. 398–9, p. 161). In fact, the novelist was probably referring, not to the whole book, but to Forster's review of it, which included numerous extended quotations, and which appeared in *The Examiner* at the time of his letter. Forster's quotations are manifestly those which would also have appealed to Dickens, above all for their stress on 'meaning by Religion what the Gospel teaches us to mean by it', namely, 'a system directing and influencing our conduct, principles, and feelings, and professing to do this with sovereign authority, and most efficacious influence' (Forster, 1844, p. 644).

Dr Arnold's attitude, as mediated by Forster, is that the true function of Christianity lies in improving the moral and social life of the community as a whole, rather than in differences over doctrine, or modes of worship. This emphasis, 'Broad Church' before that label came into existence, could be found elsewhere, in particular among the Unitarians. Perhaps the most significant act from the religious point of view taken by Dickens was when he decided to attend the Little Portland Street chapel of Edward Tagart (1804–58). He had begun to attend Thomas Madge's Essex Street Unitarian chapel on his return from America, but it was Tagart's funeral sermon on W. E. Channing, whom Dickens had met in Boston, which attracted him to Little Portland Street on 20 November 1842. There he found that he and Tagart shared 'that religion which has sympathy for men of every creed and ventures to pass judgment on none' (Pilgrim *Letters*, Vol. 4, p. 173), and a long friendship was established. Dickens's American visit helped crystallise feelings of unease about the Established Church; but the root cause of his open departure from it was sheer disgust with 'its Puseyisms, and daily outrages on common sense and humanity'. As he put it to Felton, one of the many prominent liberals he had met in America, he had therefore carried into effect 'an old idea of mine, and joined the Unitarians, who *would* do something for human improvement if they could; and who practise Charity and Toleration' (Pilgrim *Letters*,Vol. 3, pp. 455–6: 2 March 1843).

What outraged Dickens most was the Church's attitude to education, always a sensitive issue for him, and never more so than in the 1840s, when he was involved both in the upbringing of his own children, and (in collaboration with Miss Burdett Coutts) in the Ragged School movement. According to Forster, it was precisely Dickens's 'impatience' with Anglican clergymen's views on education which led him to join Tagart's congregation for 'two or three years' (1928, p. 298; an understatement, since the family continued to attend regularly, when in England, until 1847, and Dickens afterwards occasionally, alone).[5] While the establishment argued that Christianity should be taught as part of a traditional creed and system of worship in the schools, the more radical view was that only the broad essentials, common to all denominations based on the Bible, should be taught. Dickens proposed to write on the Ragged Schools for the *Edinburgh Review* if, as he put it, the *Review* were 'not afraid to take ground against the church catechism and other mere formularies and subtleties, in reference to the education of the young and ignorant' (Forster, 1928, p. 298). It was of 'vital importance' to him that 'no persons, however well intentioned', should 'perplex' the minds of Ragged children 'with religious Mysteries that young people with the best advantages, can but imperfectly understand'. He had heard 'a lady visitor' at S. R. Starey's Field Lane Ragged School 'propounding questions in reference to the "lamb of God" which I most unquestionably would not suffer anyone to put to my children: recollecting the immense absurdities that were suggested to my own childhood by the like injudicious catechizing' (Pilgrim *Letters*, Vol. 3, p. 574: 24 September 1843).

For his own children, Dickens wrote simple prayers and a plain version of *The Life of Our Lord* (1846-9, not published until 1934) which, he said, they knew 'from having it repeated to them, long before they could read, and almost as soon as they could speak' (Dexter*Letters*, Vol. 3, p. 784: 8 June 1870). *The Life of Our Lord* has been called a Unitarian work, but this is to read into it a theological significance hardly applicable, unless this simply means having a moral emphasis. It is a narrative account of the life of Christ from Nativity to Ascension, which concludes:

> Remember! - It is christianity TO DO GOOD always - even to those who do evil to us. It is christianity to love our neighbour as ourself, and to do to all men as we would have them Do to us. It is christianity to be gentle, merciful, and forgiving, and to keep those qualities quiet in our own hearts, and never make a boast of them, or of our prayers or of our love of God, but always to shew that we love Him by humbly trying to do right in everything. If we do this, and remember the life and lessons of Our Lord Jesus Christ, and try to act up to them, we may confidently hope that God will forgive us our sins and mistakes, and enable us to live and die in Peace. (Dickens, 1934 edn, pp. 127-8)

In teaching his children, Dickens chose not to dwell on the supernatural element of Christianity, but rather upon its essentially moral features.

Like other liberal, unorthodox Christians who wished to retain their faith in what they felt was the basic message of the New Testament, while rejecting the inadequacies of the Church, the evangelicals and the 'Puseyites', Dickens found among the Unitarians a haven of reasonableness and plain thinking. Nevertheless, Forster insists, he retained 'an unswerving faith in Christianity itself', continuing to feel a strong sympathy with the Church upon all 'essential points' (1928, p. 298). What did Forster mean by the 'essential points', however? He came from a family of Unitarians, and in 1832 helped Leigh Hunt with the expense of printing *Christianism, or Belief and Unbelief Reconciled* - derived, perhaps, from St Simon's *Nouveau Christianisme* (1825), an expression of faith in brotherhood and benevolence in an industrial age. Hunt's book is suffused with a Romantic 'Religion of the Heart', the title he gave a later version (complete with prayers from Wordsworth and other poets),

published in 1853, and a copy of which he presented to Dickens.⁶ It is
reasonable to suppose that Forster, with Hunt, Fonblanque, the
Unitarian W. J. Fox and other contributors to the radical journals of the
1820s and 1830s, such as the *True Sun*, the *Morning Chronicle*, *The
Examiner* and the *Monthly Repository*, shared a liberal, Romantic religion
of tolerance, charity and transcendental intuitions; and, moreover, that
Dickens, who joined this group as a young man, was deeply influenced by
them. But Forster does not tell us about this.

We need to remember that Forster wrote his biography at a time when
the Church itself was moving to a broader and more liberal position
under the impact of social, political and intellectual changes. And that
what he omits is sometimes as important as what he tells us. He reports
that for Dickens in February 1841 the 'realities' of the sacrament of
baptism no longer amounted to more than 'enabling him to form a
relationship with friends he most loved' (Forster, 1928, p. 173), a
humanist interpretation of this religious 'form' reinforced by the views of
Walter Savage Landor and John Elliotson, both of whom were asked to
be godfather to Dickens's fourth child, named after Landor. 'It creates in
me a somewhat new sentiment, it makes me religious, to think of him',
replied Landor, lightheartedly accepting; Elliotson, physician and
mesmerist (and the Dickens family doctor), also accepted:

> I shall be delighted to become father in God to your little bopeep: you
> still retaining your title of his father in the flesh, with all the rights,
> privileges, perquisites & duties thereto annexed, from the moment you
> determined to construct him to the end of life.
>   I should, however, have been compelled to forego this delight had
> you not absolved me from religious duties & every thing vulgar – For
> nothing could I consent to teach him in the vulgar tongue – nor would I
> have spoiled him for arithmetic by teaching him that three are one &
> one is three, or defaced his views of the majesty of God by assuring him
> that the maker of the Universe once came down & got a little jewess in
> the family way, & so gave himself up to fun as to manage that he should
> be the little master she produced when in the way she was because she
> loved her Lord & was favoured beyond all other damsels. (Pilgrim
> *Letters*, Vol. 2, p. 210, note 1)

This high, almost Joycean irreverence is hardly what one expects of a
respectable mid-Victorian gentleman – if Elliotson was exactly that. The
fact that Dickens had 'absolved' Elliotson from godfatherly duties
suggests he knew what to expect of his friend, even if he would not have
gone so far himself. Five years later, in *Dombey and Son*, Dickens appears
to support the full Christian meaning of christening, yet, as we shall see,
he and Forster were quite consciously guarding the novel against any

charge of irreverence. It is a difficult and delicate task to determine where Dickens stood, and how far his views may have changed during his life. Defending his assertion that Dickens was unswervingly faithful to Christianity and the Church on 'essential points', Forster included in his third volume letters from Dickens to his sons and other correspondents in which he affirmed the 'all-sufficiency' of the New Testament, and his determination to avoid 'obtrusive professions of and tradings in religion, as one of the main causes why Christianity has been retarded in this world' (Forster, 1928, pp. 818-20). Dickens became weary, if not despairing, over the sectarian squabbles of his time; but Forster allows little of this to show. Dickens belonged to the local Anglican church during the Gad's Hill period of his life, but attended infrequently: Henry Dickens mentions only an 'extremely dull curate' at Higham, who irritated his father so much 'he gave up his attendance at the services' – whether temporarily or permanently is not revealed (Henry Dickens, 1934, p. 41). The novelist concluded his will by committing his 'soul to the mercy of God through our Lord and Saviour Jesus Christ', exhorting his children to guide themselves by 'the teaching of the New Testament in its broad spirit, and to put no faith in any man's narrow construction of its letter here or there' (Forster, 1928, p. 859). To discover more about Dickens's religion, there is only one source, as Forster admits: although Dickens 'bore outwardly so little of the impress of his writings, they formed the whole of that inner life which essentially constituted the man' (ibid., p. 816).

IV

Dickens was not a religious novelist; nor were any of his novels *primarily* religious in intention or effect. This is important, for it distinguishes his work from the very large number of such novels which appeared during his lifetime. 'This is the age of Religious novels', announced the *Dublin Review* in 1846, since at least a third of the novels published the previous year were 'either directly religious, or at all events possessed more of religious character than would have been sufficient, ten years ago, to damn any novel' (vol. 21, 1846, p. 261). There were 'theological romances', 'Oxford Movement' tales, 'Low Church' novels, 'Broad Church' novels, spiritual autobiographies thinly disguised as fiction, and even the testimonies of so-called Catholic 'perverts', very popular in a Protestant country (see Maison, 1961; Wolff, 1977). 'Perversion' had a religious, not sexual significance, and meant apostasy, as one could discover in the Reverend W. J. Conybeare's justly neglected classic *Perversion; or, The Causes and Consequences of Infidelity* (1856). There was even an underground press of anti-papist pornography, including

The Convent School, or Early Experiences of a Young Flagellant (Marcus, 1966, pp. 74–5). Moreover, all these books were read, if sometimes only in the manner of George Eliot's Mrs Linnet, who confined her perusal of (non-pornographic) religious works to the 'purely secular portions, which bore a very small proportion to the whole' and so could make 'rapid progress through a large number of volumes' ('Janet's Repentance', *Scenes of Clerical Life*, 1857, ch. 3).

Dickens, like George Eliot and others, thought this kind of writing a sham. Attacking Charlotte Mary Yonge's popular 'Pusey-Novel', *The Heir of Redclyffe* (1853) for its 'want of experience of human nature', he identified the two classes which, he claimed, such a book addressed: the first, 'drawn from a large and wealthy section of the so-called religious world', looked to the 'obtrusively professed intention of the book solely', knowing and caring nothing about its execution; the second, 'represented by a body of romantic young ladies', found their 'ideal Man (name and all)' in 'such a character as Sir Guy Morville' ('Doctor Dulcamara, MP', *Household Words*, 18 December 1858, repr. in Stone, *Uncollected Writings*, Vol. 2, pp. 624–5). The most notable fact about Victorian religious novels is that they are no longer widely read; and Dickens's remarks make the reason clear. Execution *does* matter, as does the ability to penetrate the beliefs and attitudes of one's readers beyond the mere expression of wish-fulfilment. Thackeray wrote that we prefer 'romances which do not treat of algebra, religion, political economy, or other abstract science' (quoted in Ray, 1966, pp. 77–8). Religious beliefs need not be abstract; indeed, they will not be, if they are to move our feelings, and it is the achievement of Dickens's fiction that he avoids the limitations of abstraction, while pursuing his own generous and comprehensive vision.

1

Mr Pickwick and the Innocent Fall

Dickens went into the Pickwick Club to scoff, and Dickens remained to pray. (Chesterton, 1906, p. 96)

Lest there should be any well-intentioned persons who do not perceive the difference (as some such could not, when OLD MORTALITY was published) between religion and the cant of religion, piety and the pretence of piety, a humble reverence for the great truths of scripture and an audacious and offensive obtrusion of its letter and not its spirit in the commonest dissensions and meanest affairs of life, to the extraordinary confusion of ignorant minds, let them understand that it is always the latter, and never the former, which is satirized here ...
(Preface to the Cheap Edition, *Pickwick Papers*, September 1847)

I

It may seem daring, not to say foolhardy, to begin an exploration of Dickens's religious position with his first complete novel, *Pickwick Papers* (1836-7). Nothing would seem to be further from the profoundly serious experience we usually associate with religion than this irreverent comedy. One cannot altogether blame Carlyle for his amused horror at the 'strange profane story' of the sick man who exclaimed, as his ministering clergyman left the room, 'Well, thank God, *Pickwick* will be out in ten days any way!' (quoted in Forster, 1928, p. 91). On the other hand, perhaps we *can* blame those who, like the 'very dyspeptic and evangelical' Reverend Duke in George Eliot's 'Amos Barton', considered 'the immense sale of *Pickwick Papers*, recently completed, one of the strongest proofs of original sin'. Or even those who, like Thomas Arnold, for all his tolerant views and broad theology, thought Dickens's early novels unduly exciting to the rising generation. For they missed something which must be understood at the outset: namely, that it is in the humorous, the eccentric, even the grotesque, at least as much as in the earnest, decorous and idealised parts of Dickens's work, that he reveals his deepest and most important convictions. And *Pickwick Papers* is no exception. As Thackeray put it in 1840, we 'would do wrong to put that

great contemporary history of *Pickwick* aside as a frivolous work'
(1898-9, Vol. 5, p. 80). Like *Tom Jones* (which Thackeray approved of
rather less), Dickens's comic masterpiece has matter for thought, for
reflection, if not exactly for deep spiritual disquiet. Despite its
delightfully innocent, often facetious surface, the novel reveals some of
the beliefs Dickens most wished to affirm, and some of those he most
wished to attack, at the start of his career.

The religious dimension of *Pickwick Papers* is expressed in two closely
related ways: by affirming the value of innocent benevolence, embodied
mainly in the character of Mr Pickwick; and by attacking certain forms of
evangelicalism, most conspicuously in the 'deputy shepherd', Stiggins.
We here witness Dickens beginning to discover what he believed, coming
to scoff but staying to pray, as Chesterton remarked, but doing so more
consciously than is usually allowed. At the same time, as Dickens may not
have been fully aware, *Pickwick Papers* also reflects a fundamental
transition in social and moral attitudes, from the carefree, coarse
profligacy of Regency manners, with all their duelling, drunkenness and
lechery, to a new refinement, a new stress on earnestness, duty and
bourgeois family values, largely brought about by the pervasive impact of
evangelicalism upon the middle and upper classes in England.

Dickens's position in relation to evangelicalism is complex; and when
he attacks its malign features, he attacks something with which he is
intimately connected. According to the *OED*, 'Evangelicalism' consisted
in the 'doctrines and mode of thought peculiar to the Evangelical party;
adherence to that party', and the doctrine of the 'Evangelical party' it
defined as a doctrine of salvation by faith in the atoning death of Christ,
denying that either good works or the sacraments have any saving
efficacy. The 'Evangelical' Protestant insists on the totally depraved state
of human nature consequent on the Fall, asserts the sole authority of the
Bible over church or cleric, denies that any supernatural gift is imparted
by ordination, and views the sacraments merely as symbolic of an
appropriate state of mind. This religion grew out of the Methodist revival
in the first half of the eighteenth century, and was associated rather with
the Calvinist than the Arminian branch of that movement. At the heart of
'Evangelical' theology, as at the heart of Methodism, stood the doctrine
of conversion, a belief in the intense and dramatic personal change which
occurred when, burdened down by a sense of sin and inadequacy, one
threw oneself on God's mercy and was regenerated. The difficulty of
applying all this to a single 'Evangelical' party within the Church of
England should be obvious. Evangelicalism, enormously important in its
influence upon English culture and society, was so complicated, so
diffuse and so widespread that it can hardly be identified solely with the
revival within Anglicanism, even if that seems to be where it began. Nor
can it be identified with any single denomination, for it was found among

different Dissenting sects as well as within the Church. And it continued to pervade the views of confessed agnostics such as George Eliot, and even influenced Christians who opposed it, such as Dr Arnold, or Dickens. The least one can do is draw a distinction between the capitalised terms, 'Evangelical' and 'Evangelicalism', designating by them the party within the Church of England, and the uncapitalised 'evangelical' and 'evangelicalism', using the latter to refer to the much broader movement of ideas and feelings which crossed religious boundaries but which yet maintained some links with the 'doctrines and mode of thought' of the original movement.

If, then, it can be said that in general Dickens is intimately connected with evangelicalism, in the sense of sharing its emphasis on earnestness, duty and family piety, in *Pickwick Papers* he is suggesting an alternative doctrine, based on a more cheerful and optimistic view of human nature than the characteristic evangelical emphasis.

II

The first impression most readers receive from the novel has little enough to do with religion, much less evangelicalism. Its initial impact is one of barely controlled anarchy, rather than of purposeful indoctrination. Indeed, the teeming proliferation of character and incident, the hazy waywardness of plot, the vast size of the work – all these make it almost unmanageable. Some would go so far as to deny it the title of novel altogether, although to assume, as, for instance, John Lucas does, that only a narrative exhibiting a certain degree of 'coherence' and 'integrity' may be so honoured (Lucas, 1970, p. 5), seems to me both aesthetically narrow and easily challenged on historical grounds. *Pickwick Papers* takes after its picaresque and semi-picaresque predecessors, from *Don Quixote* to *Gil Blas*, from *The Vicar of Wakefield* to *Jorrocks's Jaunts and Jollities*, in its looseness of form and mixture of levels. And, in this sense like all Dickens's novels, it encourages us to read it as more than simply realistic, but in terms of a rich and provoking aesthetic of its own. The critics who have come nearest to reading it in this way are those who, like G. K. Chesterton and W. H. Auden, have responded to it as myth. Auden, in particular, offered an ingenious and persuasive, if also somewhat vulnerable, account of it in his essay on 'Dingley Dell & The Fleet', in *The Dyer's Hand and Other Essays* (1963). Where he is most vulnerable, and this applies to the mythopoeic approach to Dickens in general, is in his disregarding of the contemporary reality out of which *Pickwick Papers* sprang, forgetting that myths are always generated by real life; thus he omits the Stiggins sub-plot, an omission no reader at the time would have made, as Dickens's remarks in the preface to the

Cheap Edition of 1847, in defence of his religious satire, suggest.

Auden claims that the 'real theme of *Pickwick Papers* – I am not saying that Dickens was consciously aware of it and, indeed, I am pretty certain that he was not – is the Fall of Man'; *Pickwick Papers* tells of an innocent living in an Edenic state (defined according to no less than ten categories), who then eats of the Tree of Knowledge, and falls – not from innocence into sin, but from 'an innocent child into an innocent adult' (Auden, 1963, pp. 408–11). Dingley Dell and the Fleet, respectively, represent the realms of innocence, pre- and post-lapsarian. What is one to make of this claim? An immediate difficulty is raised by the parenthetical remark that Dickens was unaware of what he was doing. Not that the suggestion is untypical, although it tends to be made more subtly nowadays. There is, of course, a familiar sense in which a novelist may be unaware of elements in his work; but can this include his 'real theme'? A novelist's themes are expressions of the way in which he sees the world, of his beliefs. In everyday usage, beliefs may be conscious or unconscious, or both; we usually judge the extent of conscious awareness according to the manner in which the beliefs are expressed. Similarly with novels: if a belief is expressed as a persistently felt theme, then it is most probably quite conscious. When Auden talks about the 'real theme' of *Pickwick Papers*, something continuously present as a shaping pattern in the work, he is, I think, talking about the expression of a belief of which Dickens was conscious. To accept that he was not conscious would also be to feed the popular misconception of Dickens as little more than an inspired journalist creating droll anecdotes in response to the demands of serial publication, an image perhaps superseded now as far as the later works are concerned, but still potent for the earlier. The achievement of *Pickwick Papers* is that of a great artist which, if it means anything, means of a conscious craftsman. The initial improvisatory impulse behind the novel is unlikely to have continued throughout its growth. And the 'cheerful', the 'Shakespearean view, of humanity' Miss Mitford identified in it (quoted in Collins, 1971, p. 36) must surely have been a reflection of conscious purpose. Dickens had explored the darker realms of life in some of his early sketches and he allowed scenes of ingratitude, heartlessness and death to resurface in the interpolated tales of *Pickwick*; but the follies of human nature represented in the main stream of the narrative, the satire against legal and religious chicanery, are conveyed in a tone predominantly good-humoured, tolerant and benevolent. If he had induced only one reader to 'think better of his fellow men, and to look upon the brighter and more kindly side of human nature', Dickens remarked, he would have felt 'proud and happy' (preface, 1837). If we can identify a 'fall' as the 'real theme' of *Pickwick Papers*, then it must not only have been intended, but intended to have been a happy one – an innocent fall.

This idea of a 'fall' raises the much-discussed question of whether or not Mr Pickwick's character does actually change. Dickens himself defended Mr Pickwick's apparent change by arguing in his later (1847) preface that in 'real life' we learn to see the 'better part' of a person as we get to know him, and that the same thing happens with his hero, a defence usually scoffed at for its naïvety, as well as for the characteristic Dickens ploy of offering realist grounds to explain a character not entirely realist in conception. But I think one can argue that it is not Mr Pickwick who changes during the course of the narrative, rather it is *our perception* of him. It is important to be clear about this point, for it throws into relief those characters in Dickens's fiction who do change, a change which, as we shall see, is usually quite startling and dramatic, a virtual 'change of heart', rather than the gradual process of growth to be found in Trollope or George Eliot. The distinction is fundamental to Dickens, and he is usually clear about which kind of change he has in mind.

If, then, Mr Pickwick does not change, but rather our attitude to him, how does this come about? It is a function of the relationship between author and reader. The principal development or transformation Dickens wants is intended to take place in *us*, his readers, leading us to a brighter, more optimistic view of mankind and its prospects. The opening account of the Pickwick Club's transactions is admittedly somewhat dusty parody; but when we next see Mr Pickwick, in his altercation with the suspicious cabbie Sam, the juxtaposition of cockney knowingness and Mr Pickwick's 'gentlemanly' naïvety begins to give the narrative that particular quality of rich humour and cheerful humanity which dominates it thereafter, and which is reinforced by the imagery of sunlight persistently associated with Mr Pickwick, from the opening lines of the novel onwards. The treatment of the drinking and duelling at Rochester confirms this lighthearted tone, as it indicates Dickens's urge to ridicule the manners of an age now passing; and the arrival of the 'loquacious' Jingle, who so farcically deceives the Pickwickians by always telling them what they want to hear, anticipates the entry of the irrepressible Boots of the White Hart Inn, Sam Weller, whose introduction initiates a stream of hilarious and deflating commentary on Mr Pickwick's otherwise stock adventures.

Sam's viewpoint directs our response to his master's story: his initially cool attitude to his new 'sitiwation' is soon transformed into a veneration for Mr Pickwick 'which nothing but death will terminate' (ch. lvii, p. 801); in the same way, our uncertain response to the ludicrous author of studies on the source of the Hampstead ponds and the nature of the Tittlebat, the shallowly philanthropic observer of the 'gallant' drunks staggering about the streets of Rochester, becomes transformed into a strong and lasting attachment to 'our old friend', last seen in 'one of those moments of unmixed happiness, of which, if we seek them, there are ever some, to cheer our transitory existence here (ch. lvii, p. 799). The process of this change in Sam's and our viewpoint is gradual but unmistakable. It is more than a function of our acceptance of the narrator's position, as he moves from detached superiority to affectionate banter towards Mr Pickwick; but of the kind of wry comment Sam makes upon discovering his master wandering helplessly in the dark passageways of the inn at Ipswich, after his misadventure with the lady in the yellow curl-papers: 'You rayther want somebody to look arter you, sir, wen your judgement goes out a wisitin'' (ch. xxii, p. 312). As this highlights Mr Pickwick's dependence on Sam, his childlike irresponsibility, so it also draws us closer to him. We laugh at his predicaments, but we are warmed by his well-meaning outlook, his assumption that everyone must be as benevolent as he is. After his innocent escapade with Miss Witherfield, Pickwick's encounter with the law is more successful than it will be later, partly because of Sam's helpful sharpness, but also because at this distance from London the law cannot withstand his stout claim to be heard 'until I am removed by force', a claim which gains Sam's and our applause: 'Pickvick and principle' (ch. xxv, p.342).

This adherence to 'principle' increasingly evident in Mr Pickwick's dealings with the world endears him yet further to Sam and us, and increases his stature in our eyes. We concur quite happily when, for instance, Sam reproves the foolish Winkle after his escape from the supposed fury of Mr Dowler, for 'inwolving your precious governor in all sorts o' fanteegs, wen he's made up his mind to go through every think for principle' (ch. xxxviii, pp. 541-2). Mr Pickwick has come to have more serious concerns than before, when he would automatically have followed Winkle on any 'fanteegs' which came up. Yet Mr Pickwick is evidently unaware of the effect the Fleet will have on him, much less the possibility that Dodson and Fogg will try elsewhere for their expenses when he refuses to pay, and so cause Mrs Bardell to be incarcerated in her turn. This implies that Mr Pickwick's innocence has its limitations, for all its initial attractiveness; and hence that he needs to 'fall' into a more mature or knowledgeable view of things.

One of Sam's functions is to clarify the weaknesses in Mr Pickwick's innocence. Thus, after the Bardell–Pickwick trial, which ought to have shown Mr Pickwick that his innocent benevolence could not succeed before Serjeant Buzfuz's expert manipulation of judge, jury and witnesses, Sam reveals his deeper insight - 'Hooroar for the principle, as the moneylender said ven he wouldn't renew the bill' (ch. xxv, p. 489). Again, more explicitly, when he joins his master in prison, he does so 'on principle' too, which puts him 'in mind o' the man as killed his-self on principle' (ch. xliv, pp. 615-16). Sam's commitment is to the principle of loyalty and affection towards Mr Pickwick, not at all the same thing as Mr Pickwick's commitment to preventing Dodson and Fogg from recovering their ill-gotten gains. Ironically, for all his worldly knowledge, Sam has been unaware of the possibility of an innocence such as Mr Pickwick's. This is the crux of the matter, and it is hard to think that Dickens was not fully aware of it. Mr Pickwick, by contrast, remains innocent of evil, although about to be rudely awakened. This experience does not entirely destroy his innocence, however; on the contrary, his innocence miraculously includes and *transcends* what happens to him when he is sent to the Fleet.

Dickens gives no explicit, theological definition of Mr Pickwick's new state, but there is no question of its force. We are led to feel that there *can* be innocent happiness in this transitory world, as Dickens calls it. We can surely agree with Dostoevsky, who thought Mr Pickwick, though a 'weaker conception' than that most perfect good type in Christian literature, Don Quixote, 'still immense' (quoted in Carr, 1962, p. 160). He is, as Sam Weller calls him, a kind of 'angel in tights and gaiters' (ch. xlv, p. 642), the necessary articles of clothing implying always his comically mortal limitations, too.

III

This point requires more detailed examination. When Sam calls Mr Pickwick an angel, he has just learnt from Jingle's hypocritical, hymn-book-carrying, chapel-going associate, Job (a contrast between Job's false religiosity and Pickwickian goodness implicit here), that it is his own master who has been providing for their former deceivers in the Fleet prison. Mr Pickwick has come to realise that the world contains dishonest, even malevolent people, like Jingle and Dodson and Fogg; and, what is more, people who suffer, like the imprisoned debtors. In Auden's terms, he becomes debtor to those less fortunate than himself, a form of guilt he expiates by forgiving his enemies, Jingle and Job, and relieving their suffering. In this way, innocent childhood becomes innocent adulthood. While this helps us understand that what is involved in Mr Pickwick's virtue is more than merely passive goodness, it creates some difficulties. For instance, how can he experience guilt, and yet remain innocent, as this implies? And why does he not forgive Dodson and Fogg, too? It is true, they do not repent, whereas Jingle and Job Trotter have 'suffered much – very' (ch. xlii, p. 598), and become contrite. Perker suggests a reason: he argues that 'the more they gain, the more they'll seek, and so the sooner be led into some piece of knavery that must end in a crash' (ch. xlvii, p. 662). In short, they can be left to Providence, with the underlying implication that evil destroys itself without direct conflict with good. This becomes a characteristic emphasis: goodness is usually unscarred by any battle with evil.

But to return to Mr Pickwick's 'guilt': it seems not so much Mr Pickwick as *we* who are made to feel guilty. For it is our view of the good man in his new context which changes. To begin with, we have been encouraged by Dickens to delight in the child-like but irresponsible innocence of parlour games at the Manor Farm or *après*-cricket drinking in Muggleton; but within that protected, idyllic scene there lurks the nefarious Jingle, the invader of this Eden, a 'Prince of Darkness' gliding after the maiden aunt (ch. viii, p. 103). The parody and joking here should not blind us to the more serious overtones, the limitations of Dingley Dell implied by this. Then, too, there are the tales told on the two occasions when we see the happy crowd at Dingley Dell, 'The Convict's Return', and 'The Story of the Goblins who Stole a Sexton'. Both reveal an aspect of life far from that celebrated so easily at the Dell, a reality of loneliness, suffering and murderous impulses which the reader cannot altogether forget, even if the Pickwickians pay it no attention. Our sympathetic enjoyment of their activities is ultimately qualified by our ironic awareness of the actualities that have been excluded from their world.

These different aspects of life are expressed in *almost* entirely secular, human terms, although Dickens also suggests a religious dimension for those willing to respond. We are certainly not *obliged* to believe in this dimension, however. Manor Farm would, it seems, be incomplete without its 'benevolent clergyman'. But what does he do? He looks 'pleasantly on; for the happy faces which surrounded the table made the good old man feel happy too; and though the merriment was rather boisterous, still it came from the heart and not from the lips: and this is the right sort of merriment after all' (ch. vi, p. 71). Trite, perhaps; but evidently a ratification of the otherwise notably pagan revels of the Dell. His song, 'The Ivy Green', tells of the decay and death associated with the local parish church, but balances this by its stress upon the ivy's capacity to survive: 'The brave old plant in its lonely days/Shall fatten upon the past' (ch. vi, p. 73). This seems to imply that the church will survive too, maintaining its links with old memories and associations. Wardle claims that, with the 'old houses and fields', the 'little church' is like a living friend to him. Dickens seems to endorse all this. In his pseudonymous pamphlet *Sunday Under Three Heads*, published at the same time as the Dingley Dell scenes (June 1836), the ideal form of religious observance is represented by a secluded little village church 'distant about seventy miles from London', to which the 'whole population' hasten with cheerful good-humour to hear the 'impressive service of the Church of England' spoken, 'not merely *read*', by the elderly, grey-headed minister, to whom they respond 'with an air of sincere devotion' (*UT & RP*, pp. 658–9).

Dickens steers a careful path between favouring extempore sermonising, as encouraged by the evangelicals (who opposed sermons *merely* read), and favouring the lazy indifference, not to say corruption, of fashionable High Anglicanism: elsewhere in *Sunday Under Three Heads* he attacks both the 'disgusting and impious familiarity' with which a 'less orthodox' preacher calls on Christ, and the complacency of a young clergyman 'notorious at Cambridge for his knowledge of horse flesh and dancers', who hurries over the 'less comfortable portions of the service', so as not to disturb his upper-class audience (ibid., pp. 640-1). The apparently anachronistic 'traditional' set-up Dickens supports in both novel and pamphlet not only existed at the time, but continued to exist well into the 1880s, when, for example, Flora Thompson experienced it (see Thompson, 1976 edn, ch. 14). And this image of an old-fashioned parish community desiring neither evangelical enthusiasm nor High Church innovations, but preferring a quietly sincere middle way, remained with Dickens throughout his life. Churches appear infrequently in his fiction; but when they do, they tend to be stable, ancient features of the landscape. Urban churches he viewed differently, as he did evangelical or 'lay' chapels.

The benevolent old clergyman's tale offers an artless expression of conventional Christian morality. But, as a tale within a tale, it is qualified from the start as a special form of discourse, anticipating Dickens's later preference for 'romance' forms for more explicitly religious expressions of belief, for instance in the Christmas Books. In strong contrast to the happy family atmosphere generated by the main narrative, the clergyman tells of a woman and her son morally and physically battered by the reprobate head of the family. Even before the death of Mary Hogarth, which interrupted the June 1837 number of *Pickwick Papers*, an event usually taken to be the source of Dickens's idealisation of women, he wished to affirm those 'feelings of forebearance and meekness under suffering' to which 'all God's creatures, but women, are strangers' (ch. vi, p. 74). Evidently a commonplace belief, but he subverts it later: 'Wot's the good o' callin' a young 'ooman a Wenus or a angel, Sammy?' (ch. xxxiii, p. 453). The woman's illness and death suggest the workings of a retributory Providence upon her son, in apparent contrast to the benign workings of Providence in the main story; and soon her soul takes flight, 'I confidently hope,' exclaims the clergyman, 'and solemnly believe, to a place of eternal happiness and rest' (ch. vi, p. 77). This was a hope, a belief and a slight confusion that Dickens shared, though this must be the only occasion on which he permits a man of the cloth to express it. Not even Frank Milvey in *Our Mutual Friend*, the novelist's most favourably depicted clergyman, is allowed more than a troubled reading out of the lines from the burial service which give thanks for delivering 'this our sister out of the miseries of this sinful world' (bk III, ch. ix, p. 514). Dickens, unlike, say, Charlotte Yonge, who always provides a ministering clergyman for a deathbed, prefers lay mediators, for instance in the scene of the Chancery prisoner's death in *Pickwick Papers*, aptly labelled the earliest instance of 'true pathos' in his works (Gissing, 1898, p. 177). The lay mediator is the 'fortunate legatee', who, in his cobbler's apron, sits 'reading from the Bible aloud' – we are not told which passages, Dickens would rather leave such things unsaid.

'Open the window,' said the sick man.

He did so. The noise of carriages and carts, the rattle of wheels, the cries of men and boys, all the busy sounds of a mighty multitude instinct with life and occupation, blended into one deep murmur, floated into the room. Above the hoarse loud hum, arose from time to time a boisterous laugh; or a scrap of some jingling song, shouted forth by one of the giddy crowd, would strike upon the ear for an instant, and then be lost amidst the roar of voices and the tramp of footsteps; the breaking of the billows of the restless sea of life that rolled heavily on, without. Melancholy sounds to a quiet listener at any time; how melancholy to the watcher by the bed of death. (ch. xliv, p. 627)

This is one of the finest passages in the novel, surprising us with what becomes a familiar experience in Dickens's fiction, of being taken by a sudden deepening of the narrative flow into a profound perception of life. The pain and loss associated with death are not mitigated by trite allusions to release from pain, or a better world to come; yet, at the same time, there *is* someone there to read the Bible's message.

The whole subject of Dickens's attitude towards and treatment of death will be taken up in a later chapter. At this point it is worth stressing that whereas the clergyman's tale reflects a conventionally expressed faith in immortality, the Chancery prisoner's death scene explores the complex feel of the event taking place, conveying both the anguish of mortality as well as an unforced suggestion of quiet faith in the source of hope for Christians in the face of death. There is no hint of a response from Mr Pickwick. Nor do we need one. He is never more transparently the innocent glass through which we are being shown what Dickens wishes us to see. His innocence is both a desirable feature of his character, a part of his benevolent attitude towards mankind, and a strategy whereby Dickens manipulates his readers. This manipulation, of course, is related to a long tradition in satire, where many a holy fool who has failed to come to grips with reality and suffered for it has at the same time implicitly offered readers a high ideal in contrast to the deceitful world he shows us.

IV

It is possible to fall into the trap of overvaluing the Dingley Dell episodes, which Steven Marcus, for one, thinks assert that the kingdom of God is within each man, no less, and that the little company at Manor Farm represents 'the life promised by the Gospels' (Marcus, 1965, p. 51). Not that Dickens explicitly denies such a reading; but he certainly does not encourage it. What he does is more modest, despite his creation of one of the most lasting depictions of innocent good cheer and companionship in English literature in the Dingley Dell idyll, with its marriages, its communal games and love rituals, its celebration of Christmas.

Indeed, this famous Christmas cheer, often referred to as containing the essence of Dickens's view of life, if not his entire religion, here obtains its first extensive treatment. He had already touched on the subject in a sketch for *Bell's Life in London*, 27 December 1835, where the cheerful spirit of Christmas was said to do 'more to awaken the sympathies of every member of the party in behalf of his neighbour, and to perpetuate their good feeling during the coming year, than all the homilies that have ever been written, by all the Divines that have ever lived'.[1] An attitude to the festival repeated in the ironic chapter heading in *Pickwick*: 'A good-humoured Christmas Chapter, containing an Account of a Wedding, and some other Sports beside: which although in their way, even as good Customs as Marriage itself, are not quite so religiously kept up in these degenerate Times' (ch. xxviii, p. 374). A hit, a palpable hit against the contemporary evangelical emphasis upon earnest piety and serious views to the exclusion of 'sports', and substituting Dickens's own form of piety, a religion of natural human relationships, of joy through love, friendship and marriage.

Not that evangelicalism was against love, friendship and marriage; but the puritan element in the revival, which Dickens attacked wherever he saw it (and perhaps also where he did not), led to an all-or-nothing contrast between the evil of man's nature and the creation on the one hand, and the redeeming offer of Christ on the other, with a consequent devaluing of ordinary human pleasures. Eating, drinking and sliding on the ice, however, are a part of what Dickens celebrates, the 'natural' human affections. The image of what he is opposed to may be found in, for example, the figure of Nicodemus Dumps in 'The Bloomsbury christening' (*Sketches by Boz*, p. 467), the surly bachelor who hates children, subscribes to Wilberforce's Society for the Suppression of Vice 'for the pleasure of putting a stop to any harmless amusements', and contributes 'towards the support of two itinerant methodist parsons'; his name suggests all. The kind of religion Dickens affirms is revealed in his decision to make the wedding of Trundle and Isabella Wardle take place at Christmas. What is sacred is less the church ritual – although Dickens is careful to include it – than the human results: 'the tears of parting between parent and child, the consciousness of leaving the dearest and kindest friends of the happiest portion of human life', the beginning of a new and untried set of relationships (ch. xxviii, p. 384). There is something hallowed about human ties, and the Church's formal recognition of this is no more than – a formal recognition. So Dickens's attitude to it is perfunctory: 'Let us briefly say, then, that the ceremony was performed by the old clergyman, in the parish of Dingley Dell, and that Mr Pickwick's name is attached to the register' (ch. xxviii, p. 384).

Now the essential features of Christmas are the same as those of a wedding, only *everyone* can share them. Thus, at Christmas, the season of 'hospitality, merriment, and open-heartedness', his emphasis is on the reunification of families and on the beginning of new and hopeful relationships all round:

> numerous indeed are the hearts to which Christmas brings a brief season of happiness and enjoyment. How many families, whose members have been dispersed and scattered far and wide, in the restless struggles of life, are then reunited, and meet once again in that happy state of companionship and mutual good-will, which is a source of such pure and unalloyed delight, and one so incompatible with the cares and sorrows of the world, that the religious belief of the most civilised nations, and the rude traditions of the roughest savages, alike number it among the first joys of a future condition of existence, provided for the blest and happy! How many old recollections, and how many dormant sympathies, does Christmas time awaken! (ch. xxviii, p. 374)

Dickens once wrote to Forster that he hoped they might enjoy together 'fifty more Christmases, at least, in this world, and eternal summers in another' (Forster, 1928, p. 162). The idea of blissful reunification after death took a powerful hold upon his mind – and not only, perhaps, because of his yearning to reunite with Mary Hogarth, for he seems seriously to have believed in it. The most notable feature of the above passage is the breadth of what he will accept as 'religious'. He seems deliberately to override the distinction between pagan superstition and Christian faith. But this is in line with something fundamental to his religious position, namely, its closeness to popular forms of belief. His views are never likely to appeal to those who think it important to distinguish between the ill defined pieties to which most people have held, and the orthodoxly Christian.

Dickens felt a very close affinity with that level of belief which involves fantasy, magic and superstition, a popular romanticism which he invokes particularly in the interpolated tale for Christmas, the story of how the aptly named Gabriel Grub (combining the hopefully angelic and the basely animal) is, like Scrooge, converted from misanthropy to a new, innocent, optimism and benevolence. That Dickens quite consciously considered it the most important tale may be gathered from its placing at the structural centre of *Pickwick Papers*, where it acts as a condensed version of the Pickwickian pilgrimage, presenting by means of a dream vision various representations of reality to persuade the protagonist to set 'all the good of the world against the evil' (ch. xxix, p. 404). Grub's vision, though 'supernatural', is by no means specifically Christian. Allusions to a Creator are only conventional. But its purpose within Dickens's evolving structure of belief is clear: the scenes of suffering and penury to which Grub is exposed, and to which we, too, will be exposed in the Fleet prison, are a part of those darker forces hovering about *Pickwick Papers*, and yet which, in this first novel, are always resisted lest they undermine a fundamental optimism. The interpolated tales, with their drunks, dying clowns, their vicious parents and children, their murders and madness, precisely because they are interpolated, filter out life's darker aspects, leaving only the light. Mr Pickwick's response to the first tale-teller's characteristically dismal comment one bright morning on Rochester Bridge, 'Did it ever strike you, on such a morning as this, that drowning would be happiness and peace?', corresponds to our own: 'God bless me, no!' he replies, 'edging a little from the balustrade, as the possibility of the dismal man's tipping him over, by way of experiment, occurred to him rather forcibly' (ch. v, p. 58). Sam Weller's series of blackly comic anecdotes are similarly qualified. It is true that they could reveal to Mr Pickwick 'Sights, sir . . . as 'ud penetrate your benevolent heart, and come out on the other side' (ch. xvi, p. 210). But they do not.

Thus if the Dingley Dell scenes suggest a paradise, it is also an earthly one, in which the brilliancy of the Pickwickian joy is moderated by the shadows of actuality, even while those shadows are prevented from darkening the whole picture.

V

The effective climax of *Pickwick Papers* occurs at the point when Mr Pickwick's innocent goodwill sympathetically involves him with the discarded humanity of the Fleet. But the novel is, in the end, about discovering evil rather than about acting upon that discovery. This is reflected in its tendency to expand into great static set-pieces which confront innocence with experience, as in the Bardell–Pickwick trial. It is also reflected in the shifting narrative focus, which begins through the eyes of a self-conscious editor revealing the limited, self-enclosed but (to

us) delightful activities of the Pickwickians, and which goes on to present
a variety of fictional viewpoints until finally we are brought into the
Fleet, to be sternly informed, 'This is no fiction' (ch. xlii, p. 595). It is
reality. But though Mr Pickwick's sympathetic involvement with the
imprisoned debtors in the Fleet is made immediately apparent by his aid
to Jingle and Job Trotter, his eventual reaction to the sight of such misery
is to do *nothing*: to shut himself up for three months in his own room. His
retiral implicitly acknowledges his 'fall' from a false view of reality to a
true one.

The Fleet scenes sharpen our sense of what constitutes a true attitude
to reality in *Pickwick Papers*, by revealing the hypocrisy and self-interest
of the law and religion. Lowten, Mr Perker's assistant, explains to Mr
Pickwick what his philosophy boils down to: 'damn hurting yourself for
anybody else, you know' (ch. liii, p. 743). Lowten has just informed
Pickwick that Job Trotter has chosen against financial advantage to
follow Jingle to Demerara. Mr Pickwick may hardly be said to have hurt
himself paying for Jingle's new lease of life in Demerara: his unspecified
but evidently ample means take care of that. But this is only true on the
material level. More important to Dickens are the impulses referred to by
the worldly-wise Perker when he remarks to Mr Pickwick that his two
former enemies are

> '... unquestionably penitent now; but then, you know, they have the
> recollection of very recent suffering fresh upon them. What they may
> become, when that fades away, is a problem that neither you nor I can
> solve. However, my dear sir,' added Perker, laying his hand on Mr
> Pickwick's shoulder, 'your object is equally honourable, whatever the
> result is. Whether that species of benevolence which is so very cautious
> and long-sighted that it is seldom exercised at all, lest its owner should
> be imposed upon, and so wounded in his self-love, be real charity or a
> worldly counterfeit, I leave to wiser heads than mine to determine. But
> if those two fellows were to commit a burglary to-morrow, my opinion
> of this action would be equally high.' (ch. liii, p. 746)

And so should ours be, is Dickens's point, made the more emphatic by
being delivered by an unexpectedly eloquent and earnest Perker, thus
ratifying Mr Pickwick's uncalculating charity. Dickens attacks again and
again 'cautious' and 'long-sighted' benevolence, a Benthamite conception which approves good actions as a matter of cold rationality based on
self-interest. Hence, to take a much later case, the approval of Mr
Jarndyce's charity towards Skimpole, good to a fault in its blindness to
the undeserving nature of the recipient. It was an attitude in which
Dickens must have carried along many readers. The *Edinburgh Review*
was quick to salute the tendency of his works to 'make us practically

benevolent' and sympathetic towards the 'aggrieved and suffering in all classes', but without the 'meretricious cant of spurious philosophy' ([Lister], 1838, p. 77). Later, Walter Bagehot explained Dickens's emphasis as the product of a temporary reaction to the 'unfeeling harshness' of the immediately post-Napoleonic period (Bagehot, 1911 edn, Vol, 2, p. 190). In fact, Dickens grew more rather than less interested in encouraging sympathetic benevolence, but he also came to allow that there were forces at work in man and society which had a terrible power to nullify its efficacy. The ambivalence of his final position is suggested by his depiction, in the last complete novel, of a character who turns suddenly from open-hearted benevolence to cunning calculation, only to have this finally revealed as – we have to believe it – a well-intentioned trick: Noddy Boffin, in *Our Mutual Friend*.

VI

The attitude of the *Edinburgh Review* towards 'spurious philosophy' was not all that Dickens would have shared with it. In the days before *Pickwick Papers*, when Dickens was probably reading this and other reviews as a young reporter intent on educating himself, the *Review* was typically fulminating against the 'immediate and intolerable mischief in turning God's service from the heart, and from actions of piety and virtue, to the improbable, unnecessary, and useless forms "of a fantastic and hypochondriacal religion"' ([Empson], 1831, p. 304). In short, against Stigginsism, or evangelical cant. It would be foolish to ignore this aspect of *Pickwick Papers*, or the contemporary reality out of which it sprang, if only because of the heated response it generated – and still generates – among the religiously committed. Even the sympathetic Methodist minister in Philadelphia who wrote to Dickens in 1867 to say that he had 'learned more of the divine in man' from his works 'than from the divines themselves' went on to complain in person that the 'satirical dress' with which the novelist had clothed some of his religious characters, namely, Stiggins, Chadband and Mrs Clennam, would lead many, 'especially the young and uncultivated, to treat the strictest types of Christian conduct with suspicion'. Dickens seems likely to have shared the suspicions of the young and uncultivated in this respect. He replied to the clergyman:

> My view has been to make transparent the design of my writings, and my belief is that by my readers generally I am perfectly understood. Ours is an age of great religious activity. There is much zeal for the common cause of Christianity, but more for the success of particular denominations. Rivalry added to zeal has led to the employment of

improper persons as Christian teachers. To endeavour to check this tendency seemed to me could not be otherwise than good service to the real truth. (Quoted in Carrow, 1967, pp. 112, 118)

In *Pickwick Papers* his aim was more specifically related to the novel's overall purpose. In contrast with Mr Pickwick, who forgives those who erred against him (although against his will with regard to Mrs Bardell, and not at all with regard to Dodson and Fogg), and tries to relieve their suffering, the representative of religion who should be most sympathetic towards the imprisoned debtors is the red-nosed hypocrite who, on his arrival in the Fleet, delivers an 'edifying discourse for the benefit of the company', adjuring Sam Weller 'in moving terms to be on his guard in that sink of iniquity into which he was cast' (ch. xlv, p. 636; see Illustration 1).

This is precisely the kind of hilarious ironic play on evangelical religious rhetoric which earned for Dickens the opprobrium of some committed readers. Not even his disclaimer a few lines later, that 'false prophets and wretched mockers of religion' such as Stiggins brought 'into partial disrepute large bodies of virtuous and well-conducted persons of many excellent sects and persuasions' (ch. xlv, p. 637), could prevent those many well-conducted persons from feeling they had been tarred with the same brush. For, as the evangelical *Eclectic Review* pointed out on the appearance of *Pickwick Papers*, Dickens had undertaken the 'dangerous task' of making sport of fanaticism when many who did not know what the 'true religion' was might be tempted to apply to 'everything which bears its impress, the name of cant, hypocrisy, and fanaticism' (*Eclectic Review*, n.s., vol. 1, April 1837, p. 354). But what was 'true religion' for the *Eclectic Review* was precisely what Dickens thought liable to lead to cant, hypocrisy and fanaticism. The 'true religion' of *Pickwick Papers*, reflected in Mr Pickwick's innocent fall, conceives of human nature as essentially innocent and benevolent; whereas the evangelical position, as enunciated by William Wilberforce's famous *Practical View* (1797), saw mankind as 'fallen creatures, born in sin, and naturally depraved', and Christianity as a system which recognised 'no innocence or goodness of heart, but in the remission of sin, and in the effects of the operation of Divine grace' (Wilberforce, 1834 edn, p. 284). This stark message was not one which Dickens could support, and so, inevitably, alluding to the Fleet as a 'sink of iniquity' could not be other than hypocritical cant for him. Later critics have obscured this fundamental point in much the same way as the *Eclectic Review*: Valentine Cunningham, for instance, who finds Dickens's treatment of cant in *Pickwick Papers* 'unalleviated' by a glimpse of 'true religion', that is, again, evangelical Christianity (Cunningham, 1975, p. 15).

1 'The red-nosed man discourseth' (*Pickwick Papers*, ch. xlv, p. 637), by 'Phiz' (Hablot K. Browne).

More serious is the charge that the novelist, in his zeal to expose fanaticism and hypocrisy, 'unconsciously' ridicules 'doctrines and expressions which do not originate with the extravagancies of enthusiasts, but are part and parcel of the sacred Scripture' (*Eclectic Review*, n.s., vol. 1, April 1837, p. 355) - namely, the idea of being 'born again', which the elder Weller claims his second wife has 'got hold of'. Humphry House remarks that the allusion made Dickens seem little more than 'a clever journalist playing to the drunk Church-and-King mobs hired to jeer at Wesleyans' (House, 1942, p. 114); and this at least recognises, what is true, that Dickens was aiming at a fairly specific area

of contemporary belief, rather than at the doctrine of rebirth itself.
Indeed, he was to make this a central theme in his work during the 1840s.
'That every man who seeks heaven must be born again, in good thoughts
of his Maker, I sincerely believe', he wrote in 1843 (Pilgrim *Letters*, Vol.
3, p. 485), defending himself in terms not necessarily heterodox: Christ
told Nicodemus, 'Except a man be born again, he cannot see the kingdom
of God', and explained the rebirth as 'of water and of the Spirit' (John 3:
3–5); Paul wrote 'be ye transformed by the renewing of your mind, that
ye may prove what is that good, and acceptable, and perfect will of God'
(Romans 12:2). Dickens was putting in plain words a complex and subtle
spiritual demand, the force of which he did seem to feel, and criticism of
him on this point has been misguided. Apart from the unlikelihood of
Dickens ever supporting a pro-Establishment mob, House (and those
who follow his line) completely misses the traditional fun which
characterises the Stiggins–Weller relationship, and which comes to an
apt conclusion when the self-seeking deputy Shepherd receives baptism
by total immersion in a horse trough from the explosive elder
Weller.

The Stiggins sub-plot is closely bound up with the Wellers from the
start. Their subversive cockney humour establishes the basic tone of
Dickens's treatment of evangelical cant in the novel, and it is a form of
humour which is rooted in a long tradition of popular anti-clerical and
anti-religious satire going back to the medieval fabliaux. It is a post-
Reformation development to associate religion inexorably with solemnity, a development which continued well into the nineteenth century,
when the new puritanism of the evangelicals reasserted the impropriety
of laughing at godliness. For the *Eclectic Review*, fanaticism and
hypocrisy might exist, but they should *never* be made the subject of 'mere
jest'. For Dickens, high seriousness and folk humour could intermingle,
especially when he wished to attack what he saw as an abuse. Thus, the
exchange between Sam Weller and his father on the subject of Sam's
'mother-in-law' must be taken as a comic interlude, as innocuous fun:

'How's mother-in-law this mornin'?'

'Queer, Sammy, queer,' replied the elder Mr Weller, with
impressive gravity. 'She's been gettin' rayther in the Methodistical
order lately, Sammy; and she is uncommon pious, to be sure. She's too
good a creetur for me, Sammy. I feel I don't deserve her.'

'Ah,' said Mr Samuel, 'that's wery self-denyin' o' you.'

'Wery,' replied his parent, with a sigh. 'She's got hold o' some
inwention for grown up people being born again, Sammy, the new
birth, I thinks they calls it. I should wery much like to see that system
in haction, Sammy. I should wery much like to see your mother-in-law
born again. Wouldn't I put her out to nurse!' (ch. xxii, p. 297)

Mr Weller's literal interpretation of the doctrine is, in fact, not far from Nicodemus's error: 'How can a man be born when he is old? can he enter the second time into his mother's womb, and be born?' (John 3:4). But Mr Weller's function here is to act as a subversive, proletarian Pickwick, equally subject to the monstrous regiment of widows.

This is also reflected in the fact that Mrs Weller turns out to be the forerunner of a whole tribe of deluded matrons, whose religious excesses perplex their menfolk and lead to domestic discord. Some are weak 'vessels', like Mrs Nubbles, others are stronger, like Mrs MacStinger or Mrs Varden, or more complex portraits such as Miss Murdstone and Mrs Clennam, cold and heartless exemplars of where evangelical rigidity might lead. But what, exactly, is Mrs Weller, theologically speaking? Mrs Nubbles and Mrs MacStinger may be Dissenters; Mrs Varden, Miss Murdstone and Mrs Clennam, Church of England; but Mrs Weller's association is 'Methodistical'. What does this term mean? According to the *OED*, 'Of or pertaining to the Methodists or Methodism; usually with a disparaging implication'. And this is how, for example, the Anglican *Christian Spectator* later took it (n.s., vol. 6, December 1865, p. 722), remarking that Dickens could only account for Methodism by 'conceiving of a Stiggins'. It may be that Anglican readers were intended to take it this way: even had he wanted to, Dickens would have found it much less acceptable to satirise a Church of England parson so brutally, whereas the Methodists were an easy target, after decades of abuse, most of it aimed at the untrained, uneducated and, to their social superiors if not their own class, often unappealing ministers. George Whitefield, former tapster at the Bell Inn, Gloucester, 'did most to create the image of the Methodist preacher'; he was a fierce and dramatic Calvinist with an unfortunate squint, rough manners, much vanity and a habit of appealing for money to supply his 'tabernacles', all of which it was only too easy for Anglican critics to attack (see Lyles, 1960). Whereas he was convinced that God had from eternity predestined the majority of mankind to damnation, and a few to salvation through Christ, the Wesleys remained convinced that Christ had died for all men. The Calvinistic Methodists therefore held a doctrine which Dickens opposed, unlike the Wesleyan or Arminian branch (a distinction House's rash comment also misses). In addition, the Calvinistic Methodists tended to be more puritanical, and were in closer contact with the development of the Evangelical party within the Church than the Wesleyans.

The earliest use of the term 'Methodistical' noted by the *OED* makes its derivation plain, as well as offering a likely source for Dickens's application of it. The word appears in *Tom Jones*, one of the works which, as we know, 'kept alive' Dickens's youthful imagination (*David Copperfield*, ch. iv, p. 55). Jones and Partridge are brought to Whitefield's actual birthplace, the Bell Inn, Gloucester, where they meet a Mrs Whitefield, wife to the brother of the famous preacher, a woman who is 'at present as free from Methodistical opinions as her husband'. But, adds Fielding,

> I say at present: for she freely confesses that her brother's documents made at first some impression upon her, and that she had put herself to the expence of a long hood, in order to attend the extraordinary emotions of the Spirit; but having found, during an experiment of three weeks, no emotions, she says, worth a farthing, she very wisely laid by her hood, and abandoned the sect. (bk 8, ch. 8)

This three-week experiment may well be the source of Mrs Weller's rather lengthier entanglement with Methodism, if that is what it is, terminated in her case only by her final illness when, as her husband reports to Sam, she began to see

> 'that if a married 'ooman vishes to be religious, she should begin vith dischargin' her dooties at home, and makin' them as is about her cheerful and happy, and that vile she goes to church, or chapel, or wot not, at all proper times, she should be wery careful not to con-wert this sort o' thing into a excuse for idleness or self-indulgence.' (ch. lii, p. 733, and see Illustration 2)

At this late stage in the narrative Dickens seems to be arguing against *any* kind of religious zeal which might interfere with wifely 'dooties'. Fielding would have agreed with Dickens's stress on muted piety as opposed to 'enthusiasm'; but he associated disruptive zeal specifically with the 'pernicious principles of Methodism',[2] whereas Dickens seems to have something broader in mind.

On the other hand, Dickens certainly encourages us to think of Mrs Weller as Methodist at first, not only by means of the allusion to the 'new birth' doctrine which was central to Methodism, but also by following this with an account of a traditionally Methodist 'love feast'. These were not fixed in form, and the 'feast' (cake and water) was of less significance than the spiritual testimony from individuals which was supposed to follow. In Tony Weller's hilarious account, we see what humbug was possible, with events initiated by a 'kiss of peace' from the Shepherd (an early Chadband, 'with a great white face, a smilin' avay like clockwork'), followed by a hymn, then 'such a grace, such eatin' and drinkin''', and finally, amidst much groaning, the cry 'Where is the sinner; where is the mis'rable sinner?' addressed to that 'wessel of wrath', the elder Weller, who responds by knocking the Shepherd down, to the utter confusion of the ladies (ch. xxii, pp. 297-9).

Contemporary confirmation of the 'screams, the shouts, the jarring

2 'Mother-in-law . . . how are you?' (*Pickwick Papers*, ch. xxvii,
p. 367). Artist unknown, *Pickwickian Illustrations* (1837). Note
print above mantelpiece, preacher addressing 'copper-coloured
people' (*Pickwick Papers*, ch. xxvii, p. 371).

songs, the disorders and indecencies' into which Methodist revival
meetings sometimes fell may be found in *The Life of Joseph Barker,
Written by Himself* ([Barker], 1880, pp. 185–91).Barker was brought up a
Wesleyan and became an itinerant preacher for the New Connexion until
in 1841 he turned to Unitarianism, then finally returned to Methodism as
a Primitive Methodist preacher. That Dickens had Methodists in mind,
and indeed quite probably the Primitive Methodists, is indicated by the
pineapple rum aspect of Stigginsism, which reaches its climax at that
meeting of the Brick Lane Branch of the United Grand Junction
Ebenezer Temperance Association which has the predictably sleek and
perspiring Anthony Humm in the chair, 'a converted fireman, now a
schoolmaster, and occasionally an itinerant preacher' (ch. xxxiii, p. 457).
In contrast to the main body of the movement, which was more moderate
about the pleasures of the flesh, the Primitive Methodists called for
complete abstinence, a call which inevitably led to dramatic backslidings
among weaker brethren (Chadwick, 1970, pt 1, pp. 390–1; Payne, 1965,
p. 113).

In response to a complaint about this 'libel', Dickens later confessed
that he knew little of the temperance movement at the time (Styles,
1909). But he was always in favour of 'moderate' drinking, and against
what he saw as the interfering puritanism of those who believed in
abstinence. This is reflected in, for example, his treatment of Stephen
Blackpool's degraded wife in *Hard Times*, or the pathetic father of the
dolls' dressmaker in *Our Mutual Friend*, as it is in his antagonism towards
those who would refuse the working man his drink on a Sunday. The
reintroduction of Sir Andrew Agnew's Bill against the 'desecration' of
the Sabbath in April 1836 was a signal example of religious hypocrisy
directed against 'the amusements and recreations of the poor' who would
be more likely to drink to excess on a Sunday made a day of 'general
gloom and austerity' than on a day of family excursions and sports (*UT &
RP*, pp. 649, 652). Tolerance and moderation were his watchwords, in
this respect as in others, although, it may be said, he hardly shows much
tolerance towards the Methodists or Methodism in *Pickwick Papers*, for
all that he seems otherwise sympathetic to popular belief. If the
exploitation of the weak and ignorant by some of these preachers was
undeniable, it was also true that 'some of them had gifts no education
could have given': while their religion was 'simple and crude', it brought
more 'comfort and support' to its followers than the Church was able to
provide (Thompson, 1976 edn, pp. 218–19). That Dickens does not
recognise this – the placing contrast is George Eliot's *Adam Bede* – seems
a failure on his part.

On the other hand, this is oversimplifying a little. The Stiggins–Weller
scenes are *satire*, and, as Swift remarked, satire is 'a sort of *glass*, wherein
beholders do generally discover anybody's face but their own' ('Preface

of the Author', *The Battle of the Books*, 1710), and Dickens was trading on this by allowing his readers to blame the Methodists (or, more easily, the Primitive Methodists), while at the same time gradually infiltrating his more fundamental objections to the misdirection of energy apparent among zealots in general. This explains the generalised nature of Mrs Weller's deathbed recantation. It also explains Tony Weller's reflections on those flocks who make clothes for 'copper-coloured people as don't want 'em', taking no notice of 'flesh-coloured Christians as do' (ch. xxvii, p. 371), which identifies an abuse hardly apparent among Methodists alone. That Dickens wished to draw in a much larger area of contemporary religious hypocrisy is suggested, too, by his outburst on Muggleton,

> an ancient and loyal borough, mingling a zealous advocacy of Christian principles with a devoted attachment to commercial rights; in demonstration whereof, the mayor, corporation, and other inhabitants, have presented at divers times, no fewer than one thousand four hundred and twenty petitions against the continuance of negro slavery abroad, and an equal number against any interference with the factory system at home; sixty-eight in favour of the sale of livings in the Church, and eighty-six for abolishing Sunday trading in the street. (ch. vii, pp. 87–8).

Dickens focuses on evangelical hypocrisy, just as Cobbett did before him – the Cobbett who wrote an *Exposure of the Pretended Friends of the Blacks* in 1830. As for the Factory Act, there had been evangelicals on both sides, although there were also some whose guilty feelings over conditions in England had perhaps been displaced to a concern for foreign blacks, as Dickens implies here (Halévy, 1961, p. 115, note 1). The novelist no doubt added to this memories of parish meetings he had reported for the *Morning Chronicle*, at which the 'odious and oppressive tithe system' was attacked for its tendency to bring religion and its ministers into contempt (5 December 1834). Muggleton's weakness upon the corruption of the Church (the sale of livings and ecclesiastical sinecures led to Peel's Ecclesiastical Commission at this time), linked with its enthusiasm for abolishing competitive street-trading on Sundays, suggests the kind of Sabbatarianism Dickens attacks in *Sunday Under Three Heads*, a mingling of commercial and religious impulses which he felt certain lay behind Sir Andrew Agnew's notorious Bill.

It is important to be clear about the aim of Dickens's satire which, although it has its specific targets, has ultimately a more general, and therefore more persuasive, object. The term 'Methodistical', which Dickens applies to Mrs Weller's association with Stiggins, had long become virtually synonymous with 'evangelical'. As long ago as 1808,

Sydney Smith's notorious and influential articles on Methodism in the
Edinburgh Review did not trouble with the 'finer shades' of 'lunacy',
treating Calvinist and Arminian, Methodist and Evangelical, as all 'in
one general conspiracy against common sense, and rational orthodox
Christianity' (Sydney Smith, 1859 edn, Vol. 1, p. 88). Without
suggesting that Dickens was quite so undiscriminating, it is evident that
he would have been considered one of those 'Men of Taste' which the
evangelical John Foster identified in 1830 as showing their aversion to his
form of religion equally by the terms 'Fanatical, Calvinistical,
Methodistical' (Foster, 1889 edn, p. 194). Stigginsism, or evangelical
cant in general, was the evil, rather than any single sect, group, or
persuasion.

VII

Evil in *Pickwick Papers* is severely limited in scope. It exists only in the
(delightful) machinations of a strolling player using the gullibility and
snobbery of others to keep himself alive; in the hypocrisy and self-
seeking of provincial press and society; and in the scandalous, but not
overwhelming, injustices of religion and the law. Mr Pickwick is, in
effect, the innocent purveyor of his author's evangelising intentions on
behalf of a fundamentally optimistic outlook on life, an outlook which
Dickens always tried to preserve, although he could perhaps never again
do so with quite the buoyant conviction of *Pickwick Papers*.

It is only in a fairly broad sense that Dickens's preoccupations in this
first novel may be called religious. The difficulty of defining his position
with any accuracy is the same as with the eighteenth-century novelists
upon whose works he was nurtured, and some of whose basic
assumptions he absorbed, in the absence of any more powerful guidance
from his Laodicean family. Like Henry Fielding (after whom he was to
name one of his sons), he believed that innocent good nature rather than a
subtle moral intelligence on the one hand, or an ardent belief in the
depravity of unredeemed man on the other, was what made the good
man. As Fielding defined it:

> Good-Nature is that benevolent and amiable Temper of Mind which
> disposes us to feel the Misfortunes and enjoy the Happiness of others;
> and consequently pushes us on to promote the latter, and prevent the
> former; and that without any abstract Contemplation on the Beauty of
> Virtue, and without the Allurements or Terrors of Religion. (Quoted
> in B. Harrison, 1975, p. 89)

This may seem pre-religious, hardly a part of any recognisable structure of belief. Yet there is a specific religious dimension to it; the innate predisposition to virtue underlying Fielding's Parson Adams or Squire Allworthy derives from the doctrines of Latitudinarian divines such as John Tillotson – whom Dickens knew of (Coutts *Letters*, p. 106) – and who constructed an alternative to the view of this world as a vale of tears, inhabited by a race of men irremediably corrupt. The creation of Mr Pickwick, as of his several successors, Brownlow, the Cheerybles and Jarndyce, stems ultimately from the same source. Dickens's humanitarianism is not thereby unChristian, much less irreligious. It is of a kind with the broad, unorthodox position of Fielding before him. Where Dickens comes to side most obviously with the evangelicals is in his reformist urge. For him, too, in the end, cheerfulness and goodwill, though essential, are not sufficient, but must be translated into something more practical. The prime virtue becomes charity. Hence, when Mr Pickwick leaves the Fleet, turning to look at the throng of debtors gathered to see him off, we are told that in 'all the crowd of wan, emaciated faces, he saw not one which was not the happier for his sympathy and charity' (ch. xlvii, p. 666).

2

Oliver Twist and Charity

I know what charity is, better than to give to vagabonds.
(Parson Trulliber in Henry Fielding, *Joseph Andrews*, 1742, Bk 2, ch. 14)

Then cherish pity; lest you drive an angel from your door.
(William Blake, 'Holy Thursday', *Songs of Innocence and Experience*, 1789, 1794)

I

The fundamental aim of *Oliver Twist* (1837–9) is to move us, as Mr Pickwick was moved in the Fleet, into sympathy and charity for the poor. To realise this aim, Dickens reveals their sufferings to us, since, as Henry Fielding put it (1753, pp. 9–10):

> The Sufferings of the Poor are indeed less observed than their Misdeeds; not from any Want of Compassion, but because they are less known; and this is the true Reason why we so often hear them mentioned with Abhorrence, and so seldom with Pity ... They starve, and freeze, and rot among themselves; but they beg, and steal, and rob among their Betters.

Coming from a kind of good Mr Fang, a London magistrate who was an active social reformer with an expert knowledge of the poor, this has much force. Dickens, too, later wished to become a magistrate, so as to concern himself practically with the affairs of the metropolitan poor, who were always 'his clients' (Forster, 1928, pp. 347, 388). But in *Oliver Twist* this concern is expressed less directly, if no less urgently, by obliging us to observe their wretched lives through the medium of his tale of one pauper orphan set in a world of workhouse and slum barely touched on in *Pickwick Papers*.

Whereas in *Pickwick Papers* the innocent hero is only temporarily confined to prison in order to glimpse the sufferings of the poor, in *Oliver Twist* the oblivious Oliver is actually born in a kind of prison (the workhouse), and is repeatedly forced against his will into a world of indigence and vice. Taken out of the hands of the workhouse authorities who imprison him for asking for more, he is soon sold into apprenticeship to the parish undertaker, a career which begins in a 'stone cell' (ch. iv, p. 24); while his life in London may be said to start with the threat of imprisonment for theft, a threat he escapes only to be recaptured by the gang of thieves trying to train him for a criminal future. This recurrent pattern of imprisonment (vividly realised in David Lean's 1948 film version of the novel) exercises a powerful grip on us, so that we are quite ready to allow Oliver escapist fantasies of 'a calm and lasting sleep in a churchyard ground: with the tall grass waving gently above his head: and the sound of the old deep bell to soothe him in his sleep' (ch. v, p. 26). But the overall mood of *Oliver Twist* is more like one long, oppressive nightmare.

However, we should not be misled into detecting in this pervasive darkness of tone what Graham Greene called 'the eternal and alluring taint of the Manichee, with its simple and terrible explanation of our plight, how the world was made by Satan, and not by God' (Greene, 1970 edn, p. 86). It is true, as Greene points out, that this forbidding atmosphere is strikingly reinforced by the diabolic overtones surrounding the red-haired 'old gentleman' Fagin, Oliver's main antagonist, and by the comparatively weak depiction of goodness in his benefactors, Mrs Brownlow and the Maylies. But it is unlikely that Dickens should so soon – indeed, almost simultaneously – contradict the ultimately hopeful view of human destiny expressed in *Pickwick Papers*. More probably, the orderly, tolerant, finally *secure* world of *Pickwick Papers* has been overtaken by the novelist's awareness that reality is more varied and unstable, even frightening, than he was at first prepared to admit. Moments in which evil becomes terrifyingly close as a force in life are no longer relegated to interpolated tales, subsidiary fictions, but are made central to the main narrative itself. Evil is now directly faced, and by no means easily subdued. It is one of the abiding strengths of Dickens's vision of life that, unlike most of his great contemporaries in the English novel, such as Thackeray, George Eliot, or Trollope, he had a profound apprehension of evil which extended beyond the domestic or even social.

This is not to ignore (as Greene and later critics ignore) the fact that the hero of *Oliver Twist* is, finally, *saved*. He is saved by the sympathy and charity, the freely given loving aid of those good Christians (explicitly identified as such) into whose hands he is cast 'by a stronger hand than chance' (ch. xlix, p. 335). If God permits evil to flourish in *Oliver Twist* – and there can be no denying the *initial* power of the parish authorities, of Fagin and his gang – then he also ensures its ultimate failure and destruction. The turning-point is quite clear: not only do we see Bumble, symbol of parish authority, reduced and humbled by his wife (ch. xxxvii), but Sikes and Nancy pale, cadaverous and ill (ch. xxxix, pp.

256–7), after Oliver's recovery with the Maylies. Thenceforward, evil is set on a downward path. It is too simple to be overwhelmed by Oliver's earlier suffering, and to forget that, far from sharing the fate of that other parish orphan, little Dick, he is to survive and flourish in the end. Dickens's intention is expressed in the 1841 Preface, the most extended defence of any of his works. He 'wished to show', he said, 'in little Oliver, the principle of Good surviving through every adverse circumstance, and triumphing at last'. He continues to believe not only in the ultimately hopeful ordering of human affairs, despite the suffering of the poor and destitute, but also in the existence of good as a transcendental value, a 'principle' to be embodied in symbolic or 'romantic', rather than realistic form. In *Oliver Twist* Dickens moves towards the expression of both good and evil as forces having their origin beyond the material world, so that in reading the novel we are often aware of some metaphysical drama hovering about the events of the surface-narrative. When Fagin tells Sikes of his plan for using the innocent Oliver for the Chertsey robbery which will in fact turn into their downfall, he cries:

> '... Once let him feel that he is one of us; once fill his mind with the idea that he has been a thief; and he's ours! Ours for his life! Oho! It couldn't have come about better!'
> 'Ours!' said Sikes. 'Yours, you mean.'
> 'Perhaps I do, my dear,' said the Jew, with a shrill chuckle. (ch. xix, p. 126)

Fagin is interested in more than the exploitation of one 'chalk-faced kid' (which is all he is, in realistic terms) for gain: he wants Oliver's soul.

It is by means of charity that goodness ultimately triumphs in *Oliver Twist*. This is the central theme, explored in both its private and (no less important) public aspects. Dickens expresses the belief that, at the last, acts of individual love, sympathy and goodwill may provide for the suffering poor, if not the thoroughly wicked, and that it is the duty of good Christians to carry out such acts; while the public manifestation of this duty, supposedly encouraged by church and state amd embodied in the Poor Laws, he shows to derive from no truly Christian spirit, but rather from the coldly well-meaning, yet inhumane attitudes sponsored by Malthusian and Benthamite 'philosophy'. As John Overs, the working man whom Dickens helped with his literary endeavours, put it: 'Better to sin on the side of sympathy and benevolence than with the ferocious spirit of Utilitarianism and Expedience. *That* is indeed a poisoned valley from which Hope flies, Love enters not; and which Charity and a good honest heart fears and detests' (quoted in Sheila Smith, 1974, p. 203).

Charity is, of course a Christian virtue, and Dickens treats it as such.

In so far as *Oliver Twist* insists upon its importance in meeting the needs of the poor, the novel carries a more noticeably Christian hue than most of his fictional works, except perhaps the Christmas Books and the last novels. The term means more than the simple human virtue of benevolence, or giving alms to the poor; it implies the more general motive of Christian love, expressed as a love of God and one's neighbour. This distinction has been used (for example, by Houghton, 1957, p. 275) to argue that Dickens's charitable characters are not strictly Christian in their performance of benevolent acts towards others, since these seem no more than spontaneous expressions of their good nature, rather than reflections of a will dedicated to God. But Dickens wishes to avoid the premeditativeness of doing good as a duty, as well as any hint of excess – or even merely open – piety, preferring a modest, self-effacing, yet direct goodness which emerges as the natural expression of the personality. He reveals virtue implicitly, in terms of the essential being of a character, rather than in terms of its motivation. If his good people love God – and he often implies that they do – this is revealed only implicitly, through imagery and action, and not by allotting characters overtly Christian motives.

For Dickens, charity is 'the one great cardinal virtue, which, properly nourished and exercised, leads to, if it does not necessarily include, all the others' (*Nicholas Nickleby*, ch. xviii, p. 215). Nourishing and exercising charity involves other people: it is a social as well as a Christian virtue. St Paul (I Corinthians 13) provides a comprehensive account of it as an impulse directed primarily towards God, but Christ made it clear that we owe it to ourselves, and our neighbours too, as the objects of God's love (Matthew 22:37-40). Who exactly are our neighbours? Dickens pointedly alludes to the parable Christ used to supply the answer, when he has the parish beadle explain that the 'porochial seal' on the brass buttons embellishing his coat is a representation of the Good Samaritan 'healing the sick and bruised man' (ch. iv, p. 21). The parable enjoins us to succour him who 'fell among thieves' (Luke 10:29-37). Oliver, plainly, falls among thieves. But his needs are evident before he does so: from the moment of his arrival in the world, a nameless, illegitimate orphan, he is left to 'the tender mercies of churchwardens and overseers' (ch. i, p. 3). The opening chapters of the novel constitute a fiercely satirical attack upon those public authorities who signally fail to care for the poor in their charge, in direct contradiction to the message of their seal. The social dimension of this has been well accounted for, but the religious dimension has been largely ignored. This is despite Dickens's attempts to suggest it, by means of his allusion to the Good Samaritan, despite, too, the involvement of contemporary religious figures in the revision of the Poor Laws which was particularly the object of his attack.

II

To understand and respond to this aspect of *Oliver Twist*, it is essential to clarify the immediately topical, historical situation which inspired the opening chapters. It may seem that this has been sufficiently expounded by, for instance, Humphry House, whose very thorough analysis in *The Dickens World* has been adopted by most later critics. But there is more to Dickens's attack upon the Poor Laws than has so far been made apparent. Dickens was tapping a specific contemporary source in the newspapers of the time for the views, even, to some extent, the techniques, adopted in his anti-Poor Law satire; and the way in which he transformed fact into fiction has not been fully accounted for, much less the relation of all this to a growing distrust of the religious establishment.

It is generally assumed that Dickens, as a young parliamentary reporter, must have heard, and so drawn on for *Oliver Twist*, the debates on the New Poor Law. In fact, debates on this new legislation during the period when he was actually in Parliament (1834–6) were relatively slight, since the Whig government hurried the reform through in a mere six months early in 1834, and thorough parliamentary discussion began only with the motion (proposed by John Walter of *The Times*) in February 1837 for a Select Committee to inquire into the working of the new law (see Young and Hancock, 1956, p. 695). This was the month in which *Oliver Twist* began appearing in *Bentley's Miscellany*, which reveals in what sense exactly Dickens's 'glance at the new poor Law Bill' (Pilgrim *Letters*, Vol. 1, p. 231: 28 January 1837) was topical. The early months of 1837 marked the extension of the New Poor Law into the London metropolitan area, arousing great popular controversy, as the pages of the *Morning Chronicle* or *The Times* testify.[1] It seems likely that it was these events, rather than the early debates on, or even the actual passing of, the new law, which directly inspired the writing of the novel. Dickens must have been very soon aware of the broader implications of the Bill: he later recalled how he and the editor of the *Morning Chronicle*, John Black, used to quarrel about its effects, the paper having been acquired in 1834 by the Whig John Easthope in order to support the Bill (Pilgrim *Letters*, Vol. 3, p. 275: 29 April 1841). His views were much closer to those of *The Times* which, under Walter's direction, consistently opposed the Bill and its results, becoming a veritable 'compendium of poor-law crimes', not all of them based on real evidence (see Roberts, 1963, p. 98). A typical leader of February 1837 refers to the 'BENTHAMITE cant' then current according to which the policy designed to produce '*the greatest happiness to the greatest number*' was 'unquestionably' the best, yet was 'most difficult to reconcile with Christianity or civilization' (2 February 1837, p. 4). This contrast between the utilitarian cant of the 'philosophers' and the claims of Christian civilisation runs right through *The Times*'s criticism, in leading articles, letters, even fiction – extracts from *Oliver Twist*'s opening chapters were published as soon as they appeared. Even if Dickens did attend some of the early debates on the new law, most of his information, as well as a confirmation of his basic position, was probably derived from *The Times*. The narrator who remarks of the members of the 'board' who bring in the new 'system' in *Oliver Twist* that they are 'very sage, deep, philosophical men' (ch. ii, p. 9) shares the tone and attitude of the newspaper which opened its extracts from the novel with the same words ([Dickens], 1837, p. 3).

At the same time, Dickens is careful to purge his work of specific dates, places, or names – even the fictional 'Mudfog', used for Oliver's place of birth, he drops after its first appearance. He tries to avoid the accusation of bias and sensationalism inevitable when dealing with such a live issue, by avoiding the explicitness of a journalist – or of a typical 'social problem' novelist such as Frances Trollope, who clumsily attempted to deal with the renewed New Poor Law in her *Jessie Phillips* (1843). Dickens could not entirely avoid such accusations – *The Examiner* criticised his 'unworthy' use of the 'bugbears of popular prejudice' ([Forster?], 1837, p. 581) – but he was successful in preferring symbolic generalisation to detailed analysis in his treatment of the law. His art is an art of implication, not explication.

This does not mean that our reading of the novel cannot be helped by teasing out some of its more specific implications – for instance, in relation to the bastardy issue, of obvious relevance to Oliver's plight. The new law set out to abolish the traditional duty laid on parishes since Elizabethan times to 'search for the father' of illegitimate children in their care. Oliver, it seems, is born before the passing of the new law, so 'the most superlative, and, I may say, supernat'ral exertions', if we can believe Bumble, have been made to discover 'who is his father, or what was his mother's settlement, name or con-dition' (ch. ii, p. 7) – but in vain (a glance at the complicated unravelling of Oliver's family history towards the end of his story suggests a reason for this failure). However, the new 'system' which comes into being after Oliver's return from the branch workhouse introduces, in addition to the notorious dietary restrictions, regulations which 'instead of compelling a man to support his family, as they had heretofore done, took his family away from him, and made him a bachelor!' (ch. ii, p. 10). Fathers need no longer be sought after, and so the 'natural' Christian ties between parents and children are denied. Dickens emphasises the sanctity of the family in such a way as to *include* illegitimate children such as Oliver – or Rose Maylie, who carries the 'shame' of illegitimacy despite the fact that, as we later learn, this was a mere slander (ch. li, p. 355). When the truth about Oliver and Rose finally emerges, they share a 'sacred' embrace, for 'A father, sister, and mother, were gained, and lost, in that one moment' (ch.

li, p. 356). Dickens endorses Harry Maylie's sacrifice of parliamentary ambition in order to marry the apparently 'stained' Rose, just as he endorses Mr Brownlow's correction of Monks's use of the phrase 'bastard child' for Oliver, a reproach to those 'long since passed beyond the feeble censure of the world', reflecting 'disgrace on no one living, except you who use it' (ch. li, p. 350). Not for Oliver or Rose – any more than for other illegitimates such as Esther Summerson in *Bleak House* – the stigma laid down by the Old Testament: 'A bastard shall not enter into the congregation of the Lord; even to his tenth generation shall he not enter into the congregation of the Lord' (Deuteronomy 23:2). Dickens consciously aligns himself against the contemporary puritan attitude to sexual morality which had developed since the seventeenth century, but which was given new force by the evangelicals, to the effect that children begotten in sin would inherit their parents' weakness. So he concludes *Oliver Twist* by having his two orphans visit a memorial stone 'within the altar' of the old village church, a stone hallowed to the memory of Oliver's mother, and where her 'shade' may hover, for all that she was 'weak and erring' (ch. liii, p. 368).

The strength of contemporary feeling about the bastardy clause, and, indeed, about the whole attempt of the New Poor Law to 'break those bonds which naught but death should break', may be gauged from the complaint of 'Honest Jack' to John Gotch, first guardian elected under the new law in Northamptonshire, in a letter of 26 March 1838: it was difficult to understand, he wrote, 'how High Professors of the religion of him who went about doing good, can act like those brutal beings in the West Indies and tear asunder Fathers, Mothers, and Children the same time they read the command to love one another' (quoted in Tate, 1951, pp. 237–8). Most conspicuous of these 'High Professors' was Bishop Blomfield of London, since it was he who chaired the commission whose report into the Poor Laws recommended throwing out 'search for the father', and the separation of families in the new workhouses; it was he who, when it came to debate the new Bill in the House of Lords with fellow prelate Phillpotts of Exeter, argued as strongly as he could in favour of the report's original recommendations on bastardy, and against any compromise. As *The Times* reported, he was in favour of regulations which 'would make workhouses schools of moral reformation, and not of moral degradation' (1 August 1834, p. 3). Doubtless Blomfield had in mind the familiar horrors of the old 'general mixed' workhouse, in which the sick, the elderly, the insane, the unemployed and children all lived together. For him, the old law regarding illegitimacy put a premium on perjury and unchastity; the new law would sweep all this away in a wave of righteousness. And he carried the day, despite having roused so much feeling against himself that he had his speeches corrected and published, hoping to explain to the growing number of critics of the Church how he and several episcopal colleagues could endorse the unChristian measure of driving mothers to the workhouse to support their illegitimate children, thereby separating the family from the father and ruining any future prospects for them.

Blomfield was known to Dickens, who must have been aware that his defence of the bastardy clause was only one facet of 'a continuing campaign to pass legislation correcting the wanton and dissolute behaviour of the lower orders' (Soloway, 1969, p. 174). Although a High Churchman, Blomfield was as dourly moralistic in his attitude to the behaviour of the poor as any evangelical within or outside the Church. His prominence as a Sabbatarian, for instance, earned him the ironic dedication of *Sunday Under Three Heads*, which appeared two years after the clashes over the bastardy issue in the Lords, and eight months before *Oliver Twist*. The dedication concluded:

> That your Lordship would ever have contemplated Sunday recreations with so much horror, if you had been at all acquainted with the wants and necessities of the people who indulged in them, I cannot imagine possible. That a Prelate of your elevated rank has the faintest conception of the extent of those wants, and the nature of those necessities, I do not believe. (*UT & RP*, p. 636)[2]

Dickens's suspicion of the religious establishment's attitude towards the poor, whose spiritual guardian it was supposed to be, is clearly reflected in *Oliver Twist*, where it is a *sin* as well as a crime for an illegitimate pauper orphan to demand charity. Oliver's famous demand for more is followed by a passage generally overlooked: 'For a week after the commission of the impious and profane offence of asking for more, Oliver remained a close prisoner in the dark and solitary room to which he had been consigned by the wisdom and mercy of the board' (ch. iii, p. 12).

'Impious', 'profane', 'wisdom', 'mercy': responsibility extends beyond the politicians and administrators; it is evidently an offence *against Christianity* to ask for more. Churchmen who nominally represented the interests of the poor on the Poor Law Commission and in the House of Lords were quite as eager as Benthamite 'philosophers' like Nassau Senior or Edwin Chadwick to transform workhouses from refugees for the needy and infirm into houses of correction in which unemployed and able-bodied paupers were treated as if they were depraved criminals. What happens to Oliver is an indication of wider social and religious attitudes, of the wider lack of sympathy and charity towards the poverty-stricken.

III

The connection between social and religious implication is central to
Oliver Twist. When the new board interviews Oliver on his arrival from
the branch workhouse:

> 'I hope you say your prayers every night,' said another gentleman in a
> gruff voice; 'and pray for the people who feed you, and take care of you,
> like a Christian.'
>
> 'Yes, sir,' stammered the boy. The gentleman who spoke last was
> unconsciously right. It would have been *very* like a Christian, and a
> marvellously good Christian, too, if Oliver had prayed for the people
> who fed and took care of *him*. But he hadn't, because nobody had
> taught him. (ch. ii, p. 9)

Allowing the board unwittingly to condemn itself for its lack of Christian
charity, Dickens is obvious enough. But he hints at a further lack:
nobody has taught Oliver to pray.

For Dickens, this is a very important lack. According to section 19 of
the New Poor Law, the different religious creeds in a workhouse were to
be protected, and provided with ministers of their own persuasion should
the inmates require it. Not much of a provision. But the commissioners
to be appointed were to add further regulations where they saw fit; and
they saw fit to add considerably. Divine service had to be celebrated in
the workhouse, the Bible and catechism taught, a chaplain appointed;
and Dissenting ministers might visit to teach their own flock (see [Poor
Law Commissioners], 1839, Appendix A, pp. 71ff.). At first, it was ruled
that inmates were not to leave the workhouse on Sundays, one
commissioner reporting that there had on occasion been too many
paupers in the local church, causing complaint by the officiating
clergyman – a sorry state of things indeed ([Poor Law Commissioners],
1836, p. 495). But by 1839 paupers were again allowed to attend church
outside the workhouse. Religion was to be the groundwork of the
education of pauper children, and Edwin Chadwick made sensible
suggestions according to which, for example, clerical discourse might be
adapted to the capacities of the children ([Poor Law Commissioners],
1839, Appendix A, p.79).

Dickens does not completely ignore these provisions. But he hardly
represents them as being favourably executed. Oliver, so far from being
denied 'the advantages of religious consolation' after his offence of asking
for more, finds himself

> kicked into the same apartment every evening at prayer-time, and
> there permitted to listen to, and console his mind with, a general

supplication of the boys: containing a special clause, therein inserted by authority of the board, in which they entreated to be made good, virtuous, contented, and obedient, and to be guarded from the sins and vices of Oliver Twist: whom the supplication distinctly set forth to be under the exclusive patronage and protection of the powers of wickedness, and an article direct from the manufactory of the very Devil himself. (ch. iii, p. 13)

Oliver will shortly find himself under the exclusive patronage of Fagin, directly as a result of his ill-treatment by the parish authorities, the further irony being that this in no way affects his essential goodness. Like Blake, Dickens condemns what he sees as a false religion which imposes upon the innocent the traditional (now evangelically reinforced) doctrine of the depravity of human nature. Nothing infuriated him more than attempts to frighten little sinners into virtue. That there was some truth in his charge may be gathered from the otherwise sympathetic Assistant Commissioner Kay's insistence that some children in the workhouse might be found too depraved to mix with and contaminate their associates ([Poor Law Commissioners], 1839, Appendix A, p. 77).

Dickens shows the Christian alternative when Oliver is taken up by Mr Brownlow and Mrs Bedwin, the latter nursing the sick boy with 'a small Prayer Book and a large nightcap', after which he is revealed, for the first time 'fervently' praying to Heaven (ch. xii, p. 69). We do not actually see him being taught to pray; apparently this is the instantaneous effect of being succoured by good Christians. Later, when he finally arrives in the rural paradise presided over by the Maylies, we learn that he is not only taught his letters by a certain 'white-headed old gentleman' (evidently a retired clergyman of the Dingley Dell stamp), and present at the 'homely' local church on Sundays, after which he carries out *his* charitable duty of calling at the 'clean houses' of local labourers; but that he devotes his Sunday evenings to reading 'a chapter or two from the Bible: which he had been studying all week' (ch. xxxii, p. 211).

The insipid, ideal quality of this vision, beside the vigour of Dickens's attack upon the parish authorities, should not be allowed to obscure the novelist's clear desire to offer an alternative attitude towards teaching religion to pauper children. It will not be the last time when Dickens's conception of goodness emerges as an expression of willed rather than felt belief. But the existence of the will must be acknowledged.

Dickens was critical not only of the New Poor Law as such, but of the whole structure of beliefs concerning the poor which underlay the legal system of his time: 'this ain't the shop for justice', as the Dodger remarks (ch. xliii, p. 300). The link between the social philosophy of the utilitarian political economists and the religious outlook for the evangelicals, implicit in the new regulations, was forged long before their appearance, and not only among economists or evangelical ministers: it had long been the general conviction that the visible inequality of rewards was a part of the Providential plan; that vice and misery were God-given checks upon population growth; above all, that providing relief for the poor was simply interfering with the severe but necessary conditions for social, economic and moral progress (see Poynter, 1969, p. 229). This is implicit in all that happens before the appearance of the board's new 'system'. Oliver's first cry in the workhouse advertises the fact of 'a new burden having been imposed upon the parish' (ch. i, p. 2), a phrasing immediately suggestive of the prevailing attitude. Poverty is a vice to be cured by firmness, not compassion. Oliver's mother's death is brought about as much by the indifference of the authorities as by her fear of disapproval. Found lying in the street, and brought in by the overseer's order, her confinement has been attended by a pauper old woman 'rendered rather misty by an unwonted allowance of beer', and by the parish surgeon, who 'did such matters by contract' (ch. i, pp. 1–2). The ignorant inhumanity of the one, the uncaring professionalism of the other, are summed up in the surgeon's curt: 'It's all over, Mrs Thingummy!'(ch. i, p. 2). Oliver's condition is that of a total outcast, illegitimate and naked, without identity; as such, he represents a fundamental challenge to the authorities to do something about him; they immediately ensure he is 'badged and ticketed' a 'parish child', henceforward to be 'despised by all, and pitied by none' (ch. i, p. 3). Life at the branch workhouse to which he is farmed out confirms this prospect for him, as it does for the 'twenty or thirty other juvenile offenders against the poor-laws', rolling about the floor starving and naked (ch. ii, p. 4). By appropriating the greater part of their weekly stipend for herself, the aptly named Mrs Mann proves herself 'a very great experimental philosopher', remarks Dickens, 'finding in the lowest depth a deeper still' (ch. ii, p. 4).

The new Poor Law did not originate the practices it set out to further, any more than its underlying assumptions were limited to its acknowledged supporters. The only *entirely* new feature was the centralisation of poor relief, which does not concern Dickens in *Oliver Twist*, and the justice of which he may well have appreciated, given the chaotic state of public charity under the old laws (Dickens's opposition to utilitarian philosophy did not extend to its reformist implications; indeed, he warmly supported those such as his friend Dr Southwood Smith, formerly Bentham's private secretary, who were active in housing and public health). The workhouse, the board (as a local, not a national body), the closely watched diet, separation of the sexes, harsh treatment of children, especially the illegitimate – all were present before 1834 (see Aspinall and Smith, 1959, esp. pp. 439–68). Even the abolition of 'search for the father' represents a continuation, rather than a reversal, of earlier attitudes and treatment. It is therefore misguided to assume, as Harriet Martineau and others have done, that Dickens is uncertain or confused, mixing the abuses of the old system with those of the new. Dickens's chronology is hazy, but he was quite clear about the abuses, specific and general, that he wished to attack, as well as about the way to attack them – by a heightening and intensification of reality, not by mere journalism. Nor did his concern subside once the immediate provocation was past: in 1849 he was quick to denounce the continuing inadequacies in the system highlighted by the Tooting baby-farm scandal, calling the place a 'disgrace to a Christian community' ('The Paradise at Tooting', repr. *MP*, p. 146) and to *Our Mutual Friend* he added a postscript condemning the Poor Laws from the time of the Stuarts onwards, after showing in Betty Higden's paranoid fear of public charity what a 'Christian improvement' had been carried out by making 'a pursuing Fury of the Good Samaritan' (bk 3, ch. viii, p. 506).

Mr Bumble is hardly a pursuing Fury; but how far the parish functionary is from fulfilling the demand of the parable of the Good Samaritan may be gathered from his casual remark to the undertaker, Sowerberry, that the unwanted Oliver is 'a dead-weight; a mill-stone, as I may say; round the porochial throat' (ch. iv, p. 21). He unwittingly condemns both himself and those he represents by means of this echo: 'But whoso shall offend one of these little ones which believe in me, it were better for him that a millstone were hanged about his neck, and that he were drowned in the depths of the sea' (Matthew 18:6). As if to confirm the judgement on themselves, the parish are eager that Oliver may come to be hanged, or at least dispatched to sea to be killed (chs iii–iv, pp. 19–20). But the nearest we ever get to what might have happened to Oliver emerges in the fate of his surrogates, little Dick, who dies before escaping the baby-farm, and Noah Claypole, the 'charity-boy' who runs away to London to go on the 'kinchin lay' and who finally becomes, in ironic testimony to encroaching puritanism, an informer against 'charitable publicans' who open on Sundays (ch. liii, p. 366).

Oliver is the touchstone for the lack of mercy and charity in society. His plight absorbs the main force of the narrative, at times to a profoundly moving extent, as when he expresses the agony of his childish grief on being brought away by Bumble from the wretched baby-farm, associated only with deprivation, but containing also his companions in misery: he is, he cries, 'So lonely, sir! So very lonely!' causing even Bumble to lose his composure (ch. iv, p. 23). Isolated from those who can offer him the compassion and security for which he so desperately longs, Oliver is a pitiful and largely passive object. He lacks the vitality of Bumble or even Noah Claypole. But his primary function is to reveal the neglect and corruption of those around him. This is most obvious in the set-piece on 'death and poverty' (running title added in 1867) which follows his apprenticeship to the undertaker, Sowerberry. Taken to the squalid dwelling of a poor family who have suffered a bereavement, Oliver is simply a device whereby we are to be stirred into an awareness of the unobserved 'sufferings of the poor'. Sowerberry, the pauper woman's husband and old mother, four bearers pressed into service from the workhouse and the beadle provide the company for the pauper woman's funeral. They have to hurry, for 'it won't do, to keep the clergyman waiting'. Yet they wait for more than an hour, the two pauper mourners in the rain, before, at length,

> Mr Bumble, and Sowerberry, and the clerk, were seen running towards the grave. Immediately afterwards, the clergyman appeared: putting on his surplice as he came along. Mr Bumble then thrashed a boy or two, to keep up appearances; and the reverend gentleman, having read as much of the burial service as could be compressed into four minutes, gave his surplice to the clerk, and walked away again.
>   'Now, Bill!' said Sowerberry to the grave-digger. 'Fill up!' (ch. v, pp. 33–4)

Dickens makes no comment. He does not have to. And this failure of the Church in relation to one of its fundamental offices for the poor is grounded on more than the novelist's imaginings. According to Marcus Stone, Dickens said to him one day as they were walking in Cooling:

> You see that church? That is where I saw a pauper's funeral in *Oliver Twist*, exactly as it is written in the book. Here is something more interesting still. A few months afterwards I received a letter from the clergyman who behaved in an unseemly way on that occasion, asking me whether I conceived it possible that such a thing could ever occur. I wrote back to him and said, 'Thou art the man.' (M. Stone, 1910, pp. 62–3)[3]

Dickens's criticism of the inadequacy of religious as well as social institutions is more powerful and direct in *Oliver Twist* than in *Pickwick Papers*. Stiggins in the Fleet provides an easy scapegoat by comparison with the anonymous clergyman indicted above. Criticism of the Established Church and its representatives had already begun in Dickens, as his comments in, and dedication to, *Sunday Under Three Heads*, suggest; and there is also the peremptory behaviour of the clergyman in 'The Bloomsbury christening', who has 'two churchings, three christenings, and a funeral' to perform in less than an hour (*Monthly Magazine*, April 1834, repr. in *Sketches by Boz*, p. 476). But the novelist seems to be becoming more aware of the Church's shortcomings. Of course, he was not alone: 'The Church as it now stands, no human power can save', cried Dr Arnold (Stanley, 1845, Vol. I, p. 326: 10 June 1832). Arnold, like Dickens, felt that the narrowness and rigidity of the Evangelicals who seemed to dominate the Church militated against its ability to fulfil the practical, saving role demanded of it by the gospels. He even contemplated addressing the poor directly, by means of a magazine, 'Cobbett-like in style – but Christian in spirit' (ibid., Vol. 1, p. 294: 24 December 1830), an ambition which, in a sense, Dickens fulfilled with the writing of *Oliver Twist* for *Bentley's Miscellany* (although its audience was the more literate middle class, rather than the poor themselves).

Dickens's reproaches to all those who fail to respond to the demands made by Oliver reach their climax with the boy's 'weary catalogue of evils and calamities' which 'hard men had brought upon him', to Mr Losberne and the Maylies. 'Oh!' exclaims the narrator,

> if, when we oppress and grind our fellow-creatures, we bestowed but one thought on the evidences of human error, which, like dense and heavy clouds, are rising, slowly it is true, but not less surely, to Heaven, to pour their after-vengeance on our heads; if we heard but one instant, in imagination, the deep testimony of dead men's voices, which no power can stifle, and no pride shut out; where would be the injury and injustice: the suffering, misery, cruelty, and wrong: that each day's life brings with it! (ch. xxx, p. 193)

Fusing an almost evangelical earnestness of tone with his Romantic vision of the day of judgement, Dickens utters an appeal on behalf of our 'fellow-creatures', whose plight, he suggests, we are finally unable to ignore. For the *truly* evangelical note, and perhaps the original source of Dickens's imagery, one might compare John Newton's earlier observation of the cloud of smoke over London as suggestive of the accumulated stock of human misery rising like 'that cloud of sin which is continually ascending like a mighty cry in the ears of the Lord of hosts' (quoted in Brown, 1961, p. 27). Dickens holds to a more optimistic, Romantic, but none the less Christian notion, recognised by the Boston *Christian Examiner*, according to which 'crime and depravity everywhere' come from 'our want of sympathy with the poor, our small respect for man as man, our violation of the natural pledge of brotherhood' (vol. 27, November 1839, p. 174). We have to be brought to *see* (the visual metaphor is insistent), that looking on 'nature' and our 'fellow-men' and crying 'that all is dark and gloomy' is no more than a reflection of our own 'jaundiced eyes and hearts. The real hues are delicate and need a clearer vision' (ch. xxxiv, p. 226). This is confirmed in the novel by the indestructibility of Oliver's goodness and, by contrast, the self-destructiveness of evil, whether on the 'social' (e.g. Bumble) or more 'metaphysical' (Fagin) level.

IV

If, in *Oliver Twist*, there is little to be hoped for from public charity, at least there are signs of private sympathy and aid – Dickens could hardly deny this possibility for his readers. Yet it is hard to raise much enthusiasm for those who, like Rose Maylie and her foster-mother, offer Oliver the 'charity [which] had rescued [him] from misery, or death' (ch. xxxii, p. 205). The Maylies, Mr Brownlow and, to a lesser extent, Mr Losberne and the tedious Harry Maylie represent the unofficial, individual benevolence which alone seems capable of responding to the pauper orphan's needs. They are not especially associated with the Church, although Harry Maylie eventually becomes a clergyman; but they *are* a little more than the 'soft-hearted psalm-singers' Sikes calls them (ch. xvi, p. 102), Christian by nature rather than by formal adherence. It is this which enables them to recognise, instinctively, the 'noble nature and warm heart' planted in Oliver by 'that Power which has thought fit to try him beyond his years', and which inspires their aid (ch. xli, p. 278). It is arguable that this lessens the value of their charity, since they are not faced by the more realistic problem posed by a ragged, smelly and offensive urchin such as Jo, the crossing-sweeper of *Bleak House*. This is true, but as far as Oliver is concerned Dickens prefers a more symbolic form of characterisation, although, as we shall see, in Nancy he creates a more challenging and complex case.

The overtly 'good' characters, Brownlow and the Maylies, are not alone in offering charity to Oliver. Ironically, on his arrival in London, penniless and starving, it is the Artful Dodger who feeds and takes him in – as Fagin is quick to remind Oliver after his recapture by the gang later (ch. xviii, p. 114). It is this irony which effectively connects the Poor Law sections of the narrative with the succeeding account of Oliver's adventures in London. The criminals who aim to exploit pauper children such as Oliver are, apparently, on a par with, if not initially preferable to, the parish management. This link is made quite explicit when the Dodger and Charley Bates allow Oliver to be caught and blamed for their pickpocketing expedition: Fagin's lads thereby exhibit a selfishness corroborated, says Dickens, by those 'profound and sound-judging philosophers' for whom self-interest provides the motive behind all action, contrary to considerations of 'heart', or 'generous impulse and feeling' (ch. xii, p. 73).

On the other hand, this providentially unsuccessful robbery brings Oliver to the attention of his potential benefactor, Brownlow, a further irony. Brownlow seems a kind of Pickwick.[1] He is elderly, short-sighted, blissfully unaware of the world: 'it was plain, from his utter abstraction, that he saw not the book-stall, nor the street, nor the boys, nor, in short, anything but the book itself' (ch. x, p. 58). This limited vision is more culpable in *Oliver Twist* than in *Pickwick Papers*, however, since Mr Pickwick's blundering innocence harms no one more than himself, while Brownlow's blindness can indirectly harm others, for instance when he sends the newly recuperated Oliver on an errand, solely to satisfy the doubts engendered by his irascible friend Grimwig, and which leads (although of course he was not to know this) to the boy's recapture by Fagin's gang. Yet, when this 'absent old gentleman' is obliged to press a case against Oliver for theft, he takes pity on the fainting boy, defends him as vigorously as he can against the brutally inept Mr Fang (the law is as blindly ignorant here as in *Pickwick*), and thereafter becomes deeply involved in his fate. Cruikshank's depiction of the Good Samaritan in a print above Brownlow's fireplace (ch. xii, p. 71, see Illustration 3) reinforces our sense of the virtue of his action.

Brownlow is more interesting than has been allowed: for a start, he has a past, unlike Mr Pickwick. His previous experience provides him with the indefinable memory (of Oliver's father's only sister) which disposes him to trust Oliver; it also throws some uncertainty over this trust, since he has been 'deceived, before, in the objects whom I have endeavoured to benefit' (ch. xiv, p. 85). These ambivalent feelings reflect an advance in Dickens's conception of goodness, an advance not matched by his depiction of Rose Maylie who, like Oliver, is more of an emblem than a convincing human being. Rose never recovers from Dickens's idealising, indeed, other-worldly intentions (her pointless sickness unto death reinforces this). From the first she is a young lady 'in the lovely bloom and spring-time of womanhood', at an age when, apparently, 'if ever angels be for God's good purposes enthroned in mortal forms, they may be, without impiety, supposed to abide in such as hers' (ch. xxix, p. 186) – the unorthodoxy of which supposition does not prevent Dickens from suggesting it. Doubtless her origin lay partly in the novelist's feelings towards his recently deceased sister-in-law, Mary Hogarth. But what she offers is an image of unqualified, absolute Christian love, a spiritual ideal beside which Brownlow's more earthly benevolence seems, if more accessible, nevertheless limited. Thus, for example, when she and Brownlow are confronted by the desperate Nancy that fateful night on London Bridge, he is at first disposed simply to 'humour' her, whereas Rose unhesitatingly asks that he speak to her 'kindly ... Poor creature!' Nancy's response indicates how Dickens classifies Rose:

'Your haughty religious people would have held their heads up to see me as I am tonight, and preached of flames and vengeance ... Oh, dear lady, why ar'n't those who claim to be God's own folks as gentle and as kind to us poor wretches as you, who, having youth, and beauty, and all that they have lost, might be a little proud instead of so much humbler? (ch. xlvi, p. 312)

3 'Oliver recovering from the fever' (*Oliver Twist*, ch. xii, p. 71),
by George Cruikshank. Note print of Good Samaritan above
Brownlow's mantelpiece.

Rose represents Christian forgiveness and mercy, as opposed to the
vengeful wrath of a stricter tradition. Earlier, at the first meeting of the
two women in Rose's West End 'family hotel', we have seen Rose
appealing to Nancy: 'It is never too late . . . for penitence and atonement'
(ch. xl, p. 273). But Nancy can think only of her loyalty to Sikes, and
'God's wrath' (ch. xl, p. 274). Brownlow supports her distinction

between 'haughty religious people' who preach vengeance upon sinners, and humble Christians like Rose, who preach forgiveness, when he explains where he, too, would expect to find the true faith:

'Ah!' said the gentleman. 'A Turk turns his face, after washing it well, to the East, when he says his prayers; these good people, after giving their faces such a rub against the World as to take the smiles off, turn, with no less regularity, to the darkest side of Heaven. Between the Musselman and the Pharisee, commend me to the first!' (ch. xlvi, pp. 312–13)

Dickens seems bent on exposing the difference between the more hopeful and optimistic form of Christianity he believes in, and the evangelical stress upon the innate depravity of sinners which calls down retribution on their heads; so he deliberately overturns the evangelical commonplace, according to which the morality of the gospels is 'superior to that for which we look in a good deist, musselman, or hindoo', a superiority defined precisely by allowing for sins such as Nancy's in 'no shape' or 'composition' whatsoever (Wilberforce, 1834 edn, pp. 86, 91).

This emphasis upon the offering of Christian charity – as distinct from the condemnation of a vengeful God – to fallen women such as Nancy reappears later in the depiction of Alice Marwood in *Dombey and Son* and Emily in *David Copperfield*. It also appears in Dickens's conduct of Miss Burdett Coutts's Home for Fallen Women, Urania House, over some ten or twelve years, his most prolonged involvement in any single charitable activity. Miss Coutts tended towards a sterner approach, but Dickens was quite clear about where he stood, and insisted that his views be followed, according to which the former prostitutes were to be, as he put it, '*tempted* to virtue', not frightened off by reminders of their sinfulness and degradation; and in so far as they were to receive spiritual enlightenment, this was to be from 'the *New* Testament' (his emphasis), not by 'injudicious use of the Old' (Coutts *Letters*, pp. 102–3: 3 November 1847).[5] What is meant by this appears in the treatment of Nancy, indicating that for Dickens, as for many of his contemporaries, charity operates on the assumption of original virtue: we are created in God's image, which is good, and so there will remain at least a spark of divinity in even the most depraved. Hazlitt wrote that 'even among the most abandoned of the other sex, there is not infrequently found to exist (contrary to all that is generally supposed) one strong and individual attachment, which remains unshaken to the last. Virtue may be said to steal, like a guilty thing, into the secret haunts of vice and infamy; it clings to their devoted victim, and will not be driven away. Nothing can destroy the human heart' ('On cant and hypocrisy',1828, repr. in Blythe, 1970, p. 447); while Mrs Gaskell, in a similar context, held that 'the most

depraved have also their seed of the Holiness that shall one day overcome
their evil' (*Mary Barton*, 1848, ch. 8). Nancy is as important to Dickens as
Oliver, perhaps more so, since she reflects this belief. Hence his
passionate defence of her against those who, like Thackeray (1840, pp.
154-5), found her improbable and sentimental: 'From the first
introduction of that poor wretch', he wrote,

> to her laying her bloody head upon the robber's breast, there is not one
> word exaggerated or over-wrought. It is emphatically God's truth, for
> it is the truth He leaves in such depraved and miserable breasts; the
> hope yet lingering behind; the last fair drop of water at the bottom of
> rhe dried-up weed-choked well. (1841 Preface)

Special pleading, perhaps; but Nancy is a little more interesting than the
usual easy dismissal of her implies. She first reveals her 'soul of goodness
in things evil' in the chapter to which Dickens gave this running title in
1867, chapter xvi: there she emerges, astonishingly, as the defender of the
boy Oliver, whom she has just helped recapture for Fagin. The only real
moral battle in the novel is the one which takes place within her (it is also
one of the earliest instances in Dickens of a 'change of heart'). At first she
is merely one of a couple of young 'ladies' Oliver meets when he enters
Fagin's 'school' of hopeful young thieves, seeming to the innocent Oliver
'remarkably free and agreeable' in manner (ch. ix, p. 55); she seems as
callously disposed towards him as Sikes, to whom she reports that 'the
young brat's been ill' (ch. xv, p. 95); and when she finds him on his errand
for Brownlow, she puts on a superlative act as his long-lost sister to get
him back into Fagin's clutches (ch. xv, pp. 95-7). But when Oliver is then
tormented by his captors into breaking loose, shrieking, with Fagin, the
Dodger and Charley Bates in pursuit, she springs to the door crying,
'Keep back the dog, Bill', to Sikes's amazement, 'the child shan't be torn
down by the dog, unless you kill me first' (ch.xvi, p. 102). It is as if some
pent-up former self has emerged, with a shock that turns her almost
insane, 'not speaking, but pouring out the words in one continuous and
vehement scream' (ch. xvi, p. 104). Apparently Oliver has reminded her
of herself as a child, 'not half as old as this', swept up into evil ways by
Fagin, as the old devil hopes to sweep up Oliver; and hardened until only
the impact of seeing the child threatened with being torn to pieces can
bring back the recollection of what she once was. This is a typically
Romantic notion, which Dickens ensures we will interpret in Christian
terms: Oliver's arrival begins the erosion of Nancy's former, depraved
self, leading eventually to the climax of her dying cry to Sikes, as he
batters her down after her attempt to save the child has threatened her
lover: 'It is never too late to repent' (ch. xlvii, p. 322). Her words echo
Rose Maylie's, and the martyrdom is complete when she draws out

Rose's white handkerchief, emblem of unspotted virtue, holding it up 'in her folded hands, as high towards Heaven as her feeble strength would allow', breathing 'one prayer for mercy to her Maker' (ch. xlvii, pp. 322–3).

Nancy's death reveals 'God's truth', that good will come out of evil; this is further borne out by the events which follow it, her murder leading to the death of Sikes and the disruption and dispersal of Fagin's gang. It is not made clear what, precisely, Fagin is condemned to death for, but in terms of narrative logic, it is for his part in the corruption and death of Nancy, as well as in the attempted corruption of Oliver. It is the power of Providence, rather than the character of Brownlow, the Maylies, or Nancy, which ultimately ensures the triumph of charity and goodwill over evil; our sense of this is created by moments such as that in which Oliver, awaiting delivery to Sikes for the Chertsey robbery, prays to 'Heaven': 'if any aid were to be raised up for a poor outcast boy, who had never known the love of friends or kindred, it might come to him now: when, desolate and deserted, he stood alone in the midst of wickedness and guilt' (ch. xx, p. 130); at once Nancy arrives and, seeing him, feels confirmed in her secret, instinctual determination to save the boy, despite her fears for herself and Sikes: 'God forgive me', she cries, 'I never thought of this' (loc. cit.).

Thus prayer is answered, and charity offered, even when this involves some fairly obvious (realistically considered) plot manipulation. Oliver must be brought into the bosom of that cosy 'little society, whose condition approached as nearly to one of perfect happiness as can ever be known in this changing world' (ch. liii, p. 365), and individual, private benevolence, even at the cost which Nancy must suffer, will serve this end. Paradoxically, Dickens seems to endorse Bentham's view that one will only sacrifice individual interest to others when those others are such with whom one is 'connected by some domestic or other private and narrow tie of sympathy' (quoted in Clayre, 1977, p. 303), since Brownlow and the Maylies all turn out to be related to Oliver; but Nancy provides the sacrifice which is absolute.

V

There are some whom charity cannot reach. This is made quite clear when Oliver visits Fagin in the condemned cell. As Fagin dimly realises, the pauper orphan has been 'somehow the cause of all this', but Oliver nevertheless offers to save the doomed villain's soul alive, as it were: 'Let me say a prayer. Do! Let me say one prayer. Say only one, upon your knees, with me, and we will talk till morning' (ch. lii, pp. 363–4). But Fagin is not to be redeemed. He has already driven away priests 'of his own persuasion', even after they 'renewed their charitable efforts' (ch. lii, p. 361). He is too far gone even to understand what Oliver is trying to do, and so all that is left is for the boy to beg God's forgiveness for the man, which he does. It is indeed a 'frightful scene' (ch. lii, p. 364), but its meaning should be clear.

It has been argued that the scene 'inevitably' recalls the 'memorable' episode in *The Fairchild Family* (first published 1818; numerous later editions) in which Mr Fairchild takes his disobedient children out for a stroll to see a gibbeted criminal (Marcus, 1965, p. 69). But Oliver is brought to Fagin to ask about lost papers; Brownlow and the turnkey are well aware it is 'not a sight for children'; and Oliver himself tries to improve the occasion by persuading the evil old devil with whom he has been so deeply involved to pray. The real interest lies in the *contrast* between Dickens and those who, like Mrs Sherwood, encouraged the religious oppression of the young by their insistence on the depraved nature of man. Yet, while prepared to condemn the doctrine of total depravity when it is applied to children, or those who, like Nancy, show some glimmerings of hope, Dickens seems to accept it as a description of the soul of Fagin. This is not theological confusion: if Dickens believes in the final triumph of good, he is too strongly aware of the power of evil to allow any easy or unconditional triumph. And, as he remarked of Sikes, 'I fear there are in the world some insensible and callous natures, that do become, at last, utterly and irredeemably bad' (1841 Preface). The key word is 'become'. Dickens believed in the infinite corruptibility of human nature, while holding that it is essentially good in origin. At the same time, he evidently held that the fear of death could be a significant factor in the regeneration of *adult* sinners: witness Scrooge's confrontation by the Ghost of Christmas Yet To Come. But Fagin and Sikes cannot save themselves, or be saved.

What Dickens reveals in the later part of *Oliver Twist*, after Nancy's murder, is the working out of divine retribution upon the characters of Fagin and Sikes. At the same time he invites us to contemplate the inner workings of both men's conscience-stricken last moments, providing vivid glimpses of the humanity which persists within those we must nevertheless condemn. This is most striking in the depiction of Sikes, who first appears simply as a coarse, brutal thug, much given to shouting oaths and kicking his dog across the room; but after bludgeoning Nancy to death, he flees London, and we follow his restless wanderings in some detail, pursued relentlessly by news of the murder and the mental image of his victim's last moment –

> as he left the town behind him, and plunged into the solitude and darkness of the road, he felt a dread and awe creeping upon him which shook him to the core. Every object before him, substance or shadow,

took the semblance of some fearful thing; but these fears were nothing compared to the sense that haunted him of that morning's ghastly figure following at his heels. He could trace its shadow in the gloom, supply the smallest item of the outline, and note how stiff and solemn it seemed to stalk along. He could hear its garments rustling in the leaves; and every breath of wind came laden with that last low cry. If he stopped it did the same. If he ran, it followed – not running too: that would have been a relief: but like a corpse endowed with the mere machinery of life, and borne on one slow melancholy wind that never rose or fell. (ch. xlviii, p. 327)

Like Wordsworth's Peter Bell, Sikes is followed by a ruthless conscience, which takes on a cosmic significance (Leviticus 26:36: 'The sound of a shaken leaf shall chase him'). 'Let no man talk of murderers escaping justice, and hint that Providence must sleep', Dickens adds ominously, as Sikes continues wandering (ch. xlviii, p. 327). The next sight to meet his eyes is a huge fire: there can be little doubt of his ultimate destination, as there can be little doubt of Fagin's, sitting huddled in the condemned cell, and starting up from time to time 'with gasping mouth and burning skin', his flesh crackling with an inner fever (ch. lii, p. 361).

The idea of a divinity delivering warning messages by means of signs and portents which are in effect reflections of a guilty conscience goes back at least to *Macbeth*. Dickens is consciously working within a traditional, deeply familiar Christian cosmology in his treatment of evil-doers, as he is in his treatment of the good, especially Oliver. Hints of a supernatural dimension to the narrative, such as the thunder which accompanies Monks's meeting with the Bumbles (ch xxxviii, p. 251) confirm the suggestion in the novel's subtitle – 'The Parish Boy's Progress' – that on one level this is another version of the popular Christian tale of man's journey to salvation, beset by the competing forces of good and evil. It is easy to overstress this aspect of the novel. But to some extent there is a natural progression from the social satire of the early chapters to the deeper issues at stake later when, as Monks complains, whatever happens to Oliver seems 'contrived by Heaven, or the devil' (ch. xl, p. 273). This progression begins at a specific point in the narrative, namely, when Oliver first learns of the true nature of his London associates. It is a traumatic event, a kind of fall, comparable to Mr Pickwick's in the Fleet, only Oliver does not recover until finally settled in the rural paradise awaiting him at the conclusion. The boy is horror-struck as the Dodger and Charley Bates set to work on the unconscious Mr Brownlow:

In an instant the whole mystery of the handkerchiefs, and the watches, and the jewels, and the Jew, rushed upon the boy's mind. He stood, for a moment, with the blood so tingling through all his veins from terror, that he felt as if he were in a burning fire; then, confused and frightened, he took to his heels; and, not knowing what he did, made off as fast as he could lay his feet to the ground. (ch. x, p. 58)

The implications of Oliver's experience extend to a sudden, profound awareness of the closeness of evil, or hellfire. From now on he becomes a pawn in the hands of good and evil powers, persistently weak, ill, even unconscious. At times, he desires to join his dead mother, for all that she is in 'Heaven' which, he feels, is 'a long way off' (ch. xii, p. 68). Like hell, heaven becomes accessible, however, through strange, dream-like moments, when the 'mighty powers' of the mind spurn 'time and space' (ch. ix, p. 51) – an expression of Romantic psychology offered to account for the odd, trance-like moments of recognition between good and evil, such as when Oliver observes Fagin looking over his stolen hoard, or when Fagin and Monks appear at the window of the Maylie house (ch. ix, p. 51; ch. xxxiv, p. 228). But the transcendent imagination offers consolation too, as when Brownlow falls into a reverie of dead faces which 'the mind', superior to death's power

> still dressed in their old freshness and beauty: calling back the lustre of the eyes, the brightness of the smile, the beaming of the soul through its mask of clay: and whispering of beauty beyond the tomb, changed but to be heightened, and taken from earth only to be set up as a light, to shed a soft and gentle glow upon the path to Heaven. (ch. xi, p. 62)

And when Rose Maylie's tears fall upon the sleeping Oliver's forehead they stir a dream of 'love and affection he had never known', a dream which, like 'dim remembrances of scenes that never were, in this life', brings brief memories of 'a happier existence, long gone by' (ch. xxx, p. 191). *Oliver Twist* abounds in such intimations of immortality, visionary promises of escape from this world which are reminiscent of the writings of Carlyle and De Quincey and other inheritors of the religion of Romanticism.[6]

Thus Dickens modifies the common-sense, latitudinarian position expressed at the start of his writing career, by reaching towards a more subjective faith of inner apprehensions, of a sense of the numinous. But this should not be allowed to obscure the fact that, as he proudly remarked to the Dissenting minister, himself once a workhouse boy, who praised *Oliver Twist*,

> While you teach in your walk of life the lessons of tenderness you have learnt in sorrow, trust me that in mine, I will pursue cruelty and oppression, the Enemies of all God's creatures of all codes and creeds,

so long as I have the energy of thought and the power of giving it utterance. (To Rev. Thos Robinson, Pilgrim *Letters*, Vol. 2, p. 257: 8 April 1841)

The fundamental aim of *Oliver Twist* is to reveal the sufferings of the unknown poor, to overturn prevailing attitudes to their relief, and to elicit our sympathy and charity on their behalf. Philip Collins and others have tried to tie Dickens's religion down to a single formula, to call him a 'New Testament', a 'Four Gospels', or even just a 'Sermon on the Mount' Christian (Collins, 1965, p. 54). But to call him a man who believed in charity is not so simple: it is a belief which crossed sectarian boundaries, being based on the assumption that, as we are reminded in the penultimate paragraph of the novel, 'without strong affection, and humanity of heart, and gratitude to that Being whose code is Mercy, and whose great attribute is Benevolence to all things that breathe, true happiness can never be attained' (ch. liii, p. 368).

3

Death and *The Old Curiosity Shop*

'Do you believe such people *are* happy in the other world, sir? I'd
give a great deal to know.'
I declined answering Mrs Dean's question, which struck me as
something heterodox.
(Emily Brontë, *Wuthering Heights*, 1847, ch. 16)

Religion, in fact, for the great majority of our own race *means*
immortality, and nothing else.
(William James, *The Varieties of Religious Experience*, 1902,
Postscript)

I

The Old Curiosity Shop (1840-1) is the first of Dickens's novels with an
obviously religious subject at its centre: death and the consolation of death.
Death was a preoccupation in *Oliver Twist*, with its harrowing opening and
Oliver's experiences as an undertaker's mute, but here it becomes all-
pervasive, from the narrator's initial meditations to the long-drawn-out
decline of its heroine. Quilp also dies, and his death contrasts and complements Nell's, in line with a basic structural principle of the novel, expressed
quite baldly as that 'everything in our lives, whether of good or of evil,
affects us most by contrast'.[1] This principle is established by the opening
image of Nell, alone amidst all the 'lumber and decay and ugly age' of the
shop, 'the beautiful child in her gentle slumber, smiling through her light
and sunny dreams' (ch. i, p. 14) – an image which fired Dickens's
imagination, so that what was originally intended to be no more than one
of Master Humphrey's somewhat miscellaneous tales grew to a lengthy
narrative with a profusion of scenes and characters; but all, as Forster
pointed out (1928, p. 152), more or less conforming to this striking
contrast of Nell alone in a dream, surrounded by ugliness and grotesque
old age. Hood said it was 'like an Allegory' (1840, p. 887), and Dickens
agreed, inserting words to that effect into the first chapter of the
completed novel (ch. i, p. 13).
    It would be a mistake to read *The Old Curiosity Shop* as if it were a
realistic social novel, and to query the 'reality' of either Nell or her
setting. Of course, none of Dickens's novels can be accounted for simply

in terms of a mimetic aesthetic. But in *The Old Curiosity Shop* we have a work that is, as one contemporary reviewer recognised, 'more completely *sui generis*' than perhaps any other of his novels (*Ecclesiastic and Theologian*, vol. 17, October 1855, p. 467). A proper understanding of its achievement depends on admitting this. That Dickens himself felt the uniqueness of *The Old Curiosity Shop*, in terms related to its effect as religious consolation, is suggested by his choice of it to be reproduced in braille for the benefit of the afflicted in America in 1868, who normally had only the New Testament and Dr Watts's hymns to hand – not much, thought Dickens, despite his reverence for the gospels (Dolby, 1885, p. 229). The novel presents no easy task in the matter of teasing out the subtle strands of feeling and implication involved in bringing Dickens's religious views to light; yet the task must be faced, since it has been used again and again (from Dickens's day to our own) to denigrate the vague sentimentality of his beliefs, the 'religion of the blue sky' (quoted in [Hoey?], 1871, pp. 331–2), which he is supposed to propagate.

The power of this oddly compelling tale of a waif-like child's innocent pilgrimage to death lies essentially in its dream-like quality, a quality present from that curiously personal, ruminative opening, in which the young and successful novelist identifies himself with a lugubrious and dull old man, Master Humphrey, who reflects, typically, on the possibility of being 'condemned to lie, dead but conscious', in the midst of the city's bustle (ch. i, p. 1). Dickens has chosen to put aside the social concern evinced in his preceding novels, to move towards an inward realm of subjective apprehension and fancy. In line with this, he proposes in *The Old Curiosity Shop* a doctrine of subjective immortality, according to which the dead live on through the hearts and minds of those who remember them. This is a Romantic belief, even if it is expressed in Christian terms. It is derived from the idea of a transcendent realm which the individual may glimpse by means of a spiritualised imagination. It can be shown to have its roots in Dickens's personal experiences, and it is a part of what touched the novel's contemporary readers so deeply.

II

One level of implication in *The Old Curiosity Shop* is fairly easy to discern: Dickens's satire on Little Bethelism, which represents both a return to the campaign against narrow, cheerless religion opened in *Sunday Under Three Heads* and *Pickwick Papers*, and a new awareness of the pernicious effects such religion may have on its followers. The point of departure is familiar: he attacks the tendency of religious professors to suppress the harmless amusements of the poor. In *The Old Curiosity*

Shop he concentrates on play-going, possibly for reasons extrinsic to the novel. There is, of course, a long tradition of satiric invective against puritan attitudes towards the theatre, but, as Hood suggested, a new 'Zeal-of-the-land-Busy' spirit was abroad in the 1840s, with bigots 'ready to burn' 'Picture Galleries, Museums, Literary Institutions, Her Majesty's Theatres, and the people's Punch and Judy' (1842, p. 79). This was also the time when Dickens's sister Fanny was being drawn away from the laxness of the Dickens household on matters such as the theatre by her Congregationalist husband, Henry Burnett (Griffin, 1883, p. 170), perhaps confirming the novelist's sense of an upsurge of puritanism.

Certainly, when Kit Nubbles, up to this point a simple and not noticeably articulate lad, promises his family that they shall all go to Astley's popular playhouse on his first quarter holiday, and his mother objects ('I hope plays mayn't be sinful, Kit, but I'm a'most afraid'), his response is astonishing:

> Can you suppose there's any harm in looking as cheerful and being as cheerful as our poor circumstances will permit? Do I see anything in the way I'm made, which calls upon me to be a snivelling, solemn, whispering chap, sneaking about as if I couldn't help it, and expressing myself in a most unpleasant snuffle? on the contrairy, don't I see every reason why I shouldn't? Just hear this! Ha ha ha! An't that as nat'ral as walking, and as good for the health? Ha ha ha! An't that as nat'ral as a sheep's bleating, or a pig's grunting, or a horse's neighing, or a bird's singing? Ha ha ha! Isn't it, mother? (ch. xxii, p. 167)

The contemptuous repetition of sound and image in 'snivelling', 'sneaking' and 'snuffle', coupled with the reiterated assertion of a 'nat'ral' right to laugh, suggests an attack not just on the anti-theatre lobby, but on a total religious attitude. Many evangelicals (popularly supposed to be flat-nosed 'snufflers') held that frequenting plays afforded 'a proof of the depravity of human nature beyond most other things' (quoted in Brown, 1961, p. 445), an association of Christian dogma and repression peculiarly repellent to Dickens, for whom, of course, human nature is essentially good, because made by the beneficent Creator, as are the 'natural' emotions of joy and pleasure. It is especially the poor who are liable to be misled in this respect, and Dickens hallows their virtues, offering the Nubbles family as an index of those 'household affections and loves' which 'bear the stamp of Heaven' (ch. xxxviii, p. 281). When Kit offers his home as a refuge for the Trents, he is eulogised in terms which echo the parable of Dives and Lazarus (Luke 16:9): 'Thank Heaven that the temples of such spirits are not made with hands, and that they may be even more worthily hung with poor patchwork than with purple and fine linen' (ch. xi, p. 90). If this seems sentimental, it is worth noting the claims of a contemporary East End curate that the 'steady poor' (permanent residents) who 'occupied the free seats in his church practised the highest standard of Christianity that he had ever known' (quoted in Chadwick, 1970, pt I, p. 332).

It was on behalf of such people that Dickens opposed what he saw as the religious exploitation of Little Bethelism. We are not told that the Nubbleses contemplated attending the parish church, and occupying the free seats, but we may suppose that this is where Dickens would have preferred to see them: Barbara, Kit's future wife, is the conspicuous possessor of a prayer-book, a hymn-book and a Bible (ch. xxii, p. 170); and Kit himself conquers any bitterness in prison by 'reading the church catechism very attentively (though he had known it by heart from a little child)' (ch. lxi, p. 454). Nell attends the parish church. But that is in the country, and reflects Dickens's lack of confidence in urban religion: the 'rank confusion' of the city Nell and the old man leave includes both 'dissenting chapels', which teach 'with no lack of illustration, the miseries of the Earth', and 'new churches, erected with a little superfluous wealth, to show the way to Heaven' (ch. xv, p. 115).

By no means only the Dissenting chapels taught the miseries of the earth: there was little to choose, in this respect, between inspired evangelicals within and outside the Church. Moreover, some Dissenters were more, rather than less, liberal in doctrine than the Church, as Dickens would have realised when he began attending Unitarian meetings shortly after completing *The Old Curiosity Shop*, if not before. But the novelist locates what he objects to in the 'obnoxious conventicle' (ch. xli, p. 305) Mrs Nubbles attends. When Kit arrives there to fetch his mother the preacher capitalises on the disturbance to rouse his inert congregation by calling on Kit to 'Stay, Satan, stay!':

'Stay, Satan, stay!' roared the preacher again. 'Tempt not the woman that doth incline to thee, but hearken to the voice of him that calleth. He hath a lamb from the fold!' cried the preacher, raising his voice still higher and pointing to the baby. 'He beareth off a lamb, a precious lamb! He goeth about, like a wolf in the night season, and inveigleth the tender lambs!' (ch. xli, p. 307)

The ludicrous misapplication of scripture is underlined by Quilp's diabolic presence, a conjunction repeated in Mrs Nubbles's mind later, when he suddenly appears on the roof of her coach, suggesting 'that Evil Power, who was so vigorously attacked in Little Bethel, and who, by reason of her backslidings in respect of Astley's and oysters, was now frolicsome and rampant' (ch. xlviii, p. 361).

Dickens does not call Little Bethel a Dissenting chapel; and in *Nicholas*

Nickleby he refers to a place of the same name which could still have been attached to the Church of England (ch. xvi, p. 187). The name, Bethel, was commonly used by both Baptists and Methodists, and of course not all the latter had accepted separation from the Church (Chadwick, 1970, pt I. p. 370). But the preacher's 'favourite allusion' (contrasting the broad means of access to the parish church with the crooked ways by which his chapel is approached: ch. xli, p. 305) suggests Dickens here had Dissent in mind, and this is how most readers have taken it – including the daughter of a contemporary Baptist minister, who also suggested that Mrs Nubbles's pastor originated in a gentleman who used to hold forth in an old Baptist meeting house called Zoar Chapel, situated in Goodman's Fields, Whitechapel.[2] The main connection between Dickens's preacher and the man in question lies in them both having been shoemakers: 'by trade a Shoemaker, and by calling a Divine' (ch. xli, p. 305). But it was common for lay preachers to be drawn from the ranks of artisanship; and for evangelicals to be thought of as, in Sydney Smith's phrase, 'a nest of consecrated cobblers' (1859, Vol. 1, p. 138). Possibly this was because William Carey, first Baptist minister to India, was a cobbler; and because cobbling was a trade well known for the radicalism with which dissent was 'tainted' (Jay, 1979, p. 162). But, for Dickens, the important point was that it was all too easy for evangelical doctrine to be adopted by ignorant preachers wishing to exploit the poor. 'Punch and preaching is two different creeds – hopposition parties, I may say', observed one of Henry Mayhew's interviewees (quoted in Quennell, n.d., p. 435), and Dickens would have agreed.

It is also true that the novelist was influenced by the spirit of what he attacked: the earnestness and piety he hoped to promote by the depiction of Kit, or even Nell, derive from the same broad wave of change which produced the extremes of Little Bethelism, or Stigginsism. Dick Swiveller could have ended up like Fred Trent, we presume, killed abroad in a scuffle of doubtful circumstance; but his feelings for the Marchioness, his honesty against the Brasses and, finally, his sickness unto death, enable Dickens to rescue him at the last. Old Trent's dark vice, we notice, is gambling, which Dickens, like any Wilberforcian reformer, abhorred (see *Barnaby Rudge*, ch. xvi, p. 123). A similar complex involvement in the beliefs of his age is evident in his treatment of Nell's death, though more personal reasons contributed to this.

III

Within a few years of the first appearance of *The Old Curiosity Shop*, long before the biographical facts on which modern critics base their speculations emerged, it was said that Nell was 'meant to represent the once living and beloved object of the author's affection' ([Cleghorn?], 1845, p. 70). Perhaps we should now simply dismiss this assumption in a few well-chosen phrases: Gabriel Pearson remarks that the novel is merely 'an immense, unruly wreath laid on the clammy marble of Kensal Green Cemetery' (1966, p. 78). But the fact is that Nell's character and story have been placed firmly at the centre of the narrative, and to understand this fully, we have to consider what part Kensal Green cemetery had to play in it. Pearson is not as dismissive as he pretends: 'Undoubtedly, the death of Mary Hogarth was something like a religious crisis', he continues. 'Nell was an unsuccessful attempt to grope and feel a way through this crisis, to locate death as a human event' (ibid., p. 79). To call the death 'something like' a religious crisis is not very helpful, but one can see what is meant. Dickens was deeply disturbed by the loss, more so perhaps than by any other single event in his maturity; and the effect of this disturbance was to make him express his beliefs regarding death in a stream of letters, and in his diary, as well as in his fiction.

The novelist's immediate reaction to the tragedy of 7 May 1837 was anguished grief: 'I could have spared a much nearer relation or an older friend, for she has been to us what can never be replaced', he wrote to George Thomson, Mary's maternal grandfather, the next day (Pilgrim *Letters*, Vol. 1, p. 257). Work on his current serials, *Pickwick Papers* and *Oliver Twist*, was interrupted, and a public apology printed. Having arranged Mary's funeral, Dickens removed to a cottage in Hampstead with his wife, to try to recover. What consolatory hopes or beliefs arose to quell the grief? Dickens observed of his wife Catherine that 'she knows that if ever a mortal went to Heaven, her sister is there'; and expressed similarly pious views himself – 'she has passed quietly away to an immortality of happiness and joy' (Pilgrim *Letters*, Vol. 1, pp. 260, 268; 17 May, 8 June 1837). In the diary begun on 1 January 1838 (perhaps through a need to express these very feelings) the first entry concludes: 'she is gone, and pray God I may one day through his mercy rejoin her'; a fortnight later, he returns from Sunday morning service to write: 'She is sentient and conscious of my emotions *somewhere*; where we cannot tell – how we cannot tell; yet I would not at this moment renounce the mysterious yet certain hope that I shall see her in a better world, for all that this world can give me' (Pilgrim *Letters*, Vol. 1, pp. 629, 632).

The idea that the dead survive somewhere, in a mysterious realm where we will eventually rejoin them, is, of course, a common belief, often used as a consolation, as Dickens himself had already pointed out in *Pickwick* (ch. xxviii, p. 374) six months before Mary's death. Hood wrote to his friend Samuel Phillips on the loss of the latter's wife, that the comfort he had found 'most consolatory under the loss of dear relatives', was the thought that 'after some term, longer or shorter, but a mere vibration of the great pendulum of eternity, we shall all be re-united'

([Broderip and Hood], 1869, p. 400). Fanny Dickens told her brother on her deathbed that she could not help thinking of meeting her family when they too died, but 'she knew that was a mere human fancy, and could have no reality after she was dead' (Forster, 1928, p. 522). She had become a Congregationalist by then, and doubtless accepted the Calvinist principle that it is for God to save whom He has chosen. In fact, Jesus's teaching on the subject has been understood in more than one way: he rejected the literalism of the Sadducees about marriage in heaven, saying that the resurrected 'neither marry, nor are given in marriage; but are as the angels which are in heaven' (Mark 12:25); but the miracles of Jairus's daughter, and the raising of Lazarus, imply a hope of meeting again; a persistent hope which holds 'an exceedingly high religious value', while perhaps not to the orthodox 'religious in itself' (Temple, 1958, p. 115). Dickens evidently felt, as a novelist, that care should be exercised in providing for this hope too authoritatively, whatever his own 'mysterious' yet 'certain' feelings. Only children such as little Dick in *Oliver Twist* are permitted to articulate the idea (ch. xvii, p. 109); or, in *The Old Curiosity Shop*, the little boy who communicates to Nell his fervent belief that she will see his brother there (ch. lv, p. 412). But Nell herself has no such visions. She is permitted a dream of the favourite pupil among angels, but not the certain knowledge of meeting, say, her mother, that one might have expected. At the end of *The Old Curiosity Shop* Kit tells his children that Nell has gone to heaven, and promises them that if they are 'good, like her, they might hope to be there too, one day, and to see and know her as he had done when he was quite a boy' (chapter the last, p. 554); but he is addressing his children, not the reader; just as Dickens himself was addressing his children when he wrote, in *The Life of Our Lord*, that Jesus was 'now in Heaven, where we hope to go, and all to meet each other after we are dead, and there be happy always together' (1934 edn, p. 11). If Dickens felt the need to believe in the reunion of families after death when he was in the midst of his grief for Mary Hogarth, at other times he was only prepared to support it in the mouths of babes and sucklings. Perhaps he felt that the responsibility for accepting such a belief must finally be the reader's.

The clearest belief to emerge from the Mary Hogarth crisis, in relation to death, is what one may call the schoolmaster's consolation. If Mary's death posed the problem of how to come to terms with the premature loss of one so 'Young Beautiful and Good' (the phrase Dickens composed for her gravestone), one answer was that the memory of that person could function as a moral and spiritual guide to those who remain, drawing them together in the common bonds of humanity, and providing for them a link between this world and a better. The memory of Mary Hogarth haunted Dickens, entering his dreams, and coming so much into his thoughts, 'especially when I am successful, and have prospered in anything', that her image became an 'essential' part of him, as 'inseparable' from his existence as the beating of his heart (Pilgrim *Letters*, Vol. 3, p. 484: 8 May 1843). At the same time, he idealised her. Three weeks after her death, he wrote: 'she had not a single fault, and was in life almost as far above the foibles and vanity of her sex as she is now in Heaven'; soon she became 'the gentlest and purest creature that ever shed a light on earth' (Pilgrim *Letters*, Vol. 1, pp. 263, 323: 31 May, 26 October 1837). Nor was this idealised memory permitted to disappear, otherwise its uplifting function, and hence its ability to confer immortality, would also disappear. Dickens was determined 'never to shrink from speaking of her as if her memory were to be avoided' (Pilgrim *Letters*, Vol. 1, p. 323). This determination gives a strong sense of *willed* acceptance to the expression of belief in this form of immortality. The first time Dickens tried a fictional paradigm, he flinched away: Rose Maylie's supererogatory illness in *Oliver Twist*. By the time of *The Old Curiosity Shop*, he could allow his heroine to die. But it was also extraordinarily painful for him to kill Nell, and he admitted to Forster that his own consolatory belief was unable to counteract this (Pilgrim *Letters*, Vol. 2, p. 181; ?8 January 1841). The first important expression of the belief occurs after Nell has arrived at the old church where she will die. In distress at the sexton's suggestion that the dead are forgotten, she comes across the schoolmaster 'sitting on a green grave in the sun' – anticipating hopes of growth and renewal – and bursts into tears. The schoolmaster offers this passionate reassurance:

> Nell, Nell ... There is nothing ... no, nothing innocent and good, that dies, and is forgotten. Let us hold to that faith, or none ... There is not an angel added to the Host of Heaven but does its blessed work in those that loved it here. Forgotten! oh, if the good deeds of human creatures could be traced to their source, how beautiful would even death appear; for how much charity, mercy, and purified affection, would be seen to have their growth in dusty graves! (ch. liv, p. 406)

This is the faith Dickens wished to hold; but 'I can't preach to myself the schoolmaster's consolation, though I try' (Pilgrim *Letters*, Vol. 2, pp. 181-2).

The convincing suggestion that he arrived at is that recalling the dead is a means of preserving human ties. Nell's death reunites all the separated brothers – Trent and the single gentleman, Mr Garland and the bachelor; and her memory is supposed to confirm these ties for life. So, too, we hear of the village community coming together to mourn the girl who dies in their midst – 'the deaf, the blind, the lame, the palsied, the living dead' (ch. lxii, p. 542), an echo of Matthew 15:30-1. Dickens himself, in the 'midst of' Nell's death, 'was reminded of many old kindnesses, and was sorry in my heart that men who really liked each other [his estranged friends, Forster and Ainsworth] should waste life at arm's length' (Pilgrim *Letters*, Vol. 2, pp. 170–1: ?21 December 1840). Nell was one of those 'fictitious creatures' who had 'endeared' him and his audience to each other 'as real afflictions deepen friendship in actual life' (Fielding *Speeches*, p. 9). Of course, as this implies, Dickens was not alone in experiencing 'real affliction': his audience knew only too well what it was like to lose a child or close relative.

His 'doctrine of memory' is only part of a complex state of mind in Dickens. The novelist apparently assumed he would be buried in the same grave as Mary Hogarth; but when her brother died in October 1841, he had to relinquish the idea:

> It is a great trial to me to give up Mary's grave; greater than I can possibly express. I thought of moving her to the catacombs, and saying nothing about it; but then I remembered that the poor old lady [Mary's maternal grandmother] is buried next her at her own desire, and could not find it in my heart, directly she is laid in the earth, to take her grandchild away. The desire to be buried next her is as strong upon me now as it was five years ago; and I *know* (for I don't think there ever was love like that I bear her) that it will never diminish.

That he sensed something morbid in these reflections is attested by the exclamation, a few lines further on: 'I neither think nor hope (God forbid) that our spirits would ever mingle *there*.' But, he had to admit, it was 'very hard' to 'get the better of it' (Pilgrim *Letters*, Vol. 2, p. 410: 25 October 1841). Not for Dickens the Marvellian detachment of 'The Grave's a fine and private place,/But none I think do there embrace'. And in this he was far from extraordinary. De Quincey recorded that in 'sick, frantic yearning' for 'the darling' of his heart, he stretched himself every night for 'more than two months running' on the grave of Kate Wordsworth, who had died at the age of 3 (*Tait's Edinburgh Magazine*, August 1840, repr. in Wright, 1970, p. 372). This inability to accept death as the severing of all human ties produced the typical Victorian memorial – apparently reassuring, and often grotesque. But the Victorians were also their own most forceful critics. Dickens strongly disliked the 'sculptured horrors of the tomb', and much of his best comedy (for example, Mr Mould's arrangements in *Martin Chuzzlewit*, ch. xix, pp. 320–5) serves this view. 'Real affliction, real grief and solemnity' were too often outraged, he felt when a child at his first funeral ('Medicine men of civilisation', repr. in *UT & RP*, p. 285); and the plainness that he demanded for his own funeral in his will was what he desired of others too – even the Duke of Wellington (Forster, 1928, p. 859; Coutts *Letters*, p. 208: 23 September 1852). Nor was this view unique. Mrs Gaskell's *Mary Barton* (1848) contains many deaths, but, for example, Davenport's funeral is 'a simple walking funeral, with nothing to grate on the feelings of any; far more in accordance with its purpose', she continues, 'than the gorgeous hearses, and nodding plumes, which form the grotesque funeral pomp of respectable people' (ch. 6).

Yet many shared the view expressed in *The Old Curiosity Shop* that a form of immortality was supplied by memory of the dead. That great distiller of nineteenth-century commonplace, Samuel Smiles, instructed his readers (1888 edn, p. 363) that

> The example of a great death may be an inspiration to others, as well as the example of a good life. A great act does not perish with the life of him who performs it, but lives and grows up into like acts in those who survive the doer thereof and cherish his memory. Of some great men, it might almost be said that they have not begun to live until they have died.

Smiles, who considered himself a Christian, was convinced that 'character, embodied in thought and deed, is of the nature of immortality' ibid., p. 21). Thus Nell is raised above the community by her saintliness, and lives on in the memory of those who cherished it. George Eliot exclaimed 'O may I join the choir invisible/Of those immortal dead who live again/In minds made better by their presence' (*Jubal and Others Poems*, 1874); while Comte turned his life into 'a perpetual hymn' to the memory of his beloved Clothilde de Vaux (quoted in Willey, 1964, p. 205). The belief in a subjective version of immortality cut across the lines of those who believed in God and those who did not; Dickens was one of those who did.

IV

Yet, for many contemporary readers, the novelist's treatment of Nell's death was highly objectionable – even blasphemous. The High Church *Christian Remembrancer* (vol. 4, December 1842, p. 592) complained that

> if we except her haunting the old church, not a single christian feature is introduced. The whole matter is one tissue of fantastic sentiment, as though the growth of flowers by one's grave, and the fresh country air passing over it, and the games of children near it, could abate by one particle the venom of death's sting, or cheat the grave of any the smallest element of his victory.

This was a year after the novel appeared. Soon Harriet Beecher Stowe was writing in the *New-York Evangelist* that while Nell might talk 'sentimentally of angels and heaven', and even 'delightfully' of dying, Dickens did not appear to recognise 'such a person as Jesus Christ', or 'such a book as the Bible' (quoted in Wagenknecht, 1965, p. 150; the death of little Eva in her own *Uncle Tom's Cabin*, 1852, ch. 26, was hardly exemplary). Even the *North British Review*, less committed to a religious standpoint, was disturbed:

> When our hearts are touched, it is not right, and to a well constituted mind it is painful, to leave us with a few vague sentiments scarcely even of natural religion, and a picturesque sketch perhaps of a Bible in the background, but with no reference to the revelation it contains, and to those truths which furnish the only true ground of hope to the dying, and of consolation to the bereaved. (vol. 3, May 1845, pp. 84–5)

There is some justification for these charges. As we have seen, the doctrine of immortality articulated in the novel, with its emphasis on secular resurrection through memory, is not specifically Christian. Moreover, nowhere does Dickens appear to provide explicit support for the central Christian belief in Christ as mediator and redeemer. If Nell's 'artless prayers' are supposed to contain any such affirmation, Dickens, like old Trent, has 'no memory for the words', knowing only that 'they were very good' (ch. xv, p. 116). Nell may have been asked to 'say a prayer that night for a sick child', when the favourite scholar lies dying (ch. xxiv, p. 185); and she and the schoolmaster may have 'read some prayers aloud' in her church-home (ch. lii, p. 388); but there is little explicitly Christian belief in these details.

But Dickens does not attempt to put forward an explicit belief; nor is his religion sympathetic to the formal elements in Christianity. If the Bible is alluded to, it is not assumed to be directly inspired, or a literal guide to the faithful. The Church's role is perfunctory, its buildings are little more than fitting places in which to die, offering tolling bells and a burial service. The old clergyman attached to Nell's church 'would rather see her dancing on the green at nights' than have her 'sitting in the shadow of our mouldering arches' (ch. lii, p. 390), which suggests precisely the sentimental or 'natural' religion objected to. On the other hand, when Nell first visits the village church she is granted a vision of the dead in a state of eternal, painless sleep; and then, of joyful resurrection. To begin with, Nell picks up a Bible, which she reads (the texts unspecified), and then lays down, to think 'of the summer days and bright springtime that would come – of the rays of sun that would fall in aslant, upon the sleeping forms' (ch. liii, p. 398: see Illustration 4). The consolation of a benevolent nature whose timeless processes suggest continuity and happiness rather than mortality is in itself neither

4 'Resting among the tombs' (*The Old Curiosity Shop*, ch. liii, p. 396), by George Cattermole, chosen by Dickens for his sympathetic rendering of religious sentiment. Nell pauses, Bible in hand, to think of 'summer days'.

inspiring nor profound. The conception of death as sleep is common enough: 'After life's fitful fever, he sleeps well.' Yet it is scriptural as well as literary: in the Old Testament sleep is used to suggest a state of shadowy semi-being in which the dead continue to survive ('So David slept with his fathers, and was buried in the city of David', I Kings 2:10); and in the New, it is tied to the hope of resurrection ('But now is Christ risen from the dead and become the first fruits of them that slept', I Corinthians 15:20). And Dickens extends Nell's church experience to include a scene which points unequivocally to the hope of resurrection. After leaving the chapel, she slowly climbs the church tower, winding up through the darkness, until she stands upon the turret top:

Oh! the glory of the sudden burst of light; the freshness of the fields and woods, stretching away on every side, and meeting the bright blue sky; the cattle grazing in the pasturage; the smoke, that, coming from among the trees, seemed to rise upward from the green earth; the children yet at their gambols down below – all, everything, so beautiful and happy! It was like passing from death to life; it was drawing nearer Heaven. (ch. liii, p. 398)

Although there is no specific reference to the Bible, or to the saving efficacy of Christ, this *is* a representation of the belief that after death there is a resurrection, when man will come face to face with God, the source of all light. Nell's final 'assumption' is prefigured by that 'burst of light' – an image reinforced by recurrent references to light and sky in the novel (ch. xv, p.144; ch. xlvi, p. 345; ch. lxxi, p. 539).

Thus Dickens expresses an accepted Christian belief, by drawing on and reinforcing the common stock of literary and scriptural associations. To grasp this is to grasp one of the basic principles of his method. His beliefs are rarely explicit; they are characteristically embodied in the texture of the work. Here his expression is unsophisticated partly because a child cannot be expected to conceive of the resurrection in more adult terms. Nell 'thinks as a child', and so draws no more than a 'plain and easy moral' from death (ch. xxvi, p. 194). We have always to recall that Dickens is a novelist, and works through the medium of the novel. He is neither theologian (like, say, Newman), nor didactic essayist (such as Carlyle or Arnold). Moreover, he preferred childish expressions of a simple faith in life after death to pious familiarity with the text of the Bible, theological abstractions, or catechistic complexities.

Like Thackeray or Charlotte Brontë, Dickens especially disliked the notion of children as depraved creatures who need to be frightened by death. To the author of a collection of children's tales, he wrote:

I think it monstrous to hold the source of inconceivable mercy and goodness perpetually up to them as an avenging and wrathful God who – making them in His wisdom children before they are men and women – is to punish them awfully for every little venial offence which is almost a necessary part of that stage of life. I object decidedly to endeavouring to impress them with a fear of death, before they can be rationally supposed to become accountable creatures, and so great a horror do I feel at the thought of imbuing with strict doctrines those who have just reflection enough to know that if God be as rigid and just as they are told He is, their fathers and mothers and three fourths of their relations and friends must be doomed to Eternal Perdition, and [*sic*] if I were left to choose between the two evils I would far rather that my children acquired their first principles of religion from a contemplation of nature and all the goodness and beneficence of the Great Being Who created it, than I would suffer them with such strict construction ever to open a Bible or a Prayer Book, or enter a place of Worship (Pilgrim *Letters*, Vol. 1, p. 568: 25 July 1839)

In other words, Christianity as it is usually taught could and should be disregarded in so far as it endangered the conception of God as a benign and merciful being. Dickens is sometimes sentimental and imprecise; but it is no less religious to say that children should not have the fear of damnation held up to them as a warning than it is to insist that they should. It is no less religious, though from some points of view it may be less orthodox, to stress natural religion rather than faith in the teaching of the church.

The scenes leading up to Nell's death, with their emphasis on the benevolent processes of nature offering 'assurances of immortality' (ch. lxii, p. 543), should be read in this context, before they are criticised for lacking Christian features. A widespread literature for children had developed which characteristically proclaimed

> It's dangerous to provoke a God
> Whose power and vengeance none can tell;
> One stroke of His almighty rod
> Can send young sinners quick to hell.
> (Quoted in Ewbank, 1959, p. 7)

This comes from the *The Children's Friend*, a religious miscellany for the young, edited by the Reverend Carus Wilson (1791–1859), who will be remembered as Brocklehurst catechising little Jane Eyre on her posthumous destination, and foretelling the dread end awaiting naughty children (*Jane Eyre*, ch. 4). It has been said of Carus Wilson that 'in the business of frightening little children into being Evangelical little children he was a prodigious master' (Brown, 1961, p. 463); and the grim inevitability with which juvenile error is rewarded by death in his stories confirms this judgement. A truant Sabbath-breaker, for example, who 'dares the anger of an offended God' by sliding on the ice, is bound to fall in and drown (*Child's Companion . . .*, 1838, pp. 176–9). Mary Haldane, a girl of 16 when *The Old Curiosity Shop* first appeared, wrote of the terrors of 'extreme evangelical influences': 'We can hardly be thankful enough to Charles Dickens and Charlotte Brontë for exposing these evils' ([Haldane], n.d., pp. 54–5).

This is why Dickens omits the venom of death's sting from Nell's end. But he does not entirely remove it from the novel. Quilp's final struggle against death provides us with a glimpse of terror. The misshapen dwarf realises that he has trapped himself and, hearing potential rescuers, he cries out

– with a yell, which seemed to make the hundred fires that danced before his eyes tremble and flicker, as if a gust of wind had stirred them. It was of no avail. The strong tide filled his throat, and bore him on, upon its rapid current.

Another mortal struggle, and he was up again, beating the water with his hands, and looking out, with wild and glaring eyes that showed him some black object he was drifting close upon. The hull of a ship! He could touch its smooth and slippery surface with his hand. One loud cry now – but the resistless water bore him down before he could give it utterance, and, driving him under it, carried away a corpse. (ch. lxvii, p. 510)

The fire on the wharf becomes Quilp's premonition of hell; while the resistless Thames, frequently suggestive in Dickens of time sweeping man to death, here carries the defiant, mocking and apparently indestructible Quilp (who has already survived a premature wake) to his appropriate end. Whereas Nell dies gradually, peacefully and painlessly, surrounded by friends and religious uplift, Quilp's death is thoroughly nasty, and short. And while Nell is interred in holy ground, the dwarf's waterlogged body is buried at last 'with a stake through his heart in the centre of the four lonely roads' (chapter the last p. 549).[3] There are times when Nell succumbs to 'an involuntary chill – a momentary feeling akin to fear' (ch. lii, p. 389). But such moments are immediately overcome by consolatory thoughts, most effective when imagined in terms of visionary moments taken from what must have been a familiar source: Nell seems to see 'the roof opening, and a column of bright faces rising far away into the sky, as she had seen in some old scriptural picture once, and looking down on her, asleep' (ch. lii, p. 389). On their second day's journey out of London, Nell and her grandfather observe, in a labourer's cottage, 'a few common, coloured scripture subjects in frames upon the wall and chimney' (ch. xv, p. 119). It is striking how often Dickens conceives of his religious subjects in terms akin to those of such prints, a common feature of the home in his time (see Illustrations 5 and 18). And not only of the home: Mayhew reported a crossing-sweepers' lodging room filled with sacred prints in little black frames – including 'The Adoration of the Shepherds' matched by a portrait of Daniel O'Connell (Quennell, n.d., p. 396). When Inspector Bucket turns his lamp upon an infant lying in Tom-all-Alone's slum, his companion Snagsby 'is strangely reminded of another infant, encircled with light, that he has seen in pictures' (*Bleak House*, ch. xx, p. 312). His charitable impulses reflect the belief that the memory of such prints may survive as a reservoir of genuine religious feeling, to be tapped in later life.

Dickens's use of this visual material is related to a deep and consistent sympathy for the unsophisticated religious conceptions of ordinary

5 'The Sermon on the Mount', from a painting by W. Dobson (1610–46). A typical 'cottage print', from *Scripture Prints: Intended Chiefly for Distribution Among the Poor*, ed. Rev. H. J. Rose and Rev. J. W. Burgon (Oxford and London, 1851).

people, to their 'naturally' good impulses, denied by prevailing social and religious attitudes. Thus Nell's death sanctifies the charity of people like the prostitute at the races, who gives her some money and begs her to 'go home and keep at home for God's sake' (ch. xix, p. 151); in contrast with the respectable religiosity of, say, Miss Monflathers, associated with Evangelical religion through her approval of Hannah More, the poet Cowper and Dr Watts, as well as with the forces of utilitarianism, in her arraignment of Nell for being a mere 'wax-work child', when she might assist the progress of manufacturing technology to the extent of her 'infant powers'. It is the 'motherless and poor' teaching apprentice, Miss Edwards, who braves her employer's scorn to wipe away Nell's tears (ch. xxxi, pp. 235–7).

In his treatment of Nell, Dickens attempts to engage with a level of belief not catered for by the religious periodicals. He has primarily in mind, as one lone reviewer accurately observed, the vast number of his readers, many of whom were 'not at all, or only slightly, imbued with religious principles' (*Metropolitan Magazine*, vol. 30, March 1841, p. 78). And his religion is expressed accordingly.

V

Recent comment does not reveal much more appreciation of Dickens's purposes in *The Old Curiosity Shop* than that of contemporary religious reviewers. Q. D. Leavis remarks on

> Cattermole's sentimental picture of Nell on her death-bed, 'At Rest', with its very obvious and trite appurtenances of the Madonna and Child above her bed-head, the open window for the departing soul, the hour-glass and the song-bird on the window-sill, the prayer-book in the dead girl's hand, the contrast between her youthful simplicity and the decayed Gothic magnificence of her surroundings – all easily taken in (because conventional and hackneyed) even by the illiterate who could only listen to instalments read aloud. (Leavis and Leavis, 1970, p. 345; see Illustration 6)

It is not Cattermole's sentimentality, but Dickens's closeness to popular religion, which has charged Nell's deathbed with the familiar emblems of immortality, so 'easily taken in' by the illiterate. (He gave his illustrator unusually detailed instructions for the execution of this scene: Pilgrim *Letters*, Vol. 2, pp. 171–2, 199.)

But it is understandable that a modern reader should wish to call Dickens's treatment of Nell's death sentimental, as much as a reviewer in the *Christian Remembrancer*, though for different reasons. Apart from Mrs Leavis's intellectual snobbery, it must be said that we experience

6 'At rest' (*The Old Curiosity Shop*, ch. lxxii, p. 540), by George Cattermole.

difficulty in accepting the simplified formulations of an earlier age's conventions and beliefs. On the other hand, we have our own forms of sentimentality. Graham Greene's *The Power and the Glory* (1940) contains two child deathbeds, one of a Victorian 'sentimental' type, the other forcibly 'modern'. The 'charming story' of a girl 'dying of consumption very firm in her faith at the age of eleven', who has a vision of a figure 'with a golden crown', belongs to the world of false, conventional Christianity, according to Greene; while the boy, shot by a gangster on the run, who dies 'with a kind of fury of pain', as his mother and the priest-hero watch 'the eyeballs roll up and suddenly become fixed, like marbles in a solitaire-board, yellow and ugly with death', belongs to the 'real' world, in which the priest who attempts to provide the religious assurance expected of him finds his prayers 'weigh him down like undigested food' (pt 2, chs 1 and 4). The overemphatic imagery of disgust and ugliness indicates a characteristically modern form of sentimentality. Rather than condemning Dickens we should try to understand *The Old*

Curiosity Shop by reading it with a due sense of the expectations it was intended to satisfy.

Alongside that branch of contemporary religious writing which portrayed death as a dismal corrective, there was also a branch which stressed the happiness of death, and in which little saints, filled with the power of forgiveness, linger endlessly to provide touching farewells and moving reflections in the assembled mourners. A favourite was Legh Richmond's *The Dairyman's Daughter* (1814), which tells how the simple faith of a pure and innocent country girl sustains her through consumption and death, the whole imbued with a rustic charm strongly reminiscent of Nell's story. Richmond is more explicitly Christian than Dickens, but there is a remarkably similar emphasis upon the softening, consoling effect of nature in the face of death: after a gleam of sunlight lights up his dying heroine's room, 'emblematical of the bright and serene close of this young Christian's departing season', Richmond reflects that 'natural scenery, when viewed in a Christian mirror, frequently affords very beautiful illustrations of Divine truths' (Richmond, n.d., pp. 78–9).

Dickens's 'mirror' may not have been quite so Christian, but then nor was, say, Wordsworth's. Like the Wanderer's Friend in *The Excursion* (1814), Dickens meant to utter 'endearing words' (bk 2, l. 506) to soften the painful emotions associated with death, and especially as purveyed by the stricter Christian tradition:

> 'They to the grave
> Are bearing him, Little-one,' he said,
> 'To the dark pit; but he will feel no pain.
> His body is at rest, his soul in heaven'.
> (bk 2, ll. 508–11)

Nell is also drawn to a 'dark pit' (ch. lv, p. 413: a common scriptural and literary image for death or hell); but the stark fact of death is immediately qualified by restful suggestions ('She was dead. No sleep so beautiful and calm ...', ch. lxxi, p. 538), building up to a reiteration of the schoolmaster's consolation:

> When Death strikes down the innocent and young, for evey fragile form from which he lets the panting spirit free, a hundred virtues rise, in shapes of mercy, charity, and love, to walk the world, and bless it. Of every tear that sorrowing mortals shed on such green graves, some good is born, some gentler nature comes. In the Destroyer's steps there spring up bright creations that defy his power, and his dark path becomes a way of light to Heaven. (ch. lxxii, p. 544)

Even the more critical of Dickens's contemporaries, such as R. H. Horne, found this 'brief homily' on Nell's death 'profoundly beautiful'. Indeed, Horne quoted the exhortation in full, divided it up into blank verse, and remarked that it was 'worthy of the best passages in Wordsworth' (Horne, 1844, Vol. I, p. 67). Hardly an appreciative response to Wordsworth's best verse; but Horne is misled by the similarity of moral and religious inspiration. More recent critics have compared Dickens's conception of Nell with Wordsworth's treatment of, for example, Lucy, or the Little Maid of 'We Are Seven'. But Dickens's kinship with Romanticism is not limited to an affinity with Wordsworth. Shelley's 'A Summer Evening Church-Yard' (*Alastor; And Other Poems*, 1816) concludes:

> Thus solemnized and softened, death is mild
> And terrorless as this serenest night:
> Here could I hope, like some enquiring child
> Sporting on graves, that death did hide from human sight
> Sweet secrets, or beside its breathless sleep
> That loveliest dreams perpetual watch did keep.

While Leigh Hunt's *Literary Examiner* for 29 November 1823 (p. 349) typically reflected that

> there is something so serene, so calming, and so unworldly within the precincts of a church-yard, that to me it is impossible to pass one where the rudely built church is caught at intervals between the gloomy yews, and perchance the well-grown oaks, and where the moss-grown dwarf wall, running between the holy sanctuary and the busy road, marks the boundary of death and the never-failing sanctuary that gives peace to trouble and rest to fatigue. Here the houseless wanderer finds a home.

Hunt's two 'houseless wanderers' finally die in the serene surroundings of the remotest rural churchyard of them all.

Philip Collins thinks that Dickens owed more to Romantic 'middlemen' such as Hunt than to the poets (1965, p. 213). Certainly Dickens's form of Romanticism carries quite perceptible echoes of Hazlitt, Lamb, De Quincey, Leigh Hunt, Washington Irving and Samuel Rogers. Little examination of these echoes has been made, but to read Hazlitt's 'On cant and hypocrisy', Lamb's 'Dream children', De Quincey's 'Suspiria de profundis', Irving's *Sketches* (especially 'Rural funerals', 'The widow and her son' and 'The broken heart'), or Rogers's poetry is to discover the same tendency towards a belief that God is in nature, and religion in the heart. Children are typically blessed with a natural, untrammelled piety. No very precise connections can be made between Dickens and these writers, beyond the fact that Dickens owned some of their works, or, on occasion, wrote letters expressing a sympathy of interest and feeling. Samuel Rogers may have been one of the more important figures here, since *The Old Curiosity Shop* was dedicated to him, and there is an allusion to his 'Ginerva' (from *Italy, a Poem*) in the figure of the wandering old man in ch. xii, p. 91.[4] But it is also significant that Dickens had a copy of Leigh Hunt's *Religion of the Heart* (1853), which was inscribed to him 'from his constant admirer and obliged friend, Leigh Hunt' (Pilgrim *Letters*, Vol. 1, p. 239, note 2; Stonehouse, 1935, p. 63). The book preaches the gospel according to the Romantics, drawing freely on both the New Testament and the Romantic poets for inspiration. And on receiving a 'very hearty' letter about Nell and *The Old Curiosity Shop* from Irving, Dickens responded: 'There is no living writer, and there are very few among the dead, whose approbation I should feel so proud to earn' (Pilgrim *Letters*, Vol. 2, p. 267: 21 April 1841).[5]

The adducing of parallels, analogies and possible echoes necessarily involves assertions of a debatable kind. But one cannot read old Trent's 'we will travel afoot through the fields and woods, and by the side of rivers, and trust ourselves to God in the places where He dwells' (ch. xii, p. 94) without feeling that at this stage Dickens was drawing on a familiar current of contemporary Romanticism. His affiliations with the Romantics, contemptuously hinted at by the *Christian Remembrancer* and the *North British Review*, should be seen as part of an attempt to discover a form of religion not merely acceptable to the minority who could afford to concern themselves with the niceties of doctrine. To insist that, in his treatment of Nell's death, Dickens pays too little attention to theological issues, is to miss the point. Dickens felt he had to move away from accepted beliefs, or 'forms', when they came into conflict with the needs of the poor and ignorant. What was required was a religion 'so general in great religious principles as to include all creeds', since 'such a thing as the Church Catechism is wholly inapplicable to the state of ignorance that now prevails' (Pilgrim *Letters*, Vol. 3, p. 565: 16 September 1843). The religion of Romanticism supplied at least one channel through which this could be carried out.

VI

This does not mean that Dickens ignores the earlier, pre-Romantic Protestant tradition with which his readers continued to be familiar, as the overall shape of *The Old Curiosity Shop* reminds us: Nell and her grandfather's journey is strongly reminiscent of a religious tradition in which life, and death, are represented as a pilgrimage from this world to the next. Dickens's knowledge of Bunyan is already apparent in *Oliver Twist*, subtitled 'The Parish Boy's Progress'. In *The Old Curiosity Shop*, he has Nell remember 'an old copy of the Pilgrim's Progress, with strange plates, upon a shelf at home', as she and her grandfather pause to look back towards London, where the cross of St Paul's glitters above the smoke; 'I feel as if we were both Christian', she says, 'and laid down on this grass all the cares and troubles we brought with us; never to take them up again (ch. xv, pp. 116–17). Inevitably, the 'two pilgrims' are directed towards a path which begins at a wicket-gate (ch. xv, p. 114; xvi, p. 122), their trials and tribulations only just begun. Thomas Arnold referred to *The Pilgrim's Progress* as 'a complete reflexion of Scripture, with none of the rubbish of the theologians mixed up with it' (Stanley, 1845, Vol. 2, p. 67), and the course of Nell and her grandfather's journey is structured to include many parallels with Bunyan. The city they escape is a 'Babel', where figures dart about the 'long, deserted streets' (ch. xv, p. 114); it is a lost city, surrounded by a waste land 'blackened and blistered' by the flames of the brickfields (ch. xv, p. 115), reminiscent of Gehenna, the scriptural image of hell based on the perpetually burning waste dump outside the walls of Jerusalem, as well as Bunyan's City of Destruction. Through the wicket-gate, Nell and the old man meet the itinerant showmen who take them to the races, a kind of Vanity Fair, with all its jugglers and its cheats. Again, like Christian, they must escape, but there are further temptations; and when the old man, Nell's burden of sin, thinks of stealing from Mrs Jarley to supply funds for his renewed gambling mania, Nell cries out 'What shall I do to save him?' (ch. xlii, p. 316), echoing the opening lament of *The Pilgrim's Progress*, with this important difference, that her concern is to save the old man, not herself.

This follows from the fact that Nell, like Oliver before her, is not a sinner, but, in a sense, a child of grace. She is already saved, and therefore does not need to pray on her own behalf, but instead for the hoary old pack of sins she carries around with her. She draws the old man towards the ultimate goal, glimpsed as the 'blue Welsh mountains far away' (ch. xlvi, p. 347), like the Delectable Mountains, or that 'sudden burst of light' she finds on the church tower (ch. liii, p. 398), suggestive of the Celestial City itself. But she knows no more than that she must reject the corrupting life of the city, and take her 'sacred charge' ever farther away from the 'guilt and shame' associated with it (ch. xliv, p. 333); whereas Bunyan's Christian knows from the start that it is 'eternal life' he seeks – he knows where he is going. *The Pilgrim's Progress* opens on the traditional Christian note of a deep consciousness of sin, and the depravity of man's nature. But Dickens believes in 'natural goodness of heart': for him, some are good, and need to escape evil, while those who are bad cannot find salvation by a pilgrimage. This view is by no means orthodox; nor does he wish to express it in orthodox terms. A *range* of feelings, crossing sectarian or dogmatic boundaries, is to be evoked. Hence the peculiarly mixed, 'romance' form of *The Old Curiosity Shop*, the way it hovers uncertainly between allegory, religious fable, fairytale and surface realism.

R. H. Horne noticed that the novel 'had a sort of German look'(Horne, 1844, Vol. I, p. 49). He was not the only one of Dickens's contemporaries to notice this. Poe thought La Motte Fouqué's *Undine* (1811) the only work to have approached the pathos and 'ideality' of *The Old Curiosity Shop* (article in *Graham's Magazine*, May 1841, repr. in Ford and Lane, 1966, p. 24), while Sara Coleridge felt Dickens's novel 'a good deal borrowed from *Wilhelm Meister*', and Nell 'no doubt' suggested by Mignon (Forster, 1928, p. 723, note). We do not know if Dickens had read *Undine*, and Forster states that Wilhelm Meister was 'not then known' to the novelist. But it is significant that these readers should have sensed an affinity between *The Old Curiosity Shop* and the German romances with which they were obviously familiar. Dickens could not read German, but this was less of a disqualification than it would seem, at least for the purpose of discovering the romances, since these were very soon translated (by men such as Carlyle) and made widely available. 'The favourite writers are Fouqué, Grimm, Pichler, Richter, Spindler, and Tieck' (Morgan and Hohlfeld, 1949, p. 62).

The whole conception of Nell, 'so very young, so spiritual, so slight and fairy-like a creature' (ch. i, p. 13), smacks of their stories. One of the translated romances in Thomas Roscoe's four-volume collection *German Novelists* (1826), of which there were two copies in Dickens's library, tells of a fair, innocent and pious maiden driven by her cruel father to escape to a remote retreat in the woods where her father eventually finds her, but in vain, since she dies anyway, her deathbed involving a vision of her beloved awaiting her in heaven, sanctification by the rural folk, and angels miraculously strewing spring flowers (in autumn) upon her bier ('Notburga', in Roscoe, 1826, Vol. 2, pp. 131–40). Fouqué's 'Headmaster Rhenfried and his Family ' includes a scene of 'little Margery' falling asleep, and losing 'all recollection of the fearful occurrences of that dismal night: it had no longer power over her gentle spirit, for the smile that played upon her lips betokened innocent and angelic rest' (in ibid., Vol. 2, p. 381).

Dickens was very probably familiar with the contents of Roscoe's collection, which included work by Fouqué, Tieck, Hoffmann and the Grimms;[6] and he may well have drawn upon their writings for the general inspiration of the form of *The Old Curiosity Shop* (if not detailed passages) – which began as a short romance among others in *Master Humphrey's Clock*. Earlier interpolated tales, such as 'The Story of the Goblins who Stole a Sexton', or 'The Story of the Bagman's Uncle', in *Pickwick Papers*, or, most obviously, 'The Baron of Grogzwig' in *Nicholas Nickleby* (ch. vi, pp. 66–75), reveal an early interest on his part in transplanting the subjects and techniques of German romance to English fiction; but with *The Old Curiosity Shop* it was the first time he did this for an extended narrative.[7]

Dickens's purpose in so attempting to re-create something of the form and matter of German popular romances in *The Old Curiosity Shop* was to express their pervasive aura of primitive, 'natural' spirituality. They contain a kind of universal religion: the apprehension of powers for good and evil, of a mysterious life present in all things, reaching back to God. The traditional, popular forms of the romance made these apprehensions more immediately and widely recognisable than if couched in the conventional formulas of orthodox Christianity. If there is much that is self-consciously derivative and whimsical about Nell and her wanderings in the woods, there are also occasions on which a deeper and richer note is struck, for example, towards the end of Nell's sojourn with Mrs Jarley, when she takes a walk alone one evening, looking up at the stars and feeling 'a companionship in Nature', which develops into a waking dream or vision:

... She raised her eyes to the bright stars, looking down so mildly from the wide worlds of air, and, gazing on them, found new stars burst upon her view, and more beyond, and more beyond again, until the whole great expanse sparkled with shining spheres, rising higher and higher in immeasurable space, eternal in their numbers as in their changeless and incorruptible existence. She bent over the calm river, and saw them shining in the same majestic order as when the dove beheld them gleaming through the swollen waters, upon the mountain-tops down far below, and dead mankind, a million fathoms deep. (ch. xlii, p. 311)

Dickens expresses this vision of an eternity beyond the stars which is also within ourselves through a subtle use of scriptural echoes: the dove as the visible spirit of God moving over the dead waters of corrupt mankind is at the same time the Pauline image of man's incorruptible soul, risen to take its place in eternity (Genesis 8:8–9; I Corinthians 15:52).

Nell's dream-vision is not far from the exaltations of the German Romantics, for instance, Jean Paul Richter, whose 'most celebrated' dream (quoted by Carlyle in his essay on Richter) takes off from a churchyard on an apocalyptic voyage where 'world after world' reveals 'glimmering souls upon the Sea of Death' (Carlyle, 1871–4, Vol. 3, pp. 54–8) – a vibrantly suggestive image, which could well have fertilised Dickens's own imaginative musings during the 'solitary walk by starlight' along the cliffs at Broadstairs when, it seems, Nell's strange fancy came to him (Pilgrim *Letters*, Vol. 2, p. 131: 4 October 1840). Dickens had probably read Carlyle's essay, which first appeared in the *Foreign Review* in 1830, and was republished in the 1840 edition Dickens possessed (Pilgrim *Letters*, Vol. 4, p. 716). Richter, whose power to suggest the deep interconnectedness of things impressed many English

writers, from Dickens to Meredith, believed the fancies of childhood
provided special access to the numinous; what Dickens later called

> The dreams of childhood – its airy fables; its graceful, beautiful,
> humane, impossible adornments of the world beyond: so good to be
> believed in once, so good to be remembered when outgrown, for then
> the least among them rises to the stature of a great Charity in the heart,
> suffering little children to come into the midst of it, and to keep
> with their pure hands a garden in the stony ways of the world. (*Hard
> Times*, bk 2, ch. ix, p. 197)

Dickens resists the visionary, even as he evokes it. So, while sensing its
value, its essential link with the transcendent, he limits it to brief, even
isolated, moments like Nell's fleeting dream.

Dickens's attitude to the death of Nell was by no means confined to
himself in his weaker moments, nor merely to his more susceptible
readers: it was part of a European cultural phenomenon, originating in
Germany, but spreading until its precise origins become barely
traceable. To accept this is to accept a reinterpretation of the usual
simplistic explanations of the difference between our response to Nell's
death and that of Dickens's contemporaries. His beliefs struck far deeper
than has commonly been supposed; and although his treatment of death
contains its weak moments, an understanding of the cultural context
helps one to see that there are also occasions, such as Nell's vision of the
stars and the dead beneath the sea, when his literary imagination is as
strongly present as the desire to express a belief. If Dickens's religion is
felt to be weakly sentimental and vague, it must be seen that this is not
uniformly true even of the novel most widely taken to represent these
qualities. He was trying to establish a faith at once his own, and one
expressing beliefs and feelings widely shared. If he was unorthodox, this
was nevertheless within a recognisable, complex tradition. The Catholic
historian Lord Acton paid cynical tribute to this when he observed of
Dickens: 'Certain Germans of the last century remind me of him as to
religion.' They 'divinified humanity, or humanised religion, and taught
that man was perfectible, but childhood perfect'. They

> hated intolerance, exclusiveness, positive religion, and with a
> comprehensive charity embraced all mankind and condemned alike
> differences of faith and distinctions of rank, as insurrection against the
> broad, common humanity. Their religion was a sort of natural religion
> adorned with poetry and enthusiasm – quite above Christianity.
> Herder was a man of this stamp. Surely Dickens is very like them.
> Nothing can be more indefinite than his religion, or more human.
> (Quoted in Gasquet, 1906, pp. 241–2: 8 December 1861)

4
Dickens and the False Religious Cry

'He's a rum dog. Don't he look fierce at any strange cove that laughs
or sings when he's in company!' pursued the Dodger. 'Won't he
growl at all, when he hears a fiddle playing! And don't he hate other
dogs as ain't of his breed! - Oh, no!'
    'He's an out-and-out Christian,' said Charley.
(*Oliver Twist*, ch. xviii, pp. 116–17)

'How Abraham must be smoothing his etherial [*sic*] robes, to make a
warm place in his bosom for the Protestant champions of this time!'
(Charles Dickens, letter to W. C. Macready, 24 August 1841)

I

Lord Acton's stress on Dickens's hatred of 'intolerance, exclusiveness,
positive religion' implies a close link between anti-sectarianism and anti-
formalism. Dickens tends to reject, or at least ignore, 'positive religion',
but this does not mean his faith is negative. For Dickens, as for men such
as Herder, 'positive religion' represented a sterile reliance upon the
merely credal or doctrinal element in belief, and his opposition to it
sprang from a Romantic sense of Christianity as a religion of the heart, a
religion based upon deep feelings about man, nature and God. These
feelings by definition transcend sectarian barriers, and offer a unifying
rather than divisive faith. Dickens participates in a popular Romantic
tradition of non-dogmatic Christianity through his persistent emphasis
on dreams and the irrational, as well as a reiterated conviction of the
irrelevance of religious 'forms'. But in his hatred of 'intolerance,
exclusiveness, positive religion' he also draws on an earlier and more
specifically English, middle-class tradition – that of liberal Protestantism.
    This becomes apparent in the novel which succeeds *The Old Curiosity
Shop, Barnaby Rudge* (serialised in *Master Humphrey's Clock* from
February to November 1841). Powerful reminders of the Romantic cast
of Dickens's religious vision remain, especially in relation to the
murderer Rudge, his long-suffering wife, and their Idiot Boy, Barnaby.
But the main emphasis of the story directs us elsewhere, towards an ideal
of toleration and reasonableness in religion derived from the tradition of
Milton and Locke, champions of the free religious conscience. This is

where the novelist's obsessive centre of interest now lies. The change of emphasis is at least partly due to his new subject: whereas *The Old Curiosity Shop* was primarily concerned with the subjective aspect of belief, in dealing with the inner life of a child facing death, *Barnaby Rudge* tells of the events leading up to the anti-Catholic riots of 1780, and is therefore much more involved with the social aspect of religion. Critics have stressed the centrality of social themes in *Barnaby Rudge*, its testing exploration of the relationship between authority and rebellion, and the nature of historical change; but this does not mean that Dickens was uninterested in the cause of the riots themselves, namely, religious fanaticism. He took it as an opportunity to express his hatred of religious intolerance and oppression, and to urge the need for a positive, counteracting force of goodwill based on reason and common sense.

Dickens believed passionately in the need for reasonableness and toleration in religion. And he did so at a time when it was becoming difficult to be liberal-minded and respectful towards Catholicism in particular, as popular prejudice once again found in that faith a threat to Protestantism, morality and public order. But in *Barnaby Rudge* true Protestantism is revealed in terms of the frank and honest attitudes of the locksmith Gabriel Varden, who abhors his wife's mindless anti-popery, and resists as strongly as he can the general upsurge in religious fanaticism around him. Dickens himself, as he admits in the preface to the novel, had 'no sympathy with the Romish church', and this has led him to be generally accused as 'always a hearty and naïve anti-Papist' (A. Wilson, 1969, p. 11). Certainly a superficial reading of his works, which contain numerous asides aimed at, for instance, the monastic ideal (see *Great Expectations*, ch. xlix, pp. 377–8) supports this view. But it is too easy to place Dickens merely in terms of simple-minded anti-popery, as his open support in *Barnaby Rudge* for the right of Catholics to worship as they please, and to be free of legal restraint, suggests. As the *Salopian Journal* complained, his attack upon 'No popery' from the 'liberal' viewpoint, though it 'please a few . . . must offend many' (quoted in Pilgrim *Letters*, Vol. 2, p. 367, note 4). Dickens was capable of questioning not only his own religious proclivities, but also those of a large proportion of his contemporary audience.

On the other hand, there was a limit to how far Dickens's tolerance in religion could go (as there was for Milton and Locke before him), and he could not bring himself actively to encourage the special doctrines of Catholicism, any more than he could the pseudo-revelations of sectarian fanatics like Lord Gordon. If, in *Barnaby Rudge*, he promotes a liberal Protestant attitude towards Roman Catholics, it is evident from subsequent works, most notably *Pictures from Italy* (1846), and *A Child's History of England* (1851–3), that he came to feel powerful antipathies towards the characteristic features of the Catholic religion. A study of the religion expressed in *Barnaby Rudge* needs to be complemented by at least some analysis of these two works. For a man like Dickens, who firmly held to the basic Protestant idea that priestly mediators and ritual practices were superfluous, and pomp and hierarchy anathema, whether in the Catholic church proper, or in Laudian elements within the Anglican church, the views expressed in *Pictures from Italy* and *A Child's History of England* are not too surprising. *Pictures from Italy* reveals that it was at least partly in response to his experience of Continental Catholicism that Dickens's antagonism developed, while *A Child's History of England* shows how deeply Dickens had come to fear that the Church of England might be in danger from this 'foreign' faith, always liable to reassert itself. The novelist could even be led into the occasional exaggerated outburst – as when, in 1851, he shared contemporary hysteria over the relatively minor event (as it seems now) of the Pope's attempt to elevate Dr Wiseman to Cardinal and Archbishop of Westminster, and wrote to Miss Burdett Coutts, '*Now*, a war between the Roman Catholic Religion – that curse upon the world – and Freedom, is inevitable' (Coutts *Letters*, p. 186). But if Dickens's Protestantism overrides his liberalism at times, this should help remind us how firmly grounded his religion was in the traditional, popular faith.

II

John Locke's *A Letter Concerning Toleration* (1689), which offers the basic text for the liberal Protestant tradition to which Dickens belongs, opens:

Honoured Sir,

Since you are pleased to inquire what are my thoughts about the mutual toleration of Christians in their different professions of religion, I must needs answer you freely, that I esteem that toleration to be the chief characteristic mark of the true church. For whatsoever some people boast of the antiquity of places and names, or of the pomp of their outward worship; others, of the reformation of their discipline; all, of the orthodoxy of their faith – for every one is orthodox to himself – these things, and all others of this nature, are much rather marks of men striving for power and empire over one another, than of the church of Christ. Let any one have never so true a claim to all these things, yet if he be destitute of charity, meekness, and goodwill in general towards mankind, even to those that are not Christians, he is certainly yet short of being a true Christian himself.[1]

Dickens's fundamentally anti-sectarian stance, his 'unswerving faith in Christianity itself, apart from sects and schisms' (Forster, 1928, p. 298), is very close to this. Perhaps the most explicit expression of his views was made in his will, when he exhorted his children to be guided by the 'broad' teaching of the New Testament, 'and to put no faith in any man's narrow construction of its letter here or there' (ibid., p. 859); although it was in July 1843 that he wrote his acid parable, 'A Word in Season', on those sects who 'curse all other men, and curse each other', while the 'Christian Pariah . . . Does all the good he can, and loves his brother' (repr. in Kitton, 1903, p. 90). *Barnaby Rudge* is less explicit, but equally expressive of the evils of religious intolerance.

The novel's purpose is made abundantly clear in the preface. Dickens claims that the Gordon Riots teach 'a good lesson', namely, 'that what we call a religious cry is easily raised by men who have no religion, and who in their daily practice set at nought the commonest principles of right and wrong; that it is begotten of intolerance and persecution; that it is senseless, besotted, inveterate and unmerciful'. The sadistic hangman, Ned Dennis, provides the most obvious example of this 'lesson', although it is also imaged forth in a wide range of characters, from the Machiavellian John Chester and Lord Gordon's secretary Gashford, both of whom manipulate the prejudices of others for their own ends, to simpler figures such as the malicious Miggs, or Mrs Varden, who is finally converted to common sense and tolerance by her experience of the riots. But why should Dickens so emphasise the 'lesson', why insist that 'perhaps we do not know it in our hearts too well, to profit by even so humble an example as the "No Popery" riots?' The answer lies in the reappearance of the popular fanaticism and anti-popery of the earlier period: as Hood noted, *Barnaby Rudge* was in this respect 'particularly well-timed' (1842, p. 79).

As Dickens and his readers were well aware, the Protestant Association, so active in Gordon's time (1779–80), had been resurrected, partly as an unforeseen consequence of the 1829 legislation for the emancipation of Roman Catholics, which, although a political manoeuvre to prevent the Irish situation from deteriorating, rather than an expression of tolerance, reminded people of their traditional dread of popery. During discussion of the Bill

> Illiterate citizens were confronted with pictures of Bloody Mary burning heretics, with large-lettered placards about murder and Judge Jeffreys, with the question whether they would have a protestant or a Popish king . . . Cartoonists showed the Tory ministers responsible for the bill, the Duke of Wellington and Mr Peel, carrying rosaries and kissing the Pope's toe. (Chadwick, pt 1, p. 8)

And in the years immediately following the passing of the Act, Irish Protestant orators poured into England to ensure that the cause of Protestant Ascendancy was not lost on this side of the Irish Channel as well. The Orange Associations, at once ultra-Protestant and ultra-conservative, were reorganised, and when in 1833 the first *Tracts for the Times* appeared the cry of popery was inevitable, although it was hardly appropriate at this stage of the Oxford Movement, and it was soon raised. Wherever they looked, evangelical Protestant extremists were uncovering proofs of a 'gigantic papal conspiracy', a 'tide of despotism and superstition', against which the faithful were exhorted to rise up 'with God's blessing' (*Protestant Magazine*, vol. 1, January 1839, p. 24).

For liberal Protestants there must have been some doubt as to where exactly this tide of despotism and superstition was flowing: as *The Times* remarked (6 November 1841, p. 4), 'Any man who will look down a page of the reports of the Protestant Association, and stop his eye for a moment when he observes the word "cheers", "Hear, hear", will find them always called forth by some broad denunciation or coarse anecdote against the unrepresented Papist'. It is very unlikely that *The Times*'s reports of the Association's activities would fail to alarm Dickens, or that he would not feel drawn to respond. *Barnaby Rudge* was in its creator's mind at least from the signing of the original contract in May 1836, and that Dickens was aware of the growth of anti-Catholic feeling before its appearance is suggested by an otherwise puzzling moment in *Oliver Twist*, when the Maylies' doctor tries to bully Giles and Brittles into giving shaky evidence of the capture of Oliver, by asking them if they are Protestant: on receiving replies in the affirmative, 'Then tell me this,' he says, 'both of you – both of you! Are you going to take upon yourselves to swear that that boy upstairs is the boy that was put through the little window last night?' (ch. xxx, pp. 194–5). It was a repeated charge against Roman Catholics that their word could not be relied upon, a charge made not only by deluded extremists: out of the supposed laxity of the faith towards truth arose one of the most celebrated controversies of the time, between Charles Kingsley and John Henry Newman, eventually producing Newman's famous defence, the *Apologia Pro Vita Sua*.

For Dickens the word 'Protestant' has a real meaning: it denotes a felt belief, and its corruption through extreme evangelical prejudice was more than absurd – it was dangerous. By permitting, even encouraging, the expression of bigotry, those in authority could all the more easily exploit the ignorant. Thus Dickens was in favour of broadening the religious base of education – he believed that schools 'on the broad principles of Christianity' would be the 'best adornment' for the land (1847 Preface to *Pickwick Papers*); but the cry of popery was used to stir up opposition towards any relaxation of the laws governing the teaching of religion, and those who favoured the Church losing exclusive control over education were bracketed in a so-called 'triple alliance of Romanists, socinians, and infidels' (*The Times*, 28 October 1839, p. 3). In the end, *Barnaby Rudge* is less concerned with expressing sympathy for the Catholics (although it does so), than with reminding Protestants that, as Locke said, mutual toleration signified the true church. Once this was forgotten, and sectarianism ran rife, the 'worst passions of the worst men' disguised themselves under the 'mantle of religion' (ch. xlv, p. 339).

III

The contrast between base instincts and their religious disguise is pressed home at every level in *Barnaby Rudge*, from Westminster to Clerkenwell, from Sir John Chester, MP, whose plots and stratagems wear a pious, Protestant mask, to Miggs the maidservant, whose malice and sexual envy are expressed in an illiterate jumble of evangelical cant. Vengeance and envy are the main underlying motives: Chester, Gashford, Simon Tappertit and Miggs share a powerful desire to avenge real or imagined slights by forwarding the anti-Catholic riots where they can; while the mob itself, composed, except for a sprinkling of 'honest zealots', of the 'very scum and refuse of London, whose growth was fostered by bad criminal laws, bad prison regulations, and the worst conceivable police' (ch. xlix, p. 374), attacks churches, chapels, private houses, mansions and prisons, in what becomes an outburst of social vengeance on a vast and terrifying scale. Dickens avoids dealing with 'enthusiasts, however mistaken' (ch. xlviii, p. 367), since his attack is not directed at the genuinely religious, although this does limit his analysis of intolerance: after the first day of disturbances, the 'really honest and sincere' Protestants drop away from the mob (ch. l, p. 382). It is an unpleasant irony that when the violence finally ebbs away authority and justice are reinstated with almost equal ferocity and arbitrariness, turning many of the condemned into victims of the riots themselves: 'It was a most exquisite satire upon the false religious cry which had led to so much misery, that some of these people owned themselves to be Catholics, and begged to be attended by their own priests' (ch. lxxvii, p. 597).

The focus of Dickens's attack is clear: it is the worldly Chester who first introduces the distinction between Catholic and Protestant in the novel, using it as a reason for separating his son and Haredale's daughter (ch. xii, p. 92). It is a distinction about which he is, characteristically, quite cynical: as he asks his son, 'how could you ever think of uniting yourself to a Catholic, unless she was amazingly rich? You ought to be so very Protestant, coming of such a Protestant family as you do' (ch. xv,

p. 121). This conscious exploitation of religious difference to further his own ends makes Chester one of the most evil characters in the novel; it also enables him further to corrupt those who have less consciously taken up the false religious cry, such as Mrs Varden, through whom Dickens illustrates the development of religious bigotry from a relatively isolated, even harmless phenomenon, to a 'moral plague' (ch. liii, p. 403) infecting the whole society. At first she seems merely another of Dickens's deluded matrons, 'most devout when most ill-tempered' (ch. iv, p. 38). But when she finds herself face to face with the hatred and violence which her misuse of religion has, in its own small way, helped to foster, she is converted to tolerance.

It is worth looking at Mrs Varden's bigotry more closely. She is a 'staunch Protestant' in the same mould as Mrs Nubbles or Mrs Weller, believing, for example, that the 'publicans coupled with sinners in Holy Writ were veritable licensed victuallers' (ch. xiii, p. 103), in order to justify her opposition to the Maypole Inn, while passing cheerfully from 'the nothingness of good works' to 'the somethingness of ham and toast' when she herself is there (ch. xxi, p. 125). Dickens makes fun of her, but the ease with which anti-Catholic elements are grafted on to her evangelical cant suggests more serious issues are at stake. More deeply revealing is the scene of Chester's attempt to persuade her to prevent Dolly from acting as go-between for his son and Emma Haredale: in Gabriel's absence, he begins with a little sexual flattery, then quickly picks up his cue from Mrs Varden:

'. . . Let us be sincere, my dear Madam –'
'– and Protestant,' murmured Mrs Varden.
'– and Protestant above all things. Let us be sincere and Protestant . . .'
(ch. xxvii, p. 206)

Observing Mrs Varden leaning on the Protestant Manual, Chester knows exactly the right note to strike, justifying the separation of his son and Emma on 'points of religious difference' (ch. xxvii, p. 208). Mrs Varden is completely won over: 'this gentleman is a saint' (ch. xxvii, p. 209). Earlier, Chester reflected that the relationship between father and son was 'positively quite a holy sort of bond' (ch. xii, p. 94), but here he denies it, as he will throughout the novel, not only with respect to Edward, his legitimate son, but also, and more culpably, with respect to Hugh, his 'natural' son. His attempt to disrupt the Varden household is forcefully confirmed by Phiz's illustration of him holding Mrs Varden's Protestant Manual aloft while he leers down at her, unaware that the Manual points towards the Holy Family (ch. xxix, p. 217; Illustration 7).

Miggs instinctively recognises Chester's game as one that she, too, has been playing, and aids him by confirming the flattering insinuations

7 'Mr Chester making an impression' (*Barnaby Rudge*, ch. xxix, p. 217), by 'Phiz'. Chester inadvertently points the Protestant Manual at the Holy Family.

through which he undermines Mrs Varden's loyalty to Gabriel Varden, sidling up to agree that Mrs Varden is undervalued by her husband, 'for we never know the full value of *some* vines and fig-trees till we lose 'em. So much the worse, sir,' she continues, 'for them as has the slighting of 'em on their consciences when they're gone to be in full bloom elsewhere' – casting up her eyes, Dickens adds, 'to signify where that might be' (ch. xxvii, p. 205). Her richly absurd profanities place Miggs somewhere between Squeers and Mrs Gamp in scriptural inconsequentiality. But she is only apparently inconsequential: the vine and the fig-tree relate to the biblical conception of peaceful and happy coexistence, when every man should be able to invite his neighbour 'under the vine and under the fig-tree' (Zechariah 3:10); Dickens may also be alluding to the familiar parable of the barren fig-tree which symbolises outward piety without inner, fructifying faith (Matthew 21:19) a fitting image of Miggs's character, as well as of the hypocrisy present in the scene as a whole. Religion must be judged according to its fruits here and now; piety on its own is almost meaningless.

For Dickens, belief is a form of self-expression, apart from ecclesiastical or theological complications; a view which, although perfectly legitimate, besides coinciding nicely with the demands of the novel-form in allowing for the exploration of insights into individual and social behaviour, has limitations. Character and belief do not always coincide quite so neatly; and it is questionable whether belief need only be judged in human terms, since it is hardly logical to measure religion's fruits without considering whether the God really exists who is supposed to inspire them. But Dickens is not interested in raising this consideration; and in relation to his purpose of attacking false piety in *Barnaby Rudge*, it is appropriate that a good Christian should be someone who, like Mrs Rudge or Gabriel Varden, expresses his or her faith in action rather than word or pious gesture. Other novels, and other novelists, will have a different approach. For George Eliot, the merging of character and belief is apparently typical of the popular mind:

> It was a great anomaly to the Milby mind that a canting evangelical parson, who would take tea with tradespeople, and make friends of vulgar women like the Linnets, should have so much the air of a gentleman, and be so little like the splay-footed Mr Stickney of Salem, to whom he approximated so closely in doctrine. And this want of correspondence between the physique and the creed had excited no less surprise in the larger town of Laxeter, where Mr Tryan had formerly held a curacy; for of the two other Low Church clergymen in the neighbourhood, one was a Welshman of globose figure and unctuous complexion, and the other a man of atribiliar aspect, with lank black hair, and a redundance of limp cravat – in fact, the sort of thing you might expect in men who distributed the publications of the Religious Tract Society, and introduced Dissenting hymns into the Church. ('Janet's Repentance', *Scenes of Clerical Life*, ch. 3)

George Eliot's treatment of evangelicalism and Dissent is generally received favourably, while Dickens is reviled for his caricatures. Yet in the above passage she does stoop to the introduction of two Low Church caricatures; and she could also create William Dane of Lantern Yard, whose 'narrow slanting eyes and compressed lips' signal a canting Nonconformist hypocrite, while, more favourably, Silas Marner's 'defenceless, deer-like gaze' evidently expresses a trusting simplicity of high moral and spiritual value (*Silas Marner*, pt 1, ch. 1).

The point is that George Eliot was, in general, involved in a more realistic art than Dickens. Moreover, she was writing with the detachment of one anatomising a past society, rather than urging an awareness of present evil, as was Dickens. Certainly she was more familiar with the variety and depth of evangelical and Nonconformist life, especially in the provinces, than Dickens. But, again, Dickens is a satirist, sharpening his reader's awareness of a current evil by means of exaggeration and ridicule. The existence of the evil cannot be denied: according to *The Times*'s report of the formation of a new branch of the Protestant Association in Exeter Hall (17 June 1841, p. 5) 'the female branches of the society, as usual upon such occasions', made up 'the great majority of the assembly'. Gabriel Varden remains 'in outer darkness' (ch. xxxvi, p. 274), while the women rush to join the Protestant Association. An important reason for their attraction is implied by Miggs's commendation of Gordon: 'first, in respect of his steady Protestantism, then of his oratory, then of his eyes, then of his nose, then of his legs, and lastly of his figure generally, which she looked upon as fit for any statue, prince, or angel, to which sentiment Mrs Varden fully subscribed' (ch. xli, p. 312). Lord George Gordon himself, with his severe dress, his sense of power over female followers, and his eye for such details as Miggs's lack of physical endowments (ch. xxxvi, p. 274), suggests an association between puritan fanaticism and carnality familiar from earlier satirists such as Swift.

The danger to which Miggs's views may lead in a society coming under the sway of fanaticism is brought out in her response to the rioters. While Mrs Varden is shocked into repentance and common sense – a somewhat sudden transformation, but not unprepared for, nor unconvincing – Miggs simply relishes the opportunity provided by the rioters for venting her bitterness and hatred. She cries out to the mob from her attic:

> 'Simmun and gentlemen, I've been locked up here for safety, but my endeavours has always been, and always will be, to be on the right side –the blessed side – and to prenounce the Pope of Babylon, and all her inward and outward workings, which is Pagin. My sentiments is of little consequences, I know,' cried Miggs, with additional shrillness, 'for my position is but a servant, and as sich, of humilities, still I gives expressions to my feelings, and places my reliances on them which entertains my own opinions!' (ch. lxiii, pp. 482–3)

Miggs's Heepish railings are drawn from Revelations 17, although she cannot bring herself to use the word 'Whore', merely alluding to it indirectly with 'the Pope of Babylon'. If this manic utterance seems improbable, one need only look at a characteristic passage (by the anti-Catholic novelist, Mrs Tonna) in the *Protestant Magazine* ([Tonna], 1840, pp. 14–15):

> There sits the crowned Antichrist, supported on either side by the scarlet-robed ministers of Babylon the Great, in the very seat of her dominion; on the very soil that must, ere long, be ignited by the breath

of the Lord's hot vengeance; in the very identical place whence issued the mandate for the Vaudois' butcheries – the massacre of St Batholomew – the blazing fires of Smithfield, Oxford, Canterbury, and all our chief towns; – there, where the wine of the wrath of her fornication is brewed, and poured into the mantling cup of the harlot; – there, for the gratification of a wanton curiosity and more wanton display, do the descendants of our martyred forefathers eagerly press to do that, rather than to acquiesce in which, any enlightened protestant would yield his body to the racks of the Inquisition, that work their pullies in the dungeons beneath.

This is the authentic voice of popular anti-popery in the 1840s.

From the very beginning of *Barnaby Rudge*, self-delusion is associated with religious fanaticism; the riots only make explicit what is implicit from the start. Thus, in describing the Maypole Inn, the narrator tells an 'apocryphal' tale going back to the days of Queen Elizabeth, according to which the 'virgin monarch' spent a night at the Inn, after which, 'while standing on a mounting block before the door', she cuffed an unlucky page; some doubt this tradition, but, whenever the landlord 'appealed to the mounting block itself as evidence, and triumphantly pointed out that there it stood in the same place to that very day, the doubters never failed to be put down by a large majority, and all true believers exulted as in a victory' (ch. i, p. 1). It is a victory for superstition and irrationality, the mounting block serving as a kind of pseudo-relic of popular credulity. When Gordon and his retinue arrive at the Inn five years later, their talk reminds us of this tale and its implications: 'At a crisis like the present,' remarks Gordon, 'Queen Elizabeth, that maiden monarch, weeps within her tomb, and Bloody Mary, with a brow of gloom and shadow, stalks triumphant –' (ch. xxxv, p. 264). The point is driven home in an extended explanation of the appeal of Gordon's false religious cry:

To surround anything, however monstrous or ridiculous, with an air of mystery, is to invest it with a secret charm, and power of attraction which to the crowd is irresistible. False priests, false prophets, false doctors, false patriots, false prodigies of every kind, veiling their proceedings in mystery, have always addressed themselves at an immense advantage to the popular credulity, and have been, perhaps, more indebted to that resource in gaining and keeping for a time the upper hand of Truth and Common Sense, than to any half-dozen items in the whole catalogue of imposture . . . (ch. xxxvii, p. 277)

Gordon, the 'roaring lion' (ch. xlviii, p. 366), is a false prophet (see I Peter 5:8), to be resisted only through an appeal to reason rather than feeling, common sense rather than individual revelation. Dickens, strongly aware of the negative side of popular belief, is urging reason and common sense as forces for toleration throughout the novel, from Gabriel Varden calling on Joe Willet to turn his father's caprices aside by 'temperate remonstrance' rather than by 'ill-timed rebellion' (ch. iii, p. 24), to the good locksmith trying, equally vainly, to protect Sim Tappertit from the consequences of getting his soul 'into his head' (ch. iv, p. 34), as he does when the riots begin (ch. li, pp. 389–94). Gabriel is, as his name implies, a figure of power – literally, the muscular Christian – directed towards good. In a society corrupted by false shows of religious faith, his staunch, patient belief in God and goodwill towards men is as clear as the 'tink, tink, tink' emitted from the Golden Key workshop, 'a perfect embodiment of the still small voice' (ch. xli, p. 307). Gabriel cannot do more than offer passive resistance to the forces of discord, malice and evil, but he is one of Dickens's most persuasive images of good. Significantly, the novelist first thought of naming *Barnaby Rudge* after him. His imagination must have been fired by the idea of that one man, the Moravian locksmith, who refused to obey the demands of the rioters, under threat of death (see Butt and Tillotson, 1968, pp. 85–6). While the locksmith defies the fanatics, all the Lord Mayor can do is whimper to those Catholics who beg protection from him, 'what a pity it is you're a Catholic! Why couldn't you be a Protestant, and then you wouldn't have got yourself into such a mess?' (ch. xli, p. 467).

The corrupt state of the beliefs of a whole society, already suggested in *Oliver Twist* by the depiction of the lack of charity in those specifically responsible for providing it, is re-emphasised and extended by the prostitution of that 'noble' word, 'Protestant', to the 'vilest purposes': as that eminently 'public' figure, Ned Dennis puts it, 'If these Papists get into power, and begins to boil and roast instead of hang, what becomes of the laws in general, what becomes of my work! If they touch my work that's a part of so many laws, what becomes of the laws in general, what becomes of the religion, what becomes of the country!' (ch. xxxvii, pp. 284–5). The perverted logic of ignorance, fear and prejudice has replaced what 'the Almighty gave us', namely, 'common charity . . . common sense and common decency', in the words of the Catholic Haredale (ch. xliii, p. 329). By stressing the primacy of reasonableness in religion, as opposed to 'enthusiasm' (a word Dickens uses in the eighteenth-century sense of religious fanaticism), the novelist shows he is working within the liberal, latitudinarian tradition. If Dickens supports the Romantic emphasis upon individual, felt belief, rather than conventional formalism, for instance, in his approval of Barnaby's simple prayers, he is at the same time very much aware of the dangers inherent in this attitude: Barnaby is a creature without reason and, as the narrator remarks, there is something 'terrible' about the absence of the soul's 'noblest powers' in him (ch. iii, p. 28). Dickens's original plan was for the riots to be led by three escaped lunatics, a proposal Forster persuaded him to drop (Forster, 1928, p. 168). In fact, the combination of Barnaby's mindlessness, Hugh's animality and Dennis's sadism brings out the tyranny of unreason with as much force as Dickens could have desired. Appropriately, too, the novelist has Barnaby enticed into the Protestant movement by the deluded Lord Gordon himself, pathetically reinforcing the associations of insanity surrounding both figures (ch. xlviii, p. 366).

Dickens recognised the importance of setting rational limits to man's tendency to trust in his imagination where religion is concerned. And yet this does not mean that he believed religion should ultimately be grounded in reason. His position is paradoxical, and the paradox is most obvious in Barnaby Rudge himself: deficient in reason or common sense, and so easily misled into joining the anti-Catholic riots, he nevertheless belongs to Dickens's hallowed congregation of children and fools who alone are permitted a glimpse of a world beyond this one. Like Nell and Oliver, he is in touch with the stars:

> He, a poor idiot, caged in his narrow cell, was as much lifted up to God, while gazing on the mild light, as the freest and most favoured man in all the spacious city; and in his ill-remembered prayer, and in the fragment of the childish hymn, with which he sung and crooned himself asleep, there breathed as true a spirit as ever studied homily expressed, or old cathedral arches echoed. (ch. lxxiii, p. 563)

Barnaby's body is imprisoned, while his soul yearns for the light, a potent neo-Platonic image, suggestive of the influence upon Dickens of the Romantic vision, charged as it was with such Platonic conceptions. The more orthodox Christian view is implied by the shocked minister who witnesses Barnaby's emotional farewell to his bird Grip on the brink of the scaffold: 'For one in his condition, to fondle a bird! –' (ch. lxxvii, p. 593). The paradox is pushed further with Hugh, 'more brute than man' as he calls himself (ch. lxxvii, p. 596), who nevertheless offers his life (anticipating Sydney Carton) for his friend. He senses Barnaby's spiritual worth, even listening to Barnaby's prayers (ch. xii, p. 96). A providential hand seems to keep Hugh from murdering anyone during the riots, the redeeming streak in his nature emerging in moments such as that in which he prevents Dennis from summarily executing old John Willet (ch. liv, pp. 415–16). And although Dickens shows little respect in general for the sacramental aspect of religion, he has Hugh walk on to the scaffold 'with a careless air, though listening at the same time to the Service for the Dead, with something between sullen attention, and quickened curiosity' (ch. lxxvii, p. 596). Death requires some ceremony, or ritual, or recognition, and there is a hint of spiritual worth in the man who glimpses this.

But if these glimmerings of a religious vision granted to Barnaby and Hugh imply some faith in popular belief, the general tendency of *Barnaby Rudge* is to heap scorn on the merely superstitious and easily deluded elements among the people. John Willet's tale about the 'virgin monarch' suggests the ease with which the kind of popular beliefs Dickens was trying to speak for in *The Old Curiosity Shop* could turn into stupidity and fanaticism, leading eventually to the breakdown of society.

IV

While the 'Protestants' in *Barnaby Rudge* are ridiculed and exposed, the Catholics are allowed a sympathy which, however, falls somewhat short of their actual beliefs. The success with which Dickens manipulates plot and character to this end was admitted by the partial *Dublin Review* (vol. 21, September 1846, p. 188), which declared that the novelist had given

> a vivid sketch of the Gordon riots, putting in prominent places the character of a sturdy, highminded Catholic gentleman, and that of a mean, vindictive Protestant villain. The theme was interesting and untrodden ground, capable of furnishing excellent materials for a new novel; and having undertaken to write upon it, he conformed to the growing spirit of the age, and told a great deal of warning and unpalatable truth. His narrative is much more like history, in the first and most important ingredient thereof, than Fox's Book of Martyrs, or Robertson's View of Europe, or many portions of Hume's England; and therefore, notwithstanding certain important – and, considering the nature of the work, perhaps unavoidable – omissions, we thank him for it. For his recent libel on the Catholic religion we thank him not.

(The 'recent libel' was *Pictures from Italy*.) What the *Dublin Review* has not noticed is that it is a *false* Protestant, Chester, who is prominently contrasted with the 'sturdy, highminded Catholic' Haredale, and moreover that Haredale is in many respects unsympathetic.

But we feel for Haredale when, the first victim of the anti-Catholic mob, he is stoned on the steps to the river at Westminster. We never see him attending mass or confession, but Dickens does attempt to suggest the Catholic cast of his mind, making him urge Hugh, as the latter leads him to the fatal turret in the Warren: 'Gently with your light, friend. You swing it like a censer' (ch. xxxiv, p. 258); or, having him think of his home as 'but another bead in the long rosary of his regrets' (ch. lxi, p. 470). Even novelists much more sympathetic towards Catholicism than Dickens, such as Disraeli (for example, in *Henrietta Temple*, 1837), could omit overt as well as implicit references to Catholic characters' beliefs. Yet the overall effect of Haredale reflects negatively upon Catholicism: his temperament, as well as the murder of his brother, have led him to sin against the cardinal Dickens virtue of caring for your fellow men: he has 'mused and brooded, when my spirit should have mixed with all God's great Creation' (ch. lxxix, p. 605); and his 'atonement' for this, and for killing Chester, is to take himself off to a religious establishment 'known throughout Europe for the rigour and severity of its discipline', where he dies, 'after a few remorseful years' (chapter the last, p. 628). Asceticism is unnatural, even in a man who wishes to atone for killing someone.

Nevertheless, Dickens tries to be fair to the Catholics. Even before Haredale is introduced, the unjust nature of the old laws is suggested: on the one occasion when Haredale and Gordon meet, Haredale reflects bitterly that he, 'as good a gentleman' as Gordon, must hold his property 'by a trick at which the state connives because of these hard laws', and that he and other Catholics may not teach 'our youth in schools the common principles of right and wrong', without being 'denounced' (ch. xliii, p. 330). The riots in fact sprang from what was initially an organised attempt to petition Parliament against Sir George Savile's Act of 1778, which repealed those portions of the Act of 1699 condemning Catholics who kept schools to perpetual imprisonment, and preventing them from inheriting or purchasing land (see de Castro, 1926, for a full account). To begin with, the Catholics have little fear for their property or lives, and little indignation for wrongs already sustained; confident in the government's protection (which they lose subsequently, for a time), they have a 'well-founded reliance on the good feeling and right thinking of the great mass of the community, with whom, notwithstanding their religious differences, they were every day in habits of confidential, affectionate, and friendly intercourse', all of which reassured them that 'they who were Protestants in anything but the name, were no more to be considered as abettors of these disgraceful occurrences, than they themselves were chargeable with the uses of the block, the rack, the gibbet, and the stake in cruel Mary's reign' (ch. li, p. 387).

Yet, if Dickens supports the cause of tolerance at a time of growing anti-Catholic feeling in *Barnaby Rudge*, possibly even to the extent of alienating his readers (who did not flock to it as they had to its predecessors), this seems to mark the end of his open tolerance towards Catholics. Nor was he alone in turning against them. As long as Catholicism seemed limited to a clearly defined unconforming minority, it could be, and was, tolerated by liberals. But when the swing to Rome among the leaders of the Oxford Movement became widely known, primitive fears were aroused even among those Protestants who had been calling for reason and justice. As the *Protestant Magazine* (for once, correctly) observed (vol. 2, June 1840, p. 161), the appearance of 'this

Germ of Popery in the heart of our Established Church' made it
incalculably more difficult to defend: Sydney Smith, who had supported
the emancipation of the Catholics for the best liberal motives, wrote of
'doing duty at St Paul's, and preaching against the Puseyites'; Hood
(whom Dickens admired even more) found his earlier tolerance shaken:

> The Tories got up in England, for party purposes, fanaticism against
> the Catholics, and a cry of 'the Church in danger'; now, what is called
> 'High Church of Englandism', the higher it is carried, the nearer it
> approaches to Popery. I predicted the result, that it would end in
> making a sort of Pope of the Archbishop of Canterbury, and now there
> is actually a schism in the High Church party at Tory Oxford, a
> Popish-Protestant section writing in favour of celibacy, images, &c.,
> &c. ([Broderip and Hood], 1869, p. 346: 13 April 1841)

As for Dickens himself, he went on to write a farcical 'Report of the
Commissioners Appointed to Inquire into the Condition of the Persons
Variously Engaged in the University of Oxford', which attacked the
moral bankruptcy of those for whom 'justice, mercy, charity, kindness,
brotherly love, forbearance, gentleness, and Good Works, awaken no
ideas whatever', but who instead concerned themselves with the 'mere
terms Priest and Faith', the latter a compound of little boys, water and
lighted candles (*The Examiner*, 3 June 1843, repr. *MP*, p. 97). Identifying
Catholics within and without the Church, Dickens was coming to believe
that those who held beliefs which had so fatal a facility of being degraded
into corrupt, idolatrous practices must be excluded from even the most
comprehensive Christian community.

V

Dickens's 'libel on the Catholic religion', as the *Dublin Review* angrily
called *Pictures from Italy*, reflects a more sustained and deeply felt
opposition to that faith than anything previously written by him. The
sojourn abroad from July 1844 to June 1845 on which this, his second
travel-book, was based, evidently confirmed his growing suspicions about
the characteristic features of Roman Catholic worship. His religious
sympathies were in any case swinging towards a more radically Protestant
position at this time, and so his Continental experiences were perhaps
bound to seem evidence to him of how much a superstitious, even
fanatical reliance upon outward 'forms' tended to oppress and degrade.

Although to call *Pictures from Italy* a 'libel' is to some extent to mistake
its nature and intent, as well as to obscure what was true in its reflections
upon religion in France and Italy, the *Dublin Review* has a case, as

Dickens implicitly recognises when he defends himself by hoping not to be misunderstood by 'Professors of the Roman Catholic faith', since he has done his 'best' in 'one of my former productions' (*Barnaby Rudge*), to 'do justice to them'. 'I trust', he continues,

> in this, they will do justice to me. When I mention any exhibition that impressed me as absurd or disagreeable, I do not seek to connect it, or recognise it as necessarily connected with, any essentials of their creed. When I treat of the ceremonies of Holy Week, I merely treat of their effect, and do not challenge the good and learned Dr Wiseman's interpretation of their meaning. When I hint a dislike of nunneries for young girls who abjure the world before they have ever proved or known it; or doubt the *ex officio* sanctity of all Priests and Friars; I do no more than many conscientious Catholics both abroad and at home. ('The reader's passport', p. 260)

Dickens has Wiseman's *Four Lectures on the Offices and Ceremonies of Holy Week* (1839) in mind here. The *Lectures* criticised the common Protestant approach of stressing the 'effect' of the Holy Week ceremonies, explaining that they should be seen as 'dramatic' in the 'noblest' sense, 'if pomp and magnificence, which formerly belonged to everything royal and noble, have in modern times been confined in our country to theatres, and have thence received a reproachful name, will any one conclude that the church, which has preserved them, ought to abandon them in consequence?' (Wiseman, 1839, p. 46). Dickens's description of Holy Week is couched in the very terms objected to by Wiseman, calling the ceremonies 'shows', and constantly employing theatrical metaphor: 'There was a great eye to character'; 'The Cardinals, and other attendants, smiled to each other, from time to time, as if the thing were a great farce' ('Rome', pp. 401, 403). The novelist's scorn for what appeared to him an indulgence in pretence and pomp amidst poverty and oppression is in line with the conventional attitude of Protestant travellers. The 'mummery' (a favourite term of derision) of Catholic ceremonies was described at length by Conyers Middleton in his famous *A Letter from Rome* (1729); and John Sterling, in Rome in December 1838, stated that familiarity with the place destroyed 'all tendency to idealise the Metropolis and System of Hierarchy into anything higher than a piece of showy stage-declamation' (quoted in Carlyle, 1871–4, p. 149). Paradoxically, however, Dickens's appreciation of the theatrical in general, even when part of a religious activity he rejects, leads him to mitigate his overall criticism. Thus, during the High Mass, there is an impressive moment at the raising of the Host, 'when every man in the guard dropped on one knee instantly, and dashed his naked sword on the ground'; it had, remarks Dickens, a 'fine effect'

('Rome', p. 370). And if the novelist seems to ridicule shrines and images by comparing them to puppets, a 'plaster Punch's show', or the like ('To Parma, Modena, and Bologna', p. 318; 'To Rome by Pisa and Siena', p. 360), such comparisons have sympathetic overtones, especially if we remember Dickens's delight in popular art, whether it is Punch and Judy, Astley's Theatre, or, in relation to religion, the scripture prints which lie behind many of his religiously charged scenes, and which, as we have seen in *The Old Curiosity Shop*, he often refers to favourably.[2]

In general, *Pictures from Italy* is anti-Catholic, and conforms to the experiences related by most of the great mass of travel-books and 'impressions' which appeared after the Napoleonic Wars, when the Continent was inundated by English travellers. The conventional response complained of the loose morals of the priests, the hypocrisy of Catholic ceremonies, the superstitions of the populace, the relics of paganism in Catholic ritual, along with 'a dozen other objections' which caused Englishmen 'to turn from Catholic Italy with disgust' (Brand, 1957, p. 219). Perhaps it was not too surprising that *The Times* should have found 'nothing new' in *Pictures from Italy* (1 June 1846, p. 7). All too familiar would have been references to the streets teeming with monks and priests, to the religious orders prying into family secrets so as to establish 'a baleful ascendency' over the people ('Genoa and its Neighbourhood', p. 296), to the 'monotonous, heartless, drowsy chaunting' always going on in the churches ('Rome', p. 382), or to the ignorance and degradation of the peasantry, exploited through their superstitious reliance upon images and relics (for example, 'Genoa and its Neighbourhood', pp. 298-9); familiar, too, would have been the visible incorporation of fragments of the 'old mythology' into Christian altars, 'the false faith and the true' thus 'fused into a monstrous union' ('Rome', p. 398) – Middleton's *A Letter from Rome* was subtitled 'shewing an exact conformity between Popery and Paganism: or the Religion of the present Romans, derived from that of their Heathen Ancestors'.

But Dickens was not completely conventional, although he seems at times like Mrs General, who compares the Rialto, 'greatly to its disadvantage, with Westminster and Blackfriars Bridges' (*Little Dorrit*, bk II, ch. v, p. 460). His was the expression of a personal response, the response of a committed liberal Protestant, although of course the book lacks the strong historical sense of, say, Newman or Thomas Arnold. Thus the crudely executed votive paintings in Avignon Cathedral, which include a portrait of a lady having her toe amputated, 'an operation which a saintly personage had sailed into the room, upon a couch, to superintend', are absurd, laughable, perhaps, but 'evidently among the compromises made between the false religion and the true, when the true was in its infancy'; 'I could wish', the novelist continues, 'that all the other compromises were as harmless. Gratitude and Devotion are Christian qualities; and a grateful, humble, Christian spirit may dictate the observance' ('Lyons, the Rhone, and the Goblin of Avignon', pp. 273–4). Dickens's sympathies are available for those elements in the religious activities he encounters which promote the social and moral well-being of the people. Hence it is the Cappuccini, the lowest and least learned of the religious orders, but those most visibly concerned with ministering to the poor, whom he singles out for approval ('Genoa and its neighbourhood', p. 296); and he pays 'all Christian homage' to one saint at least – Charles Borromeo of Milan: 'A charitable doctor to the sick, a munificent friend to the poor, and this, not in any spirit of blind bigotry, but as the bold opponent of enormous abuses in the Romish church' ('By Verona, Mantua, and Milan', p. 345). Borromeo's practical, humane and reformist spirit is very appealing to Dickens: 'Heaven shield all imitators of San Carlo Borromeo as it shielded him! A reforming Pope would need a little shielding, even now', he adds. As he must have been aware, the oppressive and unpopular Gregory XVI was Pope at the time of writing (1844–5), and dissatisfaction was rife among Italian liberals and nationalists.

Dickens, like other English liberals, was openly sympathetic to the reformist and nationalist cause. 'Years of neglect and oppression' had reduced the spirit of the Italian people, and yet they were 'noble', and might be 'raised up' from the ashes of their past history ('A rapid diorama', p. 433). Chesterton calls this inspired cockneyism, but it is much more than that. What the novelist saw was real: the degradation of the peasantry, the oppression of the people under the unjust, corrupt and reactionary sway of Austria, of the Neapolitan and papal governments. Nor did his interest in Italian social and political improvement cease when he left the country: in 1849 he appealed on behalf of refugees from the fall of Rome (see M[atz], 1914, p. 320); and in 1860 his strong sympathies for the Italians against their oppressors appeared in an article in *All the Year Round* ('The Italian prisoner', repr. in *UT & RP*, pp. 169–78). Later visits evidently hardened his conviction of the reactionary, oppressive nature of Catholicism. In Switzerland in 1846 he warmly supported the Geneva revolution to overthrow the Jesuits, and found in general

> On the Protestant side, neatness; cheerfulness; industry; education; continual aspiration, at least, after better things. On the Catholic side, dirt, disease, ignorance, squalor, and misery. I have so constantly observed the like of this, since I first came abroad, that I have a sad misgiving that the religion of Ireland lies as deep at the root of all its sorrows, even as English misgovernment and Tory villainy. (Pilgrim *Letters*, Vol. 4, p. 611: 27 August 1846)

Remarks such as these have led critics such as Edward Wagenknecht to argue that Dickens's dislike of Roman Catholicism was based less on 'strictly religious grounds' than on his conviction that it was not a 'progressive' religion (Wagenknecht, 1966, p. 225). But this is an unreal distinction: Dickens's liberalism *involves* a religious attitude. He disbelieved in both doctrine and practice as far as the Roman system was concerned; it only strengthened his conviction of its folly to observe the evil results it produced, or helped produce. He might well have concluded with Charlotte Brontë:

> My advice to all Protestants who are tempted to do anything so besotted as turn Catholic is, to walk over the sea on to the Continent; to attend mass sedulously for a time; to note well the mummeries thereof; also the idiotic, mercenary aspect of all the priests; and *then*, if they are still disposed to consider Papistry in any other light than a most feeble, childish piece of humbug, let them turn Papists at once – that's all. I consider Methodism, Quakerism, and the extremes of High and Low Churchism foolish, but Roman Catholicism beats them all. At the same time, allow me to tell you, that there are some Catholics who are as good as any Christians can be to whom the Bible is a sealed book, and much better than many Protestants. (Quoted in Gaskell, 1975 edn, pp. 240–1: Brussels, 1842)

Like that of Charlotte Brontë, Dickens's religion was Protestant also in its tenacious attachment to the English church. Unimpressed by St Peter's during Holy Week, he added: 'I have been infinitely more affected in many English cathedrals when the organ has been playing, and in many English country churches when the congregation have been singing' ('Rome', pp. 367–8).

VI

By 1850 fears of the introduction into England of what he remembered as popish excesses abroad brought Dickens round to something approaching the popular Protestant position he had deplored in *Barnaby Rudge*. Less than a month after Pius IX's Bull establishing Roman Catholic sees in England in 1850, a satirical attack on Catholicism and Puseyism by Dickens appeared in *Household Words* (repr. *MP*, pp. 254–61).[3] In it 'Mrs Bull' tells her fractious youngster, 'Master C. J. London' (Bishop Blomfield), about the 'Bulls of Rome', a family who brought 'Mr John Bull' a world of trouble in the past: 'They pretended to be related to us, and to have some influence in our family; but it can't be allowed for a single moment – nothing will ever induce your poor father to hear of it;

let them disguise or constrain themselves now and then, as they will, they are, by nature, an insolent, audacious, oppressive, intolerable race' (p. 258). This note was not confined to Dickens. Everywhere Protestants waxed wrathful over 'papal aggression', Landor publishing a tract in which he claimed that no religion had 'ever done so much mischief in the world as that which falsely, among innumerable other falsehoods, calls itself the catholic' (Welby, 1927–36, Vol. 12, p. 89), the press denouncing the proposed elevation of Dr Wiseman to Cardinal and Archbishop of Westminster. One of the few to have kept his head, the liberal clergyman F. W. Robertson of Brighton, commented: 'This foolish act of the Pope has made Protestants nearly beside themselves with terror' (Brooke, 1901 edn, Vol. I, p. 248).

This was the context in which Dickens's *A Child's History of England* appeared, initially in irregular instalments in *Household Words* from 25 January 1851 to 10 December 1853, subsequently in three volumes (1852–4). Most of it was dictated to Georgina Hogarth, and it was very much a sideline for the hard-pressed novelist, who completed *David Copperfield* and wrote *Bleak House*, in addition to editing *Household Words*, during this period. To compress two thousand years of English history into about two hundred and fifty pages of popular instruction is in any case no mean feat, but the result is likely to contain (as it does) much that is flippant, crude, or ill-informed, and not necessarily the considered, overall view of the author. Moreover, it is a *child's* history, based very largely, and at times word for word, upon Thomas Keightley's simple and popular *History of England* (1839). The work first surfaces as a project in 1843, when Dickens mentions intending to write 'a little history of England' for his eldest son Charley, then 6, not knowing 'what I should do if he were to get hold of any Conservative or High church notions' (Pilgrim *Letters*, Vol. 3, p. 482: 3 May 1843). Certainly he provided an antidote in his history, which is unremittingly opposed to kings and bishops, most of whom are fools or tyrants set on exploiting the common people. Henry VIII is 'a blot of blood and grease upon the History of England' (ch. xxviii, p. 390), James I 'His Sowship' (ch. xxxii, p. 436), Wat Tyler receives high praise (ch. xix, pp. 295–7); Cromwell, despite his Puritan connections, is acclaimed as a Carlylean hero (ch. xxxiv, pp. 480–95). The Glorious Revolution concludes the work.

Typical of the narrator's tone and attitude is what he tells us about Archbishop Laud:

> Laud, who was a sincere man, of large learning but small sense – for the two things sometimes go together in very different quantities – though a Protestant, held opinions so near those of the Catholics, that the Pope wanted to make a Cardinal of him, if he would have accepted that

favour. He looked upon vows, robes, lighted candles, images and so forth, as amazingly important in religious ceremonies; and he brought in an immensity of bowing and candle-sniffing. He also regarded archbishops and bishops as a sort of miraculous persons, and was inveterate in the last degree against any who thought otherwise. Accordingly, he offered up thanks to Heaven, and was in a state of much pious pleasure, when a Scotch clergyman, named LEIGHTON, was pilloried, whipped, branded in the cheek, and had one of his ears cut off and one of his nostrils slit for calling bishops trumpery (ch. xxxiii, p. 457)

Laud lacked humanity, but was earnest and devout; High Church indeed, but nevertheless a Protestant; while the fanatical Leighton may be said to have earned the typical punishment of the time for his hysterical libel against church and state. The source of Dickens's personal and partisan approach is quite evident in Keightley's *History* (see Vol. 2, pp. 345-8). Dickens, like Keightley, urges the Protestant view throughout. Although the Puritans are, as in his novels, exposed as 'an uncomfortable people, who thought it highly meritorious to dress in a hideous manner, talk through their noses, and oppose all harmless enjoyments', he is firmly on their side when they oppose 'Popish' plots (ch. xxxi, p. 423). An interdict forbidding services to be performed in the churches, couples to be married, bells to be rung, or the dead to be buried (Dickens's conception of the essentials of religious ceremony) simply adds a papal contribution to the general store of misery, 'not very like the widow's contribution, as I think, when Our Saviour sat in Jerusalem over against the Treasury, "and she threw in two mites, which make a farthing"' (ch. xi, p. 202: see Mark 12:41-4).

Yet Dickens's earlier tolerance occasionally struggles through: the Suppression of the Monasteries is disapproved of (ch. xxviii, p. 383); Elizabeth's rejection of the idea that leading Catholics should be executed at the time of the Armada commended (ch. xxxi, p. 431); although the majority of Catholics 'recoiled with horror' from the Gunpowder Plot, they were 'unjustly put under more severe laws than before' (ch. xxxii, p. 444). If the novelist wishes his young readers to reject High Church or Catholic forms of worship and belief, he also wishes them to allow Catholics to express their own beliefs, and by no means to hate them. In terms of what he tells them is the first great 'lesson' of Christianity, he could hardly do otherwise: to be 'good in the sight of GOD', we must love our neighbours as ourselves, 'and do unto others as we would be done by' (ch. i, p. 137).

5

Dickens and the Change of Heart

It is from this hour that I incline to date my Spiritual New-birth, or
Baphometic Fire-baptism; perhaps I directly thereupon began to be
a Man.
(Thomas Carlyle, *Sartor Resartus*, 1833-4, bk 2, ch. 7)

'Well, well!' said the Doctor, 'I am too old to be converted . . .
(*The Battle of Life*, 1846, Part the First)

I

With typically deceptive casualness, George Orwell once remarked that
Dickens was essentially a 'change of heart' man: 'he is always pointing to
a change of spirit rather than a change of structure' (Orwell, 1965 edn, p.
97). Far from implying by this that Dickens was a reactionary humbug –
a change of heart is '*the* alibi of people who do not wish to endanger the
status quo' – Orwell meant to suggest that in his own way Dickens was
deeply critical of society and its accepted values. If, like Blake, Dickens
was no politician, he could be as radical as the poet in his appeal to
absolute standards. This appeal becomes overt in the notion of individual
regeneration which comes to dominate Dickens's art during the 1840s, a
time when 'the hopelessness of any true solution of either political or
social problems by the ordinary Downing-street methods' was
'startlingly impressed' upon him by Carlyle's writings, as well as by his
own observations, with the result that he began to try to 'convert Society'
by showing that its happiness rested 'on the same foundations as those
of the individual, which are mercy and charity not less than justice'
(Forster, 1928, p. 347).

The process of conversion or change – a sudden inner enlightenment
perceived as the product of external action, not necessarily divine in
origin, but tending to carry a burden of religious implication – becomes
increasingly important in the works succeeding *Barnaby Rudge*,
especially *Martin Chuzzlewit* (1843-4), *A Christmas Carol* (1843) and
Dombey and Son (1846-8). What distinguishes these works from *The
Chimes* (1845), *The Haunted Man* (1848), or *David Copperfield* (1849-50),
which to some extent hinge upon a change of heart, is their emphasis
throughout upon the deformation of the individual life by the

ruthlessness of the money ethic, only to be repudiated by a new awareness of the spiritual ties which bind mankind together. This is Dickens's personal interpretation of the gospel injunction to renounce worldly goods and follow Christ. He expresses the message in natural and secular terms, yet suggests a religious dimension by means of metaphoric or allegoric implication. His treatment is neither simply secular, nor profoundly metaphysical. The presentation of religious conversion, 'indeed of supernatural charity of any kind', is a supremely difficult task for the novelist, since it is apt to become 'either mawkish and unnatural or self-conscious and homiletic' (Jarrett-Kerr, 1954, p. 76). Dickens does not entirely avoid these dangers, but by means of his unique mixture of fantasy and realism he is usually convincing and certainly revealing.

In a sense, this interest in the notion of a change of heart represents a return to an older form of religious experience. Spiritual autobiography about the regeneration of the individual soul was a recognisable genre – as in St Augustine's *Confessions*, or Bunyan's *Grace Abounding*. Moreover, as the stock-in-trade of Methodism, the belief in sudden or instantaneous 'new births' became immensely influential in the late eighteenth and early nineteenth centuries, infiltrating the middle and upper classes through the activities of the Evangelicals – Wilberforce's conversion in 1785 providing the pattern. But Dickens was as sceptical as Carlyle's Teufelsdröckh about what was so 'clear and certain to your Zinzendorfs, your Wesleys, and the poorest of their Pietists and Methodists' (Carlyle, 1871–4, p. 136). Like Carlyle, he believed in a conception of conversion which did not primarily involve an acceptance of Christ, or the innate sinfulness of man, but which *did* involve a spiritual transformation affirming a new consciousness of oneself and one's place in the universe. *Dombey and Son* is the most impressive expression of this theory as it developed during the 1840s, a time of remarkable self-doubt, restlessness and artistic experimentation on Dickens's part; but *Martin Chuzzlewit* and *A Christmas Carol* offer clear, if not always forceful, hints of the evolving nature of his beliefs.

II

Dickens's American experience offers a good starting-point. 'What is man born for, but to be a Reformer, a Remaker of what man has made?' (quoted in J. F. C. Harrison, 1971, p. 173). Thus Ralph Waldo Emerson, expressing a characteristically optimistic faith in social progress based on individual change, which Dickens was to meet again and again during his sojourn in New England, home of liberal religion, Unitarianism and Transcendentalism – the last cruelly mocked by the novelist's account of a literary evening at the National Hotel in *Martin Chuzzlewit*:

'Mind and matter,' said the lady in the wig, 'glide swift into the vortex of immensity. Howls the sublime, and softly sleeps the calm Ideal, in the whispering chambers of Imagination. To hear it, sweet it is. But then, outlaughs the stern philosopher, and saith to the Grotesque, "What ho! arrest for me that Agency. Go, bring it here!" And so the vision fadeth.' (ch. xxxiv, p. 543)

But this was by no means the sum of Dickens's attitude to Transcendentalism, the idealist offshoot of Boston Unitarianism. Emerson, like Channing, was one of the first Americans to have a perceptible effect upon critical discussion in literary and intellectual circles in early Victorian England, and it seems likely that Dickens and his contemporaries found in his writings confirmation and stimulation of their own reformism. Dickens observed of Emerson's *Essays* (1841) that among much that was 'dreamy and fanciful (if he will pardon me for saying so)' there was much more that was 'true and manly, honest and bold' (*American Notes*, ch. iii, p. 57). '*American Notes*', observed an anonymous contributor to *Parker's London Magazine* in February 1845, 'betray with what class of religious opinions Mr Dickens has sympathy, and give us the clue to the coldness and barrenness of his philosophy' (vol. 1, p. 127). Dickens's enthusiasm for the manly and healthful qualities he found in Emerson hardly seems to justify the attribution of coldness and barrenness. But then the common view was that Unitarianism and its offshoots were coldly rational, sterile; whereas, in fact, Unitarianism, especially the American variety, had by the 1840s, if not earlier, shuffled off the severe rationalism of its eighteenth-century forebears, such as Joseph Priestley, and had taken on a warmer, more Romantic look, derived from Kant and Goethe, Wordsworth, Coleridge and Carlyle, for whom the divinity of nature, the glory of human aspiration and the power of intuition as well as reason had replaced the chilly rationalism of eighteenth-century liberal theology.

Dr Channing, in particular, brought together the different strands of liberal Christianity and Romanticism, to establish a form of religion which postulated human goodness and freewill against the doctrine of original sin and predestination, the indivisible unity of God and the necessity of employing individual reason in interpreting the Bible; for Channing, the New Testament revealed the unlimited potential of human goodness, the possibility that, by living a humane life following Christ's example and precepts, we could ultimately, like Christ, become one with God (Channing, 1840, pp. 309–23). It is quite clear that this form of religion appealed to Dickens, who, on his first day in Boston (a Sunday), was 'reluctantly obliged to forego the delight of hearing Dr Channing, who happened to preach that morning for the first time in a very long interval'; later, he became 'personally acquainted' with the

Unitarian preacher whose 'high abilities and character' he admired and respected (*American Notes*, ch. iii, pp. 25–6). Channing had developed his religion partly at least as a reaction to the evangelicalism of his upbringing and environment; Dickens observed in *American Notes* the continuing existence of the religion he opposed – the 'peculiar province of the Pulpit', 'always excepting the Unitarian ministry', appeared to be the denunciation 'of all rational and innocent amusements', those who strewed 'the Eternal Path with the greatest amount of brimstone' being voted 'the most righteous' (ch. iii, p. 56). The fanatical, sectarian spirit was (as Frances Trollope's *Domestic Manners of the Americans*, 1832, would have told him) even more prevalent in America than at home, and the appearance of this spirit in those 'gloomy madmen', the Trappists, who were massacred out in the prairie wilderness (ch. xiii, p. 184), or in the 'grim' and 'preposterous' Shakers (ch. xv, pp. 215–18), or other 'false prophets' like the Mormons (ch. v, p. 76), only confirmed his view that here were the 'worst among the enemies of Heaven and Earth, who turn the water at the marriage-feasts of this poor world, not into wine, but gall' (ch. xv, p. 218).[1] On the other hand, many of the institutions he saw (and he saw a lot) suggested 'how mindful they usually are, in America, of that beautiful passage in the Litany which remembers all sick persons and young children' (ch. vi, p. 94). If Dickens's overall response to America was a feeling of disillusion, nevertheless his liberal sympathies survived, perhaps all the more strongly for being tested by the hypocrisies and fanaticism he found. 'You know that I am, *truly*, a Liberal', he wrote to Macready; 'a man who comes to this Country a Radical and goes home again with his old opinions unchanged, must be a Radical on reason, sympathy, and reflection, and one who has so well considered the subject that he has no chance of wavering' (Pilgrim *Letters*, Vol. 3, pp. 158–9: 22 March 1842).

'What are the Great United States for, sir', as General Choke asks Martin Chuzzlewit on his journey to Eden, 'if not for the regeneration of man?' (ch. xxi, p. 349). America provided Dickens with the opportunity of showing a flawed, selfish hero – the first of such heroes in his works – transformed into a new man, generous, forgiving and charitable. Dickens's general purpose and design in *Martin Chuzzlewit* was 'to show, more or less by every person introduced, the number and variety of humours and vices that have their root in selfishness', the origin of the book lying in his notion of taking Pecksniff for a type of this (Forster, 1928, p. 291). Notwithstanding this hint of foresight and planning, however (reinforced by the preface to the first edition), the novel does not present a deeply coherent whole, as critics since, including Forster himself, have admitted; on the other hand, it does exhibit certain patterns of imagery, suggestive of a religious, if not strictly Christian, dimension to what happens.

To be aware of this means at least noticing that the opening paragraphs of the novel, for all their facetious parody of Fielding and Scott, are primarily intended to establish the idea of the Chuzzlewit family as the human family, their pedigree traceable 'in a direct line from Adam and Eve', a line, moreover, 'closely connected with the agricultural interest' (ch. i, p. 1), that is, with Cain, 'tiller of the ground', and the first murderer (Genesis 2:4–15). By no means every member of the human family is a murderer and a vagabond, but some inevitably are, it seems. 'Whosoever hateth his brother is a murderer', according to I John 3:15 and the internecine quarrelling of the Chuzzlewits is ultimately embodied in the evil, doomed figure of Jonas Chuzzlewit, at first little more than his miserly father's 'own son', as Chuffey keeps reminding us (ch. xi, p. 180), determined to grasp everything for himself, but eventually the haunted, guilty murderer that his desire to shorten his father's life leads him to become (ch. xlvii). Murder is the ultimate sin, as it was in *Oliver Twist* and *Barnaby Rudge*, to which other sins tend.

Although Jonas's upbringing is stressed as a factor in the shaping of his murderous personality, Dickens seems convinced that there is none the less a mysterious, primal source of evil, which he suggests by associating Jonas (and Tigg, whose appearance and behaviour anticipate Rigaud in *Little Dorrit*) with the traditional, popular conception of the devil. Hence Jonas's diabolic tendency to distort the Word, by adopting the 'true business precept' that you should 'Do other men, for they would do you' (ch. xi, p. 181). His occasional comic vitality, as when he bemoans his father's obstinate tendency to survive beyond three-score-and-ten, thereby 'flying in the face of the Bible' (ch. xi, p. 173), is easily outstripped by a much greater creation: Pecksniff. The sham architect exhibits a less overtly religious exterior than his progenitor, Tartuffe; nevertheless, he consistently pretends to a Christian, even evangelical, manner. He holds a Calvinist view of human nature (ch. iii, p. 34), yet he is careful to supplement his regular prayers with the names of those who offend against him (ch. iv, p. 58); he says grace at meals, characteristically commending those with nothing to eat to the care of Providence (ch. ix, p. 145), a power which confers a 'special' blessing on his own endeavours (ch. xx, pp. 328–9); the names of his daughters, Mercy and Charity, are, as he feels bound to confess, 'not unholy' (ch. ix, p. 149); he admires Dr Watts, and pretends to read theological works (ch. ix, p.152; ch. x, p. 155); and he makes an impression as a church dignitary of some sort, as well as, by proxy, through the organ-playing of his assistant, Tom Pinch (ch. xxxi, p. 488). One of his most sneaking, low moments occurs in church, when he eavesdrops on Tom and Mary Graham from behind a pew, subsequently eating the bread and wine he finds in the vestry (ch. xxxi, p. 495). Most revelatory, however, is his reproach to Mrs Todgers for worshipping 'the golden calf of Baal, for eighteen shillings a week' (ch. x, p. 168), which confuses the story of the golden calf with that of the worshippers of Baal (Exodus 32; I Kings 16:31–2), while exposing the idolatrous materialism which underlies all this pseudo-spirituality.

This is the basic theme of the novel, revealed even in Mrs Gamp, although it is a harsh critic who can condemn her for being, as she remarks of her late husband's wooden leg, 'as weak as flesh, if not weaker' (ch. xl, p. 625). Midwife, nurse and layer-out of the dead, she retains some of her humanity. Her curious locutions, which have us proceeding through 'this Piljian's Projiss of a mortal wale' to our 'long homes' (ch. xxv, p. 404), or which remind us that 'Rich folks may ride on camels, but it ain't so easy for 'em to see out of a needle's eye' (ch. xxv, p. 407), reveal how religious metaphor may retain some of its original force when re-created by the illiterate and ignorant. In this sense, she anticipates Captain Cuttle; and in fact the effect of her utterances is so strong and memorable as rather to undermine Dickens's pious apostrophes to the virtue of Tom Pinch's 'simple heart' (ch. v, pp. 62–3; ch. xxxix, pp. 616–17). But perhaps the pastoral innocence associated with Pinch has in any case become a little worn; Pinch grows disillusioned in the good old country church, and has to move to the metropolis, where there are churches by the dozen, although with churchyards 'all overgrown' from 'damp, and graves, and rubbish' (ch. ix, p. 128).

As this suggests, the forms and language of the traditional faith have become corrupted through misuse or neglect. If a way out of obsessive money-grubbing and selfishness is to be found, it must be by means of a new, non-dogmatic affirmation of the familiar spiritual values. This Dickens expresses by means of the hero's change of heart. Martin is nowhere as culpable as Pecksniff, Jonas, or, indeed, any other member of his family – a relatively hopeful state defined by his early rejection of his grandfather's money, the touchstone of corruption. He would, he tells Tom Pinch, prefer to dispose of himself in marriage, rather than be 'knocked down' by his older namesake, 'or any other auctioneer to any bidder whatsoever' (ch. vi, p. 95). Yet the terms of this dismissal of mammon in themselves indicate why he needs to be converted: he has not considered Mary Graham's situation, but is acting out of pride. And, anticipating Pip, he has 'great expectations', having always been taught to believe 'I should be, one day, very rich' (ch. vi, p. 93). The most damaging revelation of his self-centredness comes later, after his ungracious treatment of Tom, Mary and Mark Tapley: travelling steerage to America, he fails to respond to the demands of common humanity – indeed, he looks upon the poor, sick family installed beside him with contemptuous incomprehension, while the indefatigably cheerful Mark assists them in every way he can (ch. xv, pp. 248–52).

It is Martin's sickness unto death in the primeval desolation of Eden which leads to his crucial 'discovery of self'. The process takes some months, although it is presented as if it were almost instantaneous, a moment of inspiration or vision. Significantly, Martin requires more than a personal experience of suffering and despair for his new awareness: he has to learn to transcend his self-absorption through experiencing the demands upon his compassion and fellow-feeling made by others. Mark is a redemptive figure in the same category as Florence Dombey or Agnes Wickfield, in the same way essential for the emergence of a better nature in the hero. Only Scrooge requires the agency of no other person, although it could be said that the figures of his dreams represent the demands of humanity upon him, demands to which he is forced in the end to respond.

Dickens anticipates the change in Martin's character by suggesting that his self-love developed as a defensive reaction to his grandfather's selfishness (ch. vi, pp. 93–6), and that five weeks alone in near-poverty in London may dent if not permanently alter it. Indeed, he is led by Martin's London sojourn into bitter recrimination against the self-righteous, who deny the effects of environment upon character:

> Go ye, who rest so placidly upon the sacred Bard who had been young, and when he strung his harp was old, and had never seen the righteous forsaken, or his seed begging their bread; go, Teachers of content and honest pride, into the mine, the mill, the forge, the squalid depths of deepest ignorance, and uttermost abyss of man's neglect, and say can any hopeful plant spring up in air so foul that it extinguishes the soul's bright torch as fast as it is kindled! And, oh! ye Pharisees of the nineteen hundredth year of Christian Knowledge, who soundingly appeal to human nature, see first that it be human. Take heed it has not been transformed, during your slumber and the sleep of generations, into the nature of the Beasts. (ch. xiii, p. 224)

The biblical allusion is to Psalms 37:25, in which the psalmist, David, expresses the somewhat complacent view which occasionally emerges in the Old Testament to the effect that obeying the Law leads inevitably to (material) reward. It is dangerously self-satisfied to rely on an outmoded, static conception of human nature as unaffected by experience, especially harsh experience of the industrial age. But Dickens does not go on to show this in what happens to Martin; instead, his hero is propelled on a series of semi-picaresque wanderings which, when they take him to the ironically named 'earthly Paradise' (ch. xxii, p. 363), Eden, become archetypal. His swampy prison represents a state of mind, of being, rather than any particular place (such as Cairo, Illinois). His transformation is paralleled by developments in the ten chapters interposed between his arrival in the festering underworld and his departure from it a changed man: Mercy Pecksniff becomes 'sadly, strangely altered', by her experience of married bliss with Jonas (ch. xxviii, p. 456); and Tom Pinch finally realises his employer is a scoundrel (ch. xxxi, pp. 492–4). Dickens seems to visualise Martin's change of heart as the type of such changes: Martin's fever in Eden is 'only a seasoning; and we must all be seasoned, one way or another. That's religion, that is, you know' (ch. xxiii, p. 383).

III

In *Martin Chuzzlewit* Dickens handles the theme of the change of heart in a realistic manner. In *A Christmas Carol* he explores the idea of journeying, judgement and transformation in a consistently less realistic mode, which, paradoxically, makes for a more convincing impact. To further his argument that Dickens knew nothing of the 'nobler power of superstition', Ruskin observed that, for the novelist, Christmas meant no more than 'mistletoe and pudding – neither resurrection from dead, nor rising of new stars, nor teaching of wise men, nor shepherds' (Cook and Wedderburn, 1903–12, Vol. 37, p. 7). But if Dickens did not usually visualise Christmas as a nativity play, neither did he simply see it as a pagan feast. In his early Christmas writings he emphasises the feasting, joy and merrymaking characteristic of the Roman Saturnalia and other pagan festivals taken over by Christianity; but even in Dingley Dell, the development of a larger vision, Christian in tone but unrelated to dogma or conventionally religious postures, can be glimpsed through the fumes of punch.

By 1843, when Dickens wrote the first, and best, of his Christmas books, *A Christmas Carol* (composed in a month while still busy with *Martin Chuzzlewit*), Christmas had come to appear as the popular religious festival the age most needed, a time for the activation as well as the celebration of those benevolent impulses in human nature which, as Leigh Hunt set out to prove in an essay on Christmas in *The Examiner* in December 1817, the forces of puritanism, utilitarianism and 'Money-getting' were conspiring to destroy (Houtchens and Houtchens, 1962, pp. 163–4, 170–2). These forces are embodied in the figure of Scrooge, the 'squeezing, wrenching, grasping, scraping, clutching, covetous old sinner' (ch. i, p. 8), whose change of heart lies at the centre of *A Christmas Carol*.

To Scrooge, the demands of mercy and charity, like all other aspects of the Christmas spirit, are 'Humbug' (ch. i, p. 9). So, he resists the spirit animating his nephew, for whom Christmas, 'apart from the veneration due to its sacred name and origin', is 'a good time; a kind, forgiving, charitable, pleasant time'; and his clerk, Bob Cratchit, who raises a stifled cheer in support of these sentiments from his freezing 'tank'; and the portly gentlemen who arrive in expectation of a subscription for the poor; and even the owner of 'one scant young nose, gnawed and mumbled by the hungry cold as bones are gnawed by dogs', who regales his keyhole with 'God bless you, merry gentleman!/May nothing you dismay' before fleeing in terror (ch. i, pp. 10–13). The pattern of rejection is clear, as it moves through family, employee, class and society, down to the lowliest poor vagabond. Scrooge, the essence of wintry negation, the renouncer of all ties of blood and obligation, is totally isolated. But this is in accordance with the underlying principle of his behaviour expressed on the first page, when he shows himself 'an excellent man of business' at his partner Marley's funeral, having 'solemnised' the day with 'an undoubted bargain' (ch. i, p. 7). Like old Martin Chuzzlewit before him, and Mr Dombey after, he is dominated by the commercial spirit, he is the archetypal 'economic man' posited by the classical economists a man whose relationships are fundamentally self-centred, impersonal and directed towards the acquisition of material wealth. When it is put to him that the poor would rather die than go to prison or a workhouse, he callously retorts that they 'had better do it, and decrease the surplus population' (ch. i, p. 12), thereby aligning himself with the 'philosophers' attacked in *Oliver Twist*. (This is made even more explicit in *The Chimes*, the next Christmas Book, by means of the Benthamite Mr Filer, with his sums proving Trotty Veck's meal is taken from the mouths of widows and orphans; ch. i, pp. 94–6.)

Dickens wishes to convert his readers from this coldly complacent worldview to one in which love, charity and hope are dominant. He does not concern himself with the theological or institutional features of Christmas – with the Incarnation, or church attendance. That Scrooge should go to church after his traumatic night of dream-visions (ch. v, p. 74) is only important in that it shows him once again part of the human community, and able to overhear Tiny Tim hoping that people 'saw him in church, because he was a cripple, and it might be pleasant to them to remember upon Christmas Day, who made lame beggars walk, and blind men see' (ch. iii, p. 45). This is a conscious echo of Matthew 15:31, aimed as much at the reader as at Scrooge – or the Cratchits, who hope for a miracle to save their crippled child, a miracle which does occur, in Scrooge's change of heart, and which issues in a practical generosity enabling Tiny Tim, one of the disposable, surplus poor, to survive. No reader feels himself to be as miserly and mean as Scrooge; yet there were, and are, recognisable traits in him which clarify Dickens's aim: to provoke a similar, if less miraculous, change of heart in us. The tumultuous reception of *A Christmas Carol* suggests that Dickens's strategy was felt to work: Thackeray called it a 'national benefit', Lady Blessington said it would 'melt hearts and open purse strings', and Lord Jeffrey exclaimed (echoing Dickens's conclusion to 'A Christmas dinner') that it had 'fostered more kindly feelings, and prompted more positive acts of beneficence, than can be traced to all the pulpits and confessionals in Christendom since Christmas 1842' (Forster, 1928, p. 316; Madden, 1855, Vol. 2, p. 400).

The widespread appeal of *A Christmas Carol* and the other Christmas Books lay not only in the gentle rebuke and warning offered, but also in Dickens's conception of the post-conversion ideal. 'Except ye be converted, and become as little children, ye shall not enter into the kingdom of heaven' (Matthew 18:3); the saved Scrooge almost literally follows this injunction, becoming 'as merry as a school-boy', and frisking about his chambers, crying, 'I'm quite a baby' (ch. v, pp. 71–2). For the weary Victorian businessman, haunted (as Redlaw in *The Haunted Man* is haunted) by a hard-faced, selfish and competitive *alter ego*, childhood, and the emotions of human warmth and security associated with the primal hearth, offer an escape into lost humanity. In a later Christmas offering in *Household Words* (21 December 1850), there is an account of what the sounds of Christmas carols once meant to Dickens:

> What images do I associate with the Christmas music as I see them set forth on the Christmas Tree? Known before all the others, keeping far apart from all the others, they gather round my little bed. An angel, speaking to a group of shepherds in a field; some travellers, with eyes uplifted, following a star; a baby in a manger; a child in a spacious temple, talking with grave men; a solemn figure, with a mild and beautiful face, raising a dead girl by the hand; again, near a city gate, calling back the son of a widow, on his bier, to life; a crowd of people looking through the opened roof of a chamber where he sits, and letting down a sick person on a bed, with ropes; the same, in a tempest, walking on the water to a ship; again, on a sea-shore, teaching a great multitude; again, with a child upon his knee, and other children round; again, restoring sight to the blind, speech to the dumb, hearing to the deaf, health to the sick, strength to the lame, knowledge to the ignorant; again, dying upon a Cross, watched by armed soldiers, a thick darkness coming on, the earth beginning to shake, and only one voice heard, 'Forgive them, for they know not what they do.' (*Christmas Stories*, p. 11)

A solemn, almost apocalyptic note concludes this vision of the life and death of Christ, conjured up by childish Christmas associations. For Dickens, Christmas involves that 'nobler power' which reveals in well-worn, universally familiar images (they reel off like a sequence of gospel prints) how ultimately the hard heart may be softened through childhood memories.

Scrooge's conversion begins with the enforced contemplation of childhood memories, and it is one of Dickens's deeper and more convincing insights that his alienation from humanity is shown to be rooted in self-alienation. He has to experience pity for himself, and come to terms with his past, before he can be moved to pity others in the present. Sorrowfully observing himself as a solitary child in a schoolroom, he almost immediately experiences his first generous, outward-directed impulse: 'There was a boy singing a Christmas Carol at my door last night. I should like to have given him something: that's all' (ch. ii, pp. 27–8). The Ghost smiles thoughtfully at this, and takes him farther into his past, the complete process defined according to the timing and outward appearances of his visitors, concluding with the last, suggestively cloaked figure of Christmas Yet To Come.

It has been argued, with some contradiction, that this machinery of conversion is both insufficiently supernatural and insufficiently realistic: 'mere pictorial allegory without any pretence of belief in supernatural power, Grace, or anything like that'; at the same time, 'the agony' of conversion is not probed (House, 1942, p. 53). Perhaps Dickens should have heeded Fielding's caution to the Christian writer not to introduce into his works any of that heavenly host which make a part of his creed, leaving ghosts, elves and fairies, 'and other such mummery', to 'surprizing imaginations, for whose vast capacity the limits of human nature are too narrow' (*Tom Jones*, bk 8, ch. 1). But Dickens's imagination *is* 'surprizing', in that it calls on the supernatural, in dreams and semi-visionary experiences, to suggest a reality which transcends the everyday. He is sparing in his use of ghosts, elves, or fairies, confining them to works outside the main stream of his fiction, such as the Christmas writings, or the inset tales of *Pickwick Papers* or *Nicholas Nickleby*, with the partial exception of *The Old Curiosity Shop*, originally an inset tale itself. But the fusion of fantasy and realism was characteristic, and in the Christmas Books probably influenced by, once again, popular Romantic sources, such as the German tale. R. H. Horne observed that the Spirits in *A Christmas Carol* were 'high German', and the Marley-knocker derived from Hoffmann (Horne, 1844, Vol. I, p. 51); he might have added that the very title of the story, along with its division into 'staves', suggests the typically Romantic fantasy-song, such as Schiller's 'Song of the Bell', which in fact was said by the *Christian Remembrancer* to have been the source for the bell-goblins in *The Chimes*, although it went on to castigate the novelist for his 'mixed mockery of German diablerie, and fairies, and Socinianism' (vol. 9, January 1845, p. 302). While recognising the German Romantic source, and even the liberal religious outlook which permitted the use of such a source (was Dickens's Unitarianism common knowledge?), this reviewer found the Christmas Book dealing in 'nothing more than morals'. But, from Dickens's point of view, and that of his readers, it was surely quite legitimate to express a religious sense through popular, 'primitive' forms such as the traditional Christmas ghost-story or fairytale? *A Christmas Carol* has an affinity with the popular tradition of Christmas carols, too, which, since medieval times, have happily mingled pagan and Christian motifs, the sacred and the secular. Of course, this use of popular forms and motifs opens Dickens to the mockery of those such as Mrs Oliphant (1871, p. 677), who remarked that he was evidently 'the first to find out the immense spiritual power of the Christmas turkey'. But in an age of violent and continued sectarian disagreement, as well as mounting class tensions, there should be some sympathy for the point of view that, as Leigh Hunt well expressed it, 'Exclusiveness is the bane of humanity at all times, much more so at times of professed mirth and benevolence; and holidays that are kept in the true spirit, that is to say, with hearty sociality, and a feeling for whatever can contribute to it in external nature, will easily accommodate the idea of their customs to all descriptions of faith' (Houtchens and Houtchens, 1962, p. 177).

Dickens wished to express his sense that there was a reality beyond the immediate and everyday, without implying a specific, dogmatic commitment. He is concerned to upset the unimaginative, materialist mind into recognising the existence of powers beyond it. Before believing the specific revelation of Christianity, it is necessary to allow for 'fancy', if a baptised fancy. Yet again, spiritual soundings must be brought back to earth, to actual human relationships. Like the early radical, Major Cartwright, to whom Wilberforce expressed the hope that they might meet in a better world, Dickens might well have answered that he hoped 'we should first mend the world we were in' (quoted in Briggs, 1960, p. 177). Beneath the robes of the Spirit of Christmas Present two ragged and wolfish children appear: 'They are Man's', the Spirit tells Scrooge. 'And they cling to me, appealing from their fathers. This boy is Ignorance. This girl is Want. Beware them both' (ch. iii, p. 57). As Louis Cazamian long ago pointed out: 'les *Contes de Noël* rendent matérielle-ment perceptible le rapport chez Dickens entre le christianisme et la doctrine sociale' (Cazamian, 1904, p. 245).

IV

In *Dombey and Son* Dickens elaborates the conviction so forcefully expressed in *A Christmas Carol* that the salvation of a grasping, self-centred and materialistic society depends upon a conversion of the individual from sterile mammonism to love, innocence and generous fellow-feeling. But instead of a Romantic fantasy about the overnight conversion of a miserly old ogre into a gleeful lover of mankind, he offers here a sober, relatively realistic treatment, in which we follow through the subtle process whereby a coolly respectable, prosperous City merchant of the 1840s is brought to a new and saving vision of life. The whole process takes some thirteen years to accomplish. From the birth of the son and heir Mr Dombey hopes to mould into a hard-headed businessman after his own image, we follow the unfortunate education and death of the boy, the trial and failure of a second marriage, and the final collapse of all Dombey's worldly ambitions, leading to his suicidal despair and subsequent regeneration by means of the good offices of his rejected daughter Florence, 'his unknown Good Genius always', as Dickens called her (Forster, 1928, p. 472). A major part of the long, detailed and for him unprecedently well-planned narrative is devoted to the elucidation of this process. There is a parallel sub-plot change of heart in Alice Brown of Marwood, which repeats this theme in a lesser key. Mr Dombey's experience of suffering, despair and ultimate redemption is no more orthodox or specifically Christian than Scrooge's or Martin's before him, and does not bring him to a saving knowledge of Christ. But it *is* religious, and is moreover expressed at crucial moments in familiar Christian terms: 'Oh my God, forgive me, for I need it very much!' he cries in his extremity (ch. lix, p. 802).

To begin with, the novel was to have done with 'Pride' what *Martin Chuzzlewit* had done with 'Selfishness' (Forster, 1928, p. 471) – pride certainly plays a part in Mr Dombey's character, as it does in that of many others in the novel: it is 'as hard a master as the Devil in dark fables' (ch. xl, p. 538), and is ultimately associated with all the sins that flesh is heir to. Mr Dombey would even have resorted to murder in his frenzy against Carker, whose pride competes against his, but Providence wills otherwise, and the manager, in the pattern of the absolutely evil in Dickens, destroys himself, although not without a faint hint of the possibility of redemption (ch. lv, p. 743). Carker's villainy is deeper, more Satanic than that of anyone else in *Dombey and Son*. He is persistently associated with animals (ch. xiii, p. 172; ch. xvii, p. 232; ch. xlii, p. 574), and his 'meditations' are said to keep close to the earth, 'among the dust and worms', while he glides suggestively among the trees in a grove (ch. xxvii, pp. 368–9). No wonder he provokes Florence Dombey (as Fagin provoked Oliver Twist) to instinctive shivering and recoil (ch. xxiv, pp. 343–4).

But what Mr Dombey in fact suffers from is not so much pride, although that obviously is a contributory factor, as a monomania based on the delusion that material wealth is all-powerful. He is a two-dimensional man whose obsessive preoccupation with the continuation of the family firm involves a total distortion of his nature, and thus of his relationships with those around him. Only through the saving grace (the religious metaphor is insistent) of an infinitely forgiving love, embodied in his daughter Florence, who comes to him after his obsession has been broken by moral and financial ruin, can he return to anything approaching the fully human nature he has so long denied. This return is indicated by the concluding image of him as 'a white-haired gentleman, whose face bears heavy marks of care and suffering', wandering on the seashore with his grandchildren, and whose only pride lies in his daughter and her family (ch. lxii, pp. 829, 833). For Dickens, as for his contemporaries, family bonds are holy, 'given us', in Kingsley's words, 'to teach us their divine anti-types' ([Kingsley], 1904 edn, p. 101: 5 February 1851). Hence the domestic nature of the vision towards which *Dombey and Son* moves. In fact, it is a book essentially about domestic relations, rather than the business setting implied by the subtitle, 'Wholesale, Retail, and for Exportation'.

The nature of Mr Dombey's monomania is made quite explicit in his exultation over the birth of his son. 'The house will once again Mrs Dombey ... be not only in name but in fact Dombey and Son; Dom-bey and Son!' (ch. i, p. 1). The irony in this use of 'house' persists: for Mr Dombey, home and firm are identical. His son is not so much a child as the fitting object of his ambitious desire to extend the system of hereditary ownership underlying the firm. Mr Dombey has himself risen, 'as his father had before him, in the course of life and death, from Son to Dombey', and for nearly twenty years has been the 'sole representative' of the firm (ch. i, p. 2). The ultimate motivation for the Victorian industrialist was a dynastic one: 'to found a family, to endow them splendidly enough to last for ever, and to enjoy a vicarious eternal life in the seed of one's loins' (Perkin, 1969, p. 85). It is Mr Dombey's terrible mistake that in the search for this spurious immortality he ignores the ordinary human ties around him which might provide a real contact with the transcendent – the transcendent which waits beyond the everyday to receive him, as it receives his first wife, who, 'clinging fast to that slight spar within her arms', her daughter, drifts 'out upon the dark and unknown sea that rolls round all the world' (ch. i, p. 11).

Mr Dombey is deaf to the sound of this dark and unknown sea. His position as a powerful City merchant with trading connections across the seas underlines the irony of his ignorance, a point made almost too explicit with the loss of his ship, the *Son and Heir*, after his son has died. But the point may be said to bear emphasis, for it is central to the meaning of the novel. The attempt to perpetuate the firm of Dombey and Son through his son represents a refusal on Dombey's part to accept the ineluctable facts of life, a monstrously egoistic attempt to secure the present for ever. His egoism is more than merely personal: it reflects an attitude coming into being with the new, commercially oriented society of the post-Reform era, when the railway boom and the lifting of trade restrictions led to an unprecedented increase in mercantile investment and expansion, and the birth of that imperialist vision in which all the forces of nature appear to be providentially arranged for the purpose of trade and exploitation: 'To buy in the cheapest and sell in the dearest market, the supposed concentration of economical selfishness, is simply to fulfil the command of the Creator, who provides for all the wants of His creatures through each other's help; to take from those who have abundance, and to carry to those who have need . . . trade . . . does unwittingly serve agencies higher than itself' (G. Smith, 1861, pp. 32-3). Hence:

> The earth was made for Dombey and Son to trade in, and the sun and moon were made to give them light. Rivers and seas were formed to float their ships; rainbows gave them promise of fair weather; winds blew for or against their enterprises; stars and planets circled in their orbits, to preserve inviolate a system of which they were the centre. Common abbreviations took new meaning in his eyes, and had sole reference to them. A.D. had no concern with anno Domini, but stood for anno Dombei – and Son (ch. i. pp. 1-2)

The Dombey worldview reduces even the common Christian order of time to its crassly materialistic terms, an attitude made more explicit in a passage deleted (probably by Forster) from the corrected proofs of the first number, in which were given Mr Dombey's thoughts on the delay of Providence in granting him an heir, deferring his hope that his wife would give birth to a new 'partner' for the firm:

> That hope deferred, which, as the Scripture tells us (very correctly tells us, Mr Dombey would have added in a patronising way; for his highest distinct idea even of Scripture, if examined, would have been found to be, that as forming part of a general whole, of which Dombey and Son formed another part, it was therefore to be commended and upheld) maketh the heart sick. (Thus in ms.: ch. i, p. 2, note 2)

The allusion to Proverbs 13:12, 'Hope deferred maketh the heart sick; but when the desire cometh, it is a tree of life', is clumsy. But perhaps Dickens was drawn to it for the associative qualities of the 'tree of life' image, which connects with a pattern of images reinforcing the processes of Mr Dombey's inner life at several key points in the narrative, beginning: 'On the brow of Dombey, Time and his brother Care had set some marks, as on a tree that was to come down in good time' (ch.i, p. 1). 'What an old, old simile that is, between man and timber', as Thackeray remarked when he used it himself in *Vanity Fair* (1847-8, ch. 13). But it is nevertheless helpful in suggesting the process of breakdown, made possible by the mixture of strength and vulnerability in Mr Dombey. He does not bend, so he must break. When his second wife's pride neither gives way nor complements his own, 'instead of withering, or hanging down its head beneath the shock', it puts forth 'new shoots', to become more 'unyielding' than ever (ch. xl, p. 538). After she leaves him, Dombey is shaken, but 'not yet humbled to the level earth', for the 'root' is 'broad and deep, and in the course of years its fibres have spread out and gathered nourishment from everything around it. The tree is struck, but not down' (ch. li, p. 682). In his final despair and humiliation, Mr Dombey is 'fallen, never to be raised up any more' (ch. lix, p. 795); the Miltonic, biblical ring, however, adds redemptive hopes.

Such patterns of imagery in *Dombey and Son* relate to an altogether new depth of analysis in Dickens, primarily in the delineation of Mr Dombey's change of heart, although also at some moments in Edith's career. Previously, inner development of character was sudden, even arbitrary, where it was present at all. Complexity was dealt with in terms of fantasy or dream, rather than more realistic presentation, as here. The key to Mr Dombey's ultimately self-contradictory, self-destructive egoism is made clear from early on, as when he has to obtain a wet-nurse for Paul from among the apple-cheeked and prolific Toodles family. He cannot bear that they should ever claim 'some sort of relationship' with his son, and so he creates a relationship 'of bargain and sale, hiring and letting', even renaming Polly to suit (ch. ii, pp. 17–18). The pattern is repeated in his second marriage, except that the class roles are reversed. Polly's attempts to bring life and feeling to the deprived Paul result in her being sent away, and the child being further deprived, another step on his path to death; while Edith, resisting Dombey even as she mirrors his self-defeating pride, is caught up in a transaction aptly defined by Cousin Feenix as '*She* is regularly bought, and you may take your oath *he* is as regularly sold!' (ch. xxxvi, p. 493).

Dickens evidently intends us to contemplate these distorted relationships in a more than moral light. Mr Skewton's reflections on 'heart', her pseudo-Romantic, Puseyist pose (ch. xxi, pp. 283-5, ch. xxvii, p. 375), serve to remind us that it is precisely feeling from the heart that she needs, in place of the desire for wealth and power which obsesses her as it obsesses Mr Dombey. Her daughter's marriage ceremony becomes a parody of what it should be:

And will they in the sight of Heaven –?
Aye, that they will: Mr Dombey says he will. And what says Edith?
She will.
So, from that day forward, for better for worse, for richer for poorer, in sickness and in health, to love and to cherish, till death do them part, they plight their troth to one another, and are married. (ch. xxxi, p. 427)

Dickens brilliantly creates a sense of breathless haste to reinforce the sacrilegious overtones of the ceremony. Mrs Skewton squeaks shrilly in the sacred edifice, Carker 'tastes the sweets that linger' on Edith's lips; but Captain Cuttle, the representative in *Dombey and Son* of the alternative society which lives on the holiness of the heart's affections, joins in 'all the amens and responses, with a devout growl', and 'feels much improved by his religious exercises' (ch. xxxi, p. 431).

The retired sea-captain's religion is apparently an indiscriminate mish-mash of the Book of Common Prayer, navigation books, popular songs and Dr Watts; but it is sanctified by those sympathetic impulses which lead him to take in the homeless and fatherless, Florence Dombey and Walter Gay. Mr Dombey, on the other hand, fatally lacks this 'true' religion, a religion rooted in ordinary, warm human feelings and relationships. This is nowhere better shown than at his son's christening. Whatever 'realities' had gone out of the ceremony for Dickens, 'the meaning still remained in it of enabling him to form a relationship with friends he most loved' (Forster, 1928, p. 173); but in all Mr Dombey's life 'he had never made a friend. His cold and distant nature had neither sought one, nor found one' (ch. v, p. 49). His icy presence, and the reiterated motif of withered, falling leaves reflecting the blight cast on his son by the withdrawal of normal affection and warmth, turn the christening into a funeral, an effect subtly heightened by an accumulation of references to death. But the narrator breaks in:

> It might have been well for Mr Dombey, if he had thought of his own dignity a little less; and had thought of the great origin and purpose of the ceremony in which he took so formal and so stiff a part, a little more. His arrogance contrasted strangely with its history. (ch. v, p. 60)

Oddly, unnecessarily explicit, it would be pleasant to be able to blame this on Forster, in whose hand it is inserted in the proofs, and who had admonished Dickens to 'put the drag on' when he wrote the scene (Forster, 1928, p. 477). But Dickens, if he did not actually compose or dictate the passage, must have countenanced it, and he did not remove or alter it in later editions. If it exceeds the extent to which he would have wanted to commit himself to this particular religious 'form', it is not unapt in relation to his overall aim. The 'great origin and purpose' of baptism may be traced to John 3:5, where Christ announces the necessity of regeneration 'of water and of the Spirit'; and if Dickens does not ask for regeneration precisely in these terms, he does express a wish for a radical change of personality along spiritual lines, a change evidently resisted by Mr Dombey as he resists the inner meaning of the christening ceremony, its embodiment of the primitive Christian conception of a ceremony admitting a believer into the *community* of the faith.

For Dickens, it is in such broader, perhaps more humanist, but not irreligious meanings that the forms of orthodox Christianity took on reality. What was for him the theological side, the side liable to become entangled in the kind of controversy that came to a head with the Gorham case in 1848, was irrelevant, and best left alone. In a sense, this aligns him with the evangelicals, who considered the sacrament of baptism less important in itself than the idea of regeneration or conversion; and in stressing the need for conversion, Dickens was participating in the evangelical tradition. Mr Dombey could quite appropriately be described as that 'nominal' Christian who earns so much of Wilberforce's opprobrium for his coldly formal piety, indulging in the 'sober avarice' and 'sober ambition' typical of the business world, congratulating himself on not being 'a spendthrift', when all the while he lacks 'the true principle of action', allowing 'personal advancement or the acquisition of wealth' to become the object of his 'supreme desires'; but here the similarity ends, for Wilberforce insists that it is God who 'requires to set up his throne in the heart, and to reign in it without rival' (Wilberforce, 1834 edn, pp. 107-9), while for Dickens some human, non-clerical mediator seems always to be necessary. From *Dombey and Son* onwards, this role is played by women.

Dickens draws a distinction between the two female representatives of the love and forgiveness lacking in the coldly exclusive business life in *Dombey and Son*: Florence, and Harriet Carker. Florence, like Nell Trent before her, has 'no father upon earth' (ch. xlvii, p. 637) - her father's cruel rejection amounts to this - but she is sustained by her continuing awareness of 'that higher Father who does not reject his children's love, or spurn their tried and broken hearts' (ch. xliii, p. 580); and she is surrounded by that same semi-mythical, fairytale aura which creates in Nell a symbolic contact with the mysterious realm beyond, and so enables her to become the ultimate saviour of her sinful parent. Harriet, on the other hand, is a grown woman, anticipating Agnes Wickfield and Esther Summerson, and so she is capable of an adult perception of religious realities. To Morfin, chief clerk at Dombey and Son, she explains her devotion to her guilty brother, John Carker the Junior, in terms of

The humility of many years, the uncomplaining expiation, the true repentance, the terrible regret, the pain I know he has even in my affection, which he thinks has cost me dear, though Heaven knows I am happy, but for his sorrow! - oh Sir, after what I have seen, let me conjure you, if you are in any place of power, and are ever wronged, never, for any wrong, inflict a punishment that cannot be recalled; while there is a GOD above us to work changes in the hearts He made. (ch. xxxiii, p. 459)

This is the most explicit statement in the novel of the divine source of the change of heart. For ordinary mortals, however, conversions are 'a metaphysical sort of thing', Morfin points out in his hesitant, self-doubting way: 'We – we haven't leisure for it. We – we haven't courage. They're not taught at schools or colleges, and we don't know how to set about it. In short, we are so d——d business-like' (ch. xxxiii, p. 459).

Women and children are reserved for a special role in so far as they are not subject to the hardening process of business life. Edith, enslaved to mammon by her mother, is disqualified, as is Alice Marwood, her lower-class 'double'. It is Florence who 'might have changed' Edith 'long ago, and did for a time work some change even in the woman that I am' (ch. lxi, p. 824). Hers is a miraculous power, touching those it can release from their bondage to self-destructive pride 'like the prophet's rod of old, upon the rock' (ch. xxx, p. 420: see Exodus 17:6). Harriet's power is less emphatically religious, and more orthodox: she has compassion for the fallen stranger, Alice, whom she brings under her beneficent protection in a private equivalent of Urania Cottage. Alice, who remarks 'We shall all change, Mother, in our turn' (ch. lviii, p. 784: see I Corinthians 15:51), has been '*tempted* to virtue', in the felicitous phrase Dickens used in relation to Miss Coutts's Home for Fallen Women, and her deathbed provides Dickens with the opportunity for a peroration on the Bible, which Harriet agrees to read to her:

> the eternal book for all the weary, and the heavy-laden; for all the wretched, fallen, and neglected of this earth . . . the blessed history in which the blind, lame, palsied beggar, the criminal, the woman stained with shame, the shunned of all our dainty clay, has each a portion, that no human pride, indifference, or sophistry through all the ages that this world shall last, can take away, or by the thousandth atom of a grain reduce. (ch. lviii, pp. 785–6)

But if Harriet can read the Bible to Alice, no such piety is permitted to Florence in her role as her father's 'better angel' (ch. xxxv, p. 482). It would in any case be odd to find a child in Dickens's works who *does* read the Bible: even Nell, who takes the book up in her last days in the church, turns away to contemplate the processes of nature. Children are provided with a natural sense of religious realities, which is only too easily and too frequently crushed: typically, Master Bitherstone must read aloud to fellow inmates at Mrs Pipchin's 'a pedigree from Genesis (judiciously selected by Mrs Pipchin), getting over the names with the ease and clearness of a person tumbling up the treadmill' (ch. viii, p. 103).

In this sense, her father's indifference to her upbringing is in itself fortunate for Florence, who can thus develop her feeling for religious truth in a natural way; whereas his concern for her brother Paul leads to a kind of inward, spiritual disease, expressed as an ominous precocity in the child. Paul puts to his father the questions Mr Dombey cannot put to himself – such as 'what's money?' Money causes us 'to be honoured, feared, respected, courted and admired, and made us powerful and glorious in the eyes of all men', his father replies; indeed, it could 'very often, even keep off death, for a long time altogether' (ch viii, pp. 94–5). But: 'It can't make me strong and quite well', his son responds, 'can it?'

> 'Why, you *are* strong and quite well,' returned Mr Dombey. 'Are you not?'
> Oh! the age of the face that was turned up again, with an expression, half of melancholy, half of slyness, on it! (ch. viii, p. 95)

The slyness on the child's face is odd: partly it seems to represent Dickens's recognition that Paul *could* become like his father (and we have seen this process in operation with the Chuzzlewits); partly it conveys the sense of his being a sardonic visitor to the Dombey world who knows its illusions from the inside.[2]

In any case, Paul is already ailing, and soon death begins to enter his consciousness as the voice of the sea: often, 'he would break off, to try to understand what it was that the waves were always saying; and would rise up in his couch to look towards that invisible region, far away' (ch. vii, p. 111). Florence, as we should expect, can hear the waves, brother and sister linked by an awareness of time and death that excludes their father. When Paul is finally on his deathbed, his experience and viewpoint are movingly evoked in a series of foreshortened, impressionistic images, the light upon the wall opposite his window, the dark shadow creeping up to obliterate it, a shadow which is also the river running to the sea outside: 'Why will it never stop', he asks. 'It is bearing me away, I think!' (ch. xvi, p. 221):

> Sister and brother wound their arms around each other, and the golden light came streaming in, and fell upon them, locked together.
> 'How fast the river runs, between its green banks and the rushes, Floy! But it's very near the sea. I hear the waves! They always said so!'
> Presently he told her that the motion of the boat upon the stream was lulling him to rest. How green the banks were now, how bright the flowers growing on them, and how tall the rushes! Now the boat was out at sea, but gliding smoothly on. And now there was a shore before him. Who stood on the bank! –
> He put his hands together, as he had been used to do, at his prayers. He did not remove his arms to do it; but they saw him fold them so, behind her neck.
> 'Mama is like you, Floy. I know her by the face! But tell them that

the print upon the stairs at school, is not Divine enough. The light about the head is shining on me as I go!'

The golden ripple on the wall came back again, and nothing else stirred in the room. The old, old, fashion! The fashion that came in with our first garments, and will last unchanged until our race has run its course, and the wide firmament is rolled up like a scroll. The old, old fashion – Death!

Oh thank GOD, all who see it, for that older fashion yet, of Immortality! And look upon us, angels of young children, with regards not quite estranged, when the swift river bears us to the ocean! (ch. xvi, pp. 224–5)

Not every reader has felt the force of this appeal. R. H. Hutton, who heard Dickens read this passage, called it the 'pathos' of the 'Adelphi Theatre', pathos 'feeding upon itself' (Hutton, 1906 edn, pp. 56–7). But the death of Paul 'threw a whole nation into mourning' (Forster, 1928, p. 477), and even Thackeray exclaimed 'There's no writing against such power as this – one has no chance!' (quoted in Collins, 1971, p. 219).

Without reviewing the treatment of death in *The Old Curiosity Shop*, it is worth asking how Dickens could have had this effect. The answer lies in the popular nature of the beliefs expressed, as it does in the manner of their expression. To begin with, the novelist manipulates familiar images of growth and hope: green banks, bright flowers, the golden light. As with Nell (and Smike), this carries implications of future life without being specific about its source or quality. It is a part of Dickens's 'natural religion', as is the sea-river imagery, derived from a familiar Romantic symbolism suggestive of dissolution and loss merging into eternity. Again, Dickens is opposing texts of the usual 'violent and stunning character: the hero – a naughty boy – seldom, in the mildest catastrophe, being finished off by anything less than a lion, or a bear' (ch. viii, p. 103); and at the same time, participating in the tradition of happier tales in which the death of a saintly little being converts those around him or her, and in which glimpses of those already dead are granted the dying as a deathbed bonus. Paul's apparent recognition of the mother he has never seen may be intended to derive simply from 'her picture in the drawing-room down-stairs', of which he thinks one night (ch. xvi, p. 223), but it can also be understood as a hallucinatory projection of the image of Florence, which he confuses with her in anticipation of his impending death: 'Mama is like you, Floy.' The boy also remembers an image of Christ, taken from a print – a simplified, visual image drawn on for its universality and lack of mystification. Yet Dickens himself is a little mystifying here: Paul refers to 'the print upon the stairs at school' being insufficiently divine, from the vantage point of one who sees the 'light about the head' shining on him as he leaves this world; but it was the print 'that hung up in another place', unspecified (his room at home, perhaps?), that was in his mind when on the stairs at school, for it was in *that* print that the relevant image had its origin, the image of 'a wondering group', with, in their centre, 'one figure that he knew, a figure with a light about its head – benignant, mild, and merciful – [which] stood pointing upward' (ch. xiv, p. 193). The print on the school stair which makes him think of this other print is a 'portrait', which always looks 'earnestly after him' (ch. xiv, p. 193), and yet which is left inexplicit: is it also of Christ? or a benevolent founder of the school? The shortened reading version of the death is clearer: Paul simply grows fond of 'a large engraving that hung upon the staircase, where, in the centre of a group, one figure that he knew – *a figure with a light about its head – benignant, mild, and merciful – stood pointing upward*', and 'print' in his last speech becomes 'picture' (repr. in Collins, 1975, pp. 142, 152). The image itself is part of the traditional iconography of Christ, and remains a fertile source of religious implication for the novelist: 'Oh Agnes, ... so may I ... still find thee near me, pointing upward!' (*David Copperfield*, ch. lxiv, p. 771). The finger points to a power beyond our vision, to Heaven or God (see, for example, Illustration 8).

Dickens concludes on an apocalyptic note, derived from Isaiah (34:4) and Revelation (6:16), invoking the whole span of time, from the fall, which brought mortality, to the last days, when the firmament will be wrapped up like a scroll. The repeated 'old fashion' is inept, but not crippling, and reminds us that we must all face death, no matter how powerful or wealthy. Mr Dombey, of course, refuses to acknowledge this tie with ordinary humanity, despite having to witness his son's final lack of relation to him. His suffering is obliquely hinted at, he is reduced to a vague, impersonal object, a mere 'figure', in his dying son's vision (ch. xvi, p. 222).

V

Dickens offers little direct analysis of Mr Dombey's inner state, apart from the great set-piece on his train journey to Leamington. He hides his face at his son's funeral, and so, too, 'what the heart is, what the contest or the suffering: no one knows' (ch. xviii, p. 238). If we are meant to take it that he undergoes continuous inner conflict, as Dickens's 1858 Preface suggests we only feel this at critical 'yielding' moments. When he watches Florence (who believes him asleep), as she sits quietly in his presence after the arrival back in London of her father and new stepmother, Edith, 'Some passing thought that he had had a happy home within his reach – had had a household spirit bending at his feet – had overlooked it in his stiffnecked sullen arrogance, and wandered away and lost himself', softens him to her, so that, for an instant, he sees her by 'a

8 'The Apostles sent forth' (Matthew 10) from *Dr Kitto's Illustrated Bible* (1871-6), based on one of a series of 'Bible Pictures' by J. von K. Schnorr (1794-1872): 'a figure with a light about its head' stood 'pointing upward' (*Dombey and Son*, ch. xiv, p. 193).

clearer and brighter light'; but as the words, 'Florence, come here' rise to his lips, they are checked and stifled by a footstep on the stair (ch. xxv, pp. 483-4). It is Edith's step, like Destiny; her entry halts his melting conscience, and by an ironic shift he begins to experience in his turn the proud rejection inflicted on his daughter. Yet even as the possibility of his regeneration seems to disappear, subtle workings which will eventually bring it about are set in motion: 'As he looked, she became blended with the child he had loved', that is, with Paul.

The vital role of memory (and the associated moral response, guilt) is suggested from early on, when Florence attempts to embrace her father after Paul's death, only to be met with stern, freezing rejection, at which she utters a low, despairing cry: 'Let him remember it in that room, years to come' (ch. xviii, p. 253). The phrases become a poignant refrain, taken up finally when domestic misery has been followed by commercial ruin, and Mr Dombey sits alone in the empty house:

'Let him remember it in that room, years to come . . .' He did
remember it. In the miserable night he thought of it; in the dreary day,
the wretched dawn, the ghostly, memory-haunted twilight. He did
remember it. In agony, in sorrow, in remorse, in despair! 'Papa! Papa!
Speak to me, dear Papa!' He heard the words again, and saw the face.
He saw it fall upon the trembling hands, and heard the one prolonged
low cry go upward. (ch. lix, pp. 795–6)

The process of self-accusation is successfully dramatised: Mr Dombey is
the Haunted Man whose memory has returned to do its holy work, his
despair leading to a state of self-alienation which brings him to the brink
of suicide (ch. lix, pp. 798–801). Of course, he cannot save himself; the
earthly mediatrix of divine love and forgiveness has to come to him; and
she does.

How is it that Florence is able to redeem her father, and bring about a
change of heart? She has been fiercely attacked, both in Dickens's day
and our own, and we have to come to terms with her role if we are to
accept her crucial final impact upon Mr Dombey. Like Oliver and Nell,
she seems the largely passive vessel of a divinity which is unable to
intercede in worldly events by any other means. However, to Oliver, all
good things come in time; Florence must suffer and endure, pursuing her
'sacred purpose' (ch. xxiii, p. 315) to win her father, and the more she is
rejected, the more she has reason 'for saving him' (ch. xxiv, p. 338). Her
unspoken call to her father is to 'seek a refuge in my love before it is too
late!' (ch. xxxv, p. 483). Unlike Amy Dorrit, whom she anticipates, she
must *convert* her father. It is not enough that she should (as she does)
suffer and endure: she must love her father whatever he does, hoping that
'patient observation of him and trust in him would lead her bleeding feet
along that stoney road which ended in her father's heart' (ch. xxviii, p.
385). The Christ parallel is central. Like Nell, she must take on the
burden of her erring parent's sin, although she does not have to die in
order to save him.

At first her father's devaluation of her to 'a piece of base coin', a 'bad
Boy' (ch. i, p. 3), seems absolute. But there is a memory: of Florence and
her mother, 'two figures clasped in each other's arms, while he stood on
the bank above them, looking down a mere spectator – not a sharer with
them – quite shut out' (ch. iii, p. 31); and this generates an uneasiness, an
inner tension which will eventually create the potential for salvation. She
holds 'the clue to something secret in his breast, of the nature of which he
was hardly informed himself' (loc. cit.). Florence is the projection of Mr
Dombey's conscience, and if she is his daughter, she is also a symbolic
being, not to be judged in wholly realistic terms. This becomes clearer at
the death of her brother: she ministers to him, she is locked in the dying
child's arms, he sees her face as his mother's, beckoning to him from the

next world, and her sacred office as a link between this world and the next is established. But Dickens seems uncertain whether he is sanctifying Florence or the emotions he gives her. Her desolate, sorrowful remembrance of Paul, the love she continues to bear for the dead boy, is not allowed to burn 'so fiercely and unkindly long', for

> The flame that in its grosser composition has the taint of earth, may prey upon the breast that gives it shelter; but the sacred fire from Heaven, is as gentle in the heart, as when it rested on the heads of the assembled twelve, and showed each man his brother, brightened and unhurt. The image conjured up, there soon returned the placid face, and softened voice, the loving looks and words, the quiet trustfulness and peace; and Florence, though she wept still, wept more tranquilly, and courted the remembrance. (ch. xviii, p. 242)

The 'image' is the product of Florence's imagination, Dickens implies, not his own. It is a visual image of the Pentecostal flame (see Acts 2:3), derived no doubt from the religious prints likely to be found in children's books, illustrated Bibles, or upon the walls of their rooms, and so the fitting product of a child's sensibility.

This is true also of the fairytale imagery which hovers about her. It may drift towards whimsy, but it is seriously intended, drawn from the popular fantasies which sustain belief in areas where orthodoxy, much less evangelicalism, cannot or will not enter. 'Wild, weak, childish', may be her fancies, her 'enchanted vision' of having a 'kind father' to tell her of 'their common hope and trust in God'; or 'recognition in the far-off land between her brother and her mother', who, she feels, look on her with 'love and commiseration' as she weeps for her father's 'alienated heart' (ch. xxiii, pp. 313–14). But the lonely, 'sacred care' which engenders these visions will bring 'a heap of fiery coals' upon her father's head (ch. xxiv, p. 338; see Romans 12:20). And so retribution will come, not only to Mr Dombey, but also to the society which has produced him – that is, unless there is a change of heart, unless we all recognise the reality beyond the immediate, the everyday, the material; in short, the reality represented by Florence.

The challenging, broader implications of Mr Dombey's treatment of his daughter are powerfully present in the narrator's last warning to the recalcitrant father: 'Awake, unkind father! Awake, now sullen man! The time is flitting by; the hour is coming with an angry tread. Awake!' (ch. xliii, pp. 583–4). Ruin follows. And yet there is hope, too, in Florence's infinite loving forgiveness, movingly expressed on her return to the lonely, broken figure (ch. lix, p. 801). At last Mr Dombey feels 'oh, how deeply! – all that he had done', and begs God for forgiveness (ch. lix, p. 802). No Scrooge to dance around in child-like glee, exercising a new-found benevolence, he is reconciled to his daughter, to the human claims of his family, but is incapable of more. For a time an almost divine intercessor, Florence subsequently takes on the more earthly role of wife and mother: the imaginative drive towards making her a symbol of grace, of absolute values, falters in the end, as perhaps it must in terms of the deeply Protestant cast of Dickens's vision, hostile to ritual and symbology.

VI

The larger, almost cosmic implications of Dickens's warning message to Mr Dombey to 'Awake!' are more than metaphoric. Dickens is consciously echoing Romans 13:11: 'now it is high time to awake out of sleep: for now is our salvation nearer than when we believed'. He may also be echoing Carlyle's cry to the Captains of Industry in *Past and Present* (1843), to search their hearts for the 'spark of the Godlike' slumbering there: 'Awake, O nightmare sleepers; awake, arise, or be forever fallen!' (Carlyle, 1871–4, p. 233). This is, ironically, also Satan's appeal to his dazed followers in *Paradise Lost*, itself doubtless derived in part from the biblical source. Apocalypse was in the air during the 1840s – Dickens satirises it himself in the Reverend Melchizedech Howler's millenarian outbursts (*Dombey and Son*, ch. xv, p. 206; ch. lx, p. 814) – and this novel is also intended to awaken us before it is too late.

The world of the novel and the reader's world are explicitly linked in the well-known passage in which we are asked to consider the forces which have shaped Mr Dombey: 'Was Mr Dombey's master-vice, that ruled him so inexorably, an unnatural characteristic?' (ch. xlvii, p. 619). The answer, with intentional paradox, is that pride is unnatural, in that it is created by man, and not nature or God, and yet also natural, in that it is the inevitable consequence of enforced distortions of our society. Mr Dombey's perversion represents a perversion in all. Dickens goes on fiercely to attack the refusal to believe in the existence of a foul, polluted world all around us; he sarcastically bids us (especially, it seems, the evangelically inclined) to 'hold forth' on the 'unnatural sinfulness' of children brought up to be 'far away from Heaven' (ch. xlvii, p. 619) (suggesting a clear continuity with his lamentations over the maltreatment of Oliver), and goes on to imagine a 'moral pestilence' rising in dark clouds from the poor quarters of the town, to corrupt the better, culminating in a radical, Blakean conception of 'infancy that knows no innocence, youth without modesty or shame, maturity that is mature in nothing but in suffering and guilt, blasted old age that is a scandal to the form we bear' (ch. xlvii, pp. 619–20). 'Unnatural humanity!' he cries,

When we shall gather grapes from thorns, and figs from thistles; when
fields of grain shall spring up from the offal in the by-ways of our
wicked cities, and roses bloom in the fat churchyards that they cherish;
then we may look for natural humanity, and find it growing from such
seed. (ch. xlvii, p. 620)

It is entirely characteristic that the miraculous possibility of a return to
our original nature should be expressed in a fusion of Romantic, nature
imagery, and the familiar scriptural 'Ye shall know them by their fruits.
Do men gather grapes of thorns, or figs of thistles?' (Matthew 7:16).

A change of heart means ultimately a return to one's original, God-
given nature, it seems. But what are the implications for society as a
whole? Dickens expands the vision further, to include a 'good spirit' with
'a more potent and benignant hand than the lame demon in the tale',
lifting the rooftops of a nominally 'Christian people', to reveal 'dark
shapes' issuing forth 'to swell the retinue of the Destroying angel' of
Revelation, and to rain down 'tremendous social retributions' (ch. xlvii,
p. 620).[3] With an exhortatory (again, almost evangelical) emphasis,
Dickens urges us to share his basic conviction of the ultimate oneness of
humanity, which can only be rediscovered, as Mr Dombey rediscovers it,
through gaining an awareness of our ties one to the other:

> Bright and blest the morning that should rise on such a night: for men,
> delayed no more by stumbling-blocks of their own making, which are
> but specks of dust upon the path between them and eternity, would
> then apply themselves, like creatures of one common origin, owning
> one duty to the Father of one family and tending to one common end,
> to make the world a better place! (ch. xlvii, p. 620)

Dorothea's dark night of the soul in *Middlemarch* (1871-2, bk 8, ch. 80) is
followed by an awakening to awareness of her relation to her fellow
humans, too; in Dickens the religious emphasis is a vital additional
presence, confirming the more radical and disturbing nature of his
vision.

6

The Social Gospel:
David Copperfield and *Bleak House*

Crouched against the wall of the Workhouse, in the dark street, on
the muddy pavement-stones, with the rain raining upon them, were
five bundles of rags ... I address people with a respect for the spirit
of the New Testament, who do mind such things, and who think
them infamous in our streets.
('A nightly scene in London', *Household Words*, 26 January 1856)

By him that veil was rent asunder which parts the various classes of
society. Through his genius the rich man, faring sumptuously every
day, was made to see and feel the presence of the Lazarus at his
gate ...
(Dean Stanley, *Sermon [on] the Funeral of Charles Dickens*, 1870)

I

Most modern criticism of Dickens, while recognising the developing
complexity and seriousness of the social views revealed in his novels from
Dombey and Son onwards, fails to take into account the religious aspect of
those views. In fact, Dickens was increasingly concerned to warn his
audience, and to call upon it to respond to the sufferings of the poor in
terms of the gospel demand for forgiveness and charity. As he reminded
readers of the newly founded *Household Words* in an outburst prompted,
ironically enough, by a plague of begging-letter writers, they should
consider

That the crowning miracle of all the miracles summed up in the New
Testament, after the miracle of the blind seeing, and the lame walking,
and the restoration of the dead to life, was the miracle that the poor had
the Gospel preached to them. That while the poor were unnaturally
and unnecessarily cut off by the thousand, in the prematurity of their
age, or in the rottenness of their youth – for of flower or blossom such
youth has none – the Gospel was NOT preached to them, saving in
hollow and unmeaning voices. ('The begging-letter writer', 18 May
1850, repr. in *UT & RP*, p. 385)

One such hollow and unmeaning voice he embodied in the vessel Chadband, the lay preacher whose confrontation with the starving, destitute boy Jo lies at the centre of *Bleak House* (1852–3), the greatest of his social novels, and also the most powerful expression of this phase of his beliefs.

Dickens's religion is always oriented towards society and social action. But it was particularly during the early 1850s that he seems to have desired most strongly the re-enactment of what had become for him the 'crowning miracle' of the New Testament, the bringing of the gospel to the poor, despite the 'Gorham controversies, and Pusey controversies, and Newman controversies, and twenty other edifying controversies' which were, as he said, driving 'a certain large class of minds in the community . . . out of all religion' ('A sleep to startle us', *Household Words*, 13 March 1852, repr. in *MP*, p 341). If, that is, that class of minds had any religion to begin with: as the religious census of 1851 demonstrated, to the horror of church and chapel, the urban masses which had sprung up in the wake of the industrial revolution were unprecedently remote from, and ignorant of, organised religion in any form. For Dickens this could not altogether have been a surprise, although it must have reinforced his sense of the gap between the material conditions of the poor and the spiritual message offered to them. Already in 1843 he remarked the 'monstrous task' of attempting to impress the children of the poor 'even with the idea of a God, when their own condition is so desolate' (Pilgrim *Letters*, Vol. 4, p. 563), and he subsequently stressed in a public speech (in 1851) his conviction that 'even Education and Religion can do nothing where they are most needed, until the way is paved for their ministrations by Cleanliness and Decency' (Fielding *Speeches*, p. 129).

The continuity of this emphasis on relating the material to the spiritual needs of the poor is clear in Dickens. Hence his incorporation, almost word for word, of a key passage from this speech into a Christmas Story for *Household Words* two years later. The poor 'nobody' at the centre of 'Nobody's Story' responds to the approach of a 'kind preacher' who 'would have said some prayers to soften his heart in his gloom' with the same cry Dickens mimicked in the speech:

O what avails it, missionary, to come to me, a man condemned to residence in this foetid place, where every sense bestowed upon me for my delight becomes a torment, and where every minute of my numbered days is new mire added to the heap under which I lie oppressed! But, give me my first glimpse of Heaven, through a little of its light and air; give me pure water; help me to be clean; lighten this heavy atmosphere and heavy life, in which our spirits sink, and we become the indifferent and callous creatures you too often see us;

gently and kindly take the bodies of those who die among us, out of the small room where we grow to be so familiar with the awful change that even ITS sanctity is lost to us; and, Teacher, then I will hear – none know better than you, how willingly – of Him whose thoughts were so much with the poor, and who had compassion for all human sorrow! (Extra Christmas number of *Household Words*, repr. *Christmas Stories*, p. 64; cf. Fielding *Speeches*, p. 129, and Illustration 9)

Such eloquence from a dispossessed illiterate would be absurd, were it not that Dickens is using prose fantasy to appeal to the middle-class 'missionaries' to recognise the true needs of the poor.

The word 'missionary' conveys more than an ironic allusion to the gulf any 'kind preacher' or similarly philanthropically minded being must cross from his known, civilised world into the dark jungle where the poor live: it is also a reference to the new interest shown by the middle class in the 1850s in evangelising the benighted denizens of their slum areas by establishing so-called 'missions' among them. Such missions had long been a minor feature of religious activity in the metropolis: the London City Mission, patronised by Lord Shaftesbury, was founded in 1835; but it was not until more recently that middle- or upper-class urban congregations, Nonconformist and Anglican, began to support them with enthusiasm (Best, 1971, pp. 190–2). Dickens's interest began early: on 27 April 1844 he wrote to the wife of his close friend Serjeant Talfourd to say he would not fail to give his 'best attention to the subject of the Home Mission, and its report. And if its Christian aid be extended to all classes of Believers, and its Christian instruction be such as all poor creatures may receive, I will drop my mite into its treasury . . .' (Pilgrim *Letters*, Vol. 4, p. 114). The LCM was non-denominational and, moreover, its work was linked with the Ragged School movement, which Dickens had long supported; but his fictional interests were less specific, as this passionate outcry in *The Chimes* indicates –

Who turns his back upon the fallen and disfigured of his kind; abandons them as vile; and does not trace and track with pitying eyes the unfenced precipice by which they fell from good – grasping in their fall some tufts and shreds of that lost soil, and clinging to them still when bruised and dying in the gulf below; does wrong to Heaven and man, to time and to eternity. (*Christmas Books*, p. 124)

Not an orthodox version of the Fall, perhaps; but true to the novelist's understanding of the spirit of the New Testament, a spirit he tried to foster, for example, in his relationship with Miss Burdett Coutts, whose pious sympathies, 'at first inclined to be restricted to Church and religious work', he took pains to redirect 'into the broader channels

9 'Scripture reader in a night refuge', by Gustave Doré, from G.
Doré and B. Jerrold, *London* (1872). The 'crowning miracle' was
that 'the poor had the Gospel preached to them' ('The begging-
letter writer', *Household Words*, 18 May 1850).

of philanthropic effort for the masses'. Her religious rigidity was
observed by others, as was the development of what the Duke of
Wellington (no less) recognised as her 'good and just sense' of 'religious
notions': 'Christianity was intended to regulate the Social Life of Human
Creatures!' (quoted in Patterson, 1953, pp. 151–2, 79).

Yet if this notion of Christianity was beginning to make itself felt at the
duke's level of society, the fact remained that the poor were still not being
reached by the gospel. If, in 1851, it seemed easy (as Dickens himself felt)
to justify England to the Pope, it was a lot more difficult, in Charles
Kingsley's phrase, to 'justify God to the people' (quoted in Briggs, 1965,
p. 36). Kingsley, with the radical lawyer J. M. Ludlow and the liberal
theologian F. D. Maurice, took part in an organised attempt – the
Christian Socialist movement – to popularise a Christian doctrine of
social concern, based partly on the fear of godless Continental socialism
entering Britain in the wake of the 1848 revolutions, but also on the
conviction that selfish competition and class division could be replaced
by Christian love and charity. Dickens shared this conviction, although

in other respects he diverged from the Christian Socialists. He preferred operating as an individual, rather than as part of an organised movement: encouraging Miss Coutts in her 'Westminster' project to provide religious, educational and sanitary facilities for the poor, he observed that there was 'no better way of doing good, or of preparing the great mass of mankind to think of the great doctrines of our Saviour' (Coutts *Letters*, p. 206).

Dickens's form of 'social' Christianity only really began to receive full recognition and approval from the Church as it moved towards the 'Broad' position enunciated by liberals such as Dean Stanley or Benjamin Jowett. Bishop Fraser of Manchester cautiously remarked in Westminster Abbey, three days after the novelist's death, that 'Possibly we might not have been able to subscribe to the same creed in relation to God, but I think we should have subscribed to the same creed in relation to man' (*The Times*, 14 June 1870, p. 12). The idea of a 'social gospel', stressing the prime importance of improving the material conditions of the poor before attempting to bring them to Christ in any theological sense, only became widely known in the 1880s, by when a canon of Westminster could claim that what was preached in the Abbey was essentially the 'Social Gospel of Christ' (Westcott, 1888, preface). *The Bitter Cry of Outcast London*, the enormously influential anonymous pamphlet published in 1883, opened: 'There is no more hopeful sign in the Christian Church of today than the increased attention which is being given by it to the poor and outcast classes of society. Of these it has never been wholly neglectful; if it had it would have ceased to be Christian. But it has, as yet, only imperfectly realised and fulfilled its mission to the poor' (repr. in Keating, 1976, p. 90). The seal of acceptability may be said to have finally been set upon this form of Christianity in Britain when Frederick Temple became Archbishop of Canterbury in 1896 (Chad-wick, pt 2, p. 285). For Dickens, however, the idea of a social gospel expressed as a continuing deep conviction of our collective responsibility for the poor and dispossessed was potent long before it became respectable in orthodox religious circles. Touched on intermittently in his works from *Oliver Twist* onwards, by the 1850s it becomes the core belief from which all others radiate. This is especially true of *Bleak House*, although the notion may be seen developing into an essential part of his vision in the Christmas Books, *Dombey and Son* and, to some extent, *David Copperfield* (1849–50). *Hard Times* (1854) and *Little Dorrit* (1855–7) reveal, too, the first fruits of what one might call Dickens's conversion from a sense of individual to a sense of social sin.

The faith in, or at least hope for, individual regeneration expressed in *Dombey and Son* is replaced by a pervasive awareness of social evil, relieved only by the persistence of semi-divine images of deliverance embodied in the idealised female characters – Agnes Wickfield, Esther Summerson, Rachel and Amy Dorrit. These icons suggest the possibility of deliverance or redemption, but from *Bleak House* onwards Dickens's disillusionment is so strong that it sometimes seems almost to overwhelm the hopes implicit in them. The tension between the faith of the first-person narrator, Esther Summerson, and the corrosive despair of the omniscient narrator of *Bleak House* reflects the ambivalence of his final position.

Hard Times gathers up and reinforces Dickens's repugnance towards Benthamite reductionism and his faith in Christian charity across class divisions, but does not add significantly to the evolving shape of his beliefs, so will not be dealt with here. But *David Copperfield*, predecessor to *Bleak House*, and 'favourite child' (preface) of both author and his public, does require some attention, since it not only reveals a necessary taking stock on Dickens's part, a search for the roots of compassion in personal memory, but shows a favoured aspect of the social gospel in the study of the forgiveness and redemption of 'fallen' women. It is also perhaps the last convincingly optimistic novel of Dickens's career: in it, individual charity is seen to issue in success, whether it is Betsey Trotwood taking the ragged David Copperfield in, the hero and his great-aunt helping the Micawbers to migrate to Australia, Mr Peggotty taking his redeemed women to the same distant haven, or even the transformation of the poor usher of Creakle's school into Doctor Mell of Colonial Salem-House Grammar School. In *Bleak House* such hopes are, like Miss Flite's birds, trapped and doomed to die.

II

In *David Copperfield* Dickens makes plain the personal basis of his struggle against social injustice by contemplating, in fictional form, the painful rejection and isolation which he experienced as a child. He thus fulfils the doctrine of *The Haunted Man* (written in the autumn of 1848, while he was brooding on *David Copperfield*), according to which it is the 'beneficent design of Heaven' that the 'softening memory of sorrow, wrong or trouble' should lodge in one's mind, there to exercise a redeeming influence upon the understanding, and one's actions: to deny the pain of the past is to deny the Heavenly attribute of forgiveness to oneself, and hence the source of one's compassion for others (*Christmas Books*, pp. 378-9). This doctrine, intimately related to Dickens's view of how to cope with death through memory and charity, is not very effectively realised in *The Haunted Man*, although it is plain that for some time the novelist's own return to his past had led to an intensification of his concern for the sufferings of the poor and outcast. It was expressed in letters and articles on education, crime and other social issues: even as he was engaged on the first monthly number of *David Copperfield* in April 1849, he found time for a bitter attack on Drouet, proprietor of the infamous Tooting 'baby-farm' ('The verdict for Drouet', *The Examiner*, 21 April 1849, repr. in *MP*, pp. 149–50); and further articles followed, until in March 1850 he founded *Household Words* partly in order to continue troubling the conscience of his readers.

But, as has been observed (for example, Monod, 1968, p. 317), *David Copperfield* seems in the first place intended to offer an account of what one might call, on the analogy of Wordsworth's great poem (published July 1850), 'The growth of a novelist's mind'. Yet this is to imply pretensions which are hardly realised, since not only is there little sense of David's vocation as a writer, but the truncated account of his three-year sojourn abroad, during which he is consoled by 'great Nature' after the double loss of his 'bad angel' Steerforth and his 'child-wife' Dora (ch. lviii, pp. 814–15), can hardly compare with Wordsworth's narrative of the complex movements of his moral consciousness. Moreover, in line with his ties to the liberal, latitudinarian approach of the author most in his mind when he began the novel, Henry Fielding (Forster, 1928, p. 524), Dickens is attempting to pursue a middle path between the demands of feeling and reason, and not merely to offer an account of the development of a sensibility in his hero – hence his emphasis upon David's 'undisciplined heart', for instance, at the death of Dora (ch. liii, p. 768). *David Copperfield* is a Romantic novel in so far as it shows Dickens's fruitless yearning for individual self-fulfilment, in the form of his hero's recurrent sense of an 'old unhappy loss or want of something' – a theme first mentioned when his great-aunt hints Dora may not offer all he rapturously expects (ch. xxxv, p. 504), and repeated as a refrain thereafter. As Forster observed, this yearning took on a new intensity for the grown man who later asked his friend, 'Why is it, that as with poor David, a sense always comes crushing on me now, when I fall into low spirits, as of one happiness I have missed in life, and one friend and companion I have never made?' (Forster, 1928, p. 639). It is a kind of *Sehnsucht* or desire for meaning and security which can never be satisfied, and which has religious overtones. In the novel, perhaps reflecting Dickens's marital difficulties, perhaps reflecting his persistent tendency to idealise young, unattainable women, it is Agnes Wickfield, the love he has blindly ignored since the days of his youth, who offers David the ultimate happiness: 'Clasped in my embrace, I held the source of every worthy aspiration I had ever had; the centre of myself, the circle of my life, my own, my wife; my love of whom was founded on a rock' (ch. lxii, p. 864; see Matthew 7:25).

Hillis Miller (1968, p. 157) explains this as

> a late example of that transposition of religious language into the realm of romantic love which began with the poets of courtly love, and which finds its most elaborate Victorian expression in *Wuthering Heights*.

David has that relation to Agnes which a devout Christian has to God, the creator of his selfhood, without whom he would be nothing.

But this is forcing a modern interpretation, even if it is generally true that Dickens's fiction represents a stage on the path of secularisation in literature begun in the twelfth century. (Thackeray's *Pendennis*, 1850, offers another example.) Agnes's exalted self-sacrifice sanctifies her love for David; but she is not quite the creator of his 'selfhood', since, as is quite evident to us, if not to him, he has made himself to a large extent, ploughing through every 'forest of difficulty' (ch. xxxvi, p. 520) with the utmost energy and determination. Dickens has not yet reached the position of, say, D. H. Lawrence, who expresses an entirely secularised version of the Christian's relation to God, for example, in the coming together of Lydia and Tom Brangwen: 'their flesh was one rock from which the life gushed, out of her who was smitten and rent, from him who quivered and yielded' (*The Rainbow*, 1915, ch. 2). More important in *David Copperfield* is the role of the woman as semi-divine mediator of wisdom or 'truth' for the chronically insecure young hero, who gropes blindly for the love and companionship denied him as a child (see Illustration 10). Agnes points upwards to heaven for consolation when David collapses at Dora's death (ch. liii, p. 768), and it is this image of her which remains with him, a source of faith and hope (ch. lxiv, p. 877). She has become assimilated with 'that spirit' which Dickens felt directed his life, 'and through a heavy sorrow has pointed upward with unchanging finger', namely, Mary Hogarth (Forster, 1928, p. 206), the words of whose epitaph are echoed in his description of Agnes, 'so true . . . so beautiful . . . so good' (ch. lx, p. 839).

Once again, this image of a figure pointing upward to Heaven may be said to derive from a familiar Christian iconographic tradition. Dickens seems to acknowledge this by showing David consciously creating his vision of Agnes in terms of a memory of a 'stained glass window' in church (presumably Blunderstone Church), as well as of a picture of her dead mother on the stair at her home in Canterbury (ch. xv, p. 223). The negative, sterile overtones suggested by the sources of David's vision, however, reveal an ambivalence in the novelist's attitude which is not resolved. The young boy David re-creates the objects of his love in simplified, visual terms, as when he first meets Emily, and 'my fancy raised up something round that blue-eyed mite of a child, which etherealised, and made a very angel of her' (ch. iii, p. 37); similarly Dora is more of an 'idea', a bright and distant 'image', than a real (and flawed) young woman (ch. xxxiii, p. 474). He then has to learn to reject these false images of women. But he goes on to etherealise Agnes, whose name, suggestive of the lamb of God, indicates that she is, miraculously, able to fulfil his requirements in a way not possible for Emily or Dora. Dickens

10 'My child-wife's old companion' (*David Copperfield*, ch. liv, p. 771), by 'Phiz'. The church-steeple and moon behind Agnes suggest the chaste, 'transcendent' love to which David must now turn.

wants to show the survival of the childish imaginative faculty which persists as an essential part of the adult's ability to imagine transcendence, even at the cost (unconscious, no doubt) of creating a woman as sexless as she is transcendent. David, like Oliver or Nell or Paul Dombey before him, is aware of the existence of another world, 'the land of dreams and shadows, the tremendous region whence I had so lately travelled; and the light upon the window of our room shone out upon the earthly bourne of all such travellers, and the mound above the ashes and dust, that once was he, without whom I had never been' (ch. i, p. 12). An evocative blend of Shakespeare (*Hamlet*, III, i:78-80), the Bible (Genesis 18:27) and Tennyson ('To J.S.', ll. 23-4), suggests how the imagination provides one route towards a religious apprehension of reality; a route confirmed by his contemporary, Newman, who recalled his own boyish imagination running 'on unknown influences, on magical powers', thinking 'life might be a dream, or I an Angel, and all this world a deception' (*Apologia Pro Vita Sua*, 1864, ch. 1).

But if David Copperfield's early life seems at times representative, this is, as Matthew Arnold observed (1881, pp. 1034-42), much more the case with Dickens's depiction of the negative, destructive influence upon him of the Murdstones and their religion. Part of David's fear of his stepfather is based on what we would now call oedipal jealousy, as Dickens subtly indicates when the boy is sent from home so that his mother can remarry in his absence, and he wonders if his nurse Peggotty 'were employed to lose me like the boy in the fairy tale' (ch. ii, p. 27); more important, it is also his response to the Murdstones' unrelenting will to dominate and exploit, a will made worse by being embodied in a religion, shown as blasphemous and extreme. Their creed is revealed as a function of their personality: 'The gloomy taint that was in the Murdstone blood, darkened the Murdstone religion, which was austere and wrathful', 'a vent for their bad humours and arrogance' (ch. iv, p. 52; ch. lix, p. 834). Their rigid, cold insistence upon 'firmness' towards poor David helps destroy his mother and, by implication, helps make him sensitive and vulnerable (Mrs Joe has the same effect upon Pip). Their 'theology' is based on the assumption Dickens always opposed, according to which 'all children' are 'a swarm of little vipers (though there *was* a child once set in the midst of the Disciples)' (ch. iv, p. 55: see Matthew 18:2).

The Murdstones bring a rude incursion of Calvinist fervour into the sleepy Anglicanism of Blunderstone Church (see Illustration 11), picking out the darker phrases of the traditional prayers (such as 'miserable sinners', from the Litany), with 'cruel relish' (ch. iv, p. 52). It is a long way from Mrs Weller's 'methodistical' cant, or the obscure 'ranting' connections of Mrs MacStinger. Dickens asks us to take the Murdstones more seriously, while drawing back from more explicit, direct attack upon prevailing evangelicalism - indeed, he excised an

11 'Our pew at church' (*David Copperfield*, ch. i, p. 10), by 'Phiz'. Mr Murdstone stares fiercely over his prayer-book across the sleeping congregation at David and Mrs Copperfield.

allusion connecting the bullying headmaster, Creakle, with this form of religion (quoted in Collins, 1965, pp. 114–15), perhaps realising he would antagonise readers such as David Masson, who had had enough of the novelist's 'antipathy to Puritanism', the product, he supposed, of Dickens's Unitarianism (1851, p. 89). Yet the continuity between the grim religion of the Murdstones, the brutal kind of education they prefer, and the ruthless business ethos embodied in Murdstone and Grinby's, where David is sent to be degraded as 'a little labouring hind' (ch. xi, p. 154), is clear.

It is this experience of the common toil of the urban working class, feelingly recounted in chapter xi, and evidently based on Dickens's own sufferings at Warren's Blacking, which creates the man who, when he treads this 'old ground' again, seems to 'see and pity' himself (ch. xi, p. 169). To 'see' and thus to 'pity' are the central motives of this phase of Dickens's art, and the whole movement of *David Copperfield* is away from the self-regarding life, towards compassion and service to others. Evangelicalism did not necessarily discourage this, as Dickens well knew; but the spirit of egoistic self-denial which helped produce the bullying hypocrisy of the Murdstones was all too liable to deflect Christian impulses, he believed, and not without reason.

Agnes provides the selfless exemplar of his ideal in the domestic world which is the main focus of the narrative; but Mr Peggotty shows how it can be expressed in the larger world into which Emily's 'fall' takes him. In so far as the religious dimension of *David Copperfield* has attracted discussion, this has concentrated on Mr Peggotty: his apparent transformation from a vengeful angry father into some kind of prophet of mercy constituting 'the event with the richest religious significance in the novel' (Pearlman, 1972, p. 20). This involves a serious oversimplification of what happens to Mr Peggotty: he is by no means a vengeful father-figure to begin with, even if, as critics who take this line point out, he is associated with the Old Testament by name (Daniel) and in the detail of his surroundings – living with his nephew, Ham, in a kind of 'ark' with 'common coloured pictures' on the walls, depicting 'Abraham in red going to sacrifice Isaac in blue, and Daniel in yellow cast into a den of green lions' (ch. iii, pp. 30, 32). But he has already fulfilled the requirements of merciful fatherhood, having brought together into his 'ark' the orphaned and neglected, the outcast and dispossessed. David asks him: 'Haven't you *any* children, Mr Peggotty?' (ch. iii, p. 33). And the answer is no, for he has made Emily, Ham and Mrs Gummidge his family.

Yet there is a moment when Mr Peggotty comes temporarily under the sway of Old Testament wrath, and a desire to punish the wicked; and it is at this moment that the underlying theme of the development of forgiveness and charity towards the sinful and outcast makes itself most strongly felt. Significantly, the moment occurs at the end of the tenth

number, the structural centre of the novel, as Emily's elopement with
Steerforth comes to light. At first Mr Peggotty tries to rush out in wild
pursuit of his niece, prepared even to drown her seducer. Ham interposes
himself between his adopted father and the door. Then, in a totally
unexpected outburst, the 'lone lorn' Mrs Gummidge, up to now always
isolated in her self-pity, cries:

> 'No, no, Dan'l, not as you are now. Seek her in a little while, my lone
> lorn Dan'l, and that'll be but right! but not as you are now. Sit ye
> down, and give me your forgiveness for having ever been a worrit to
> you, Dan'l – what have *my* contrairies ever been to this! – and let us
> speak a word about them times when she was first an orphan, and when
> Ham was too, and when I was a poor widder woman, and you took me
> in. It'll soften your poor heart, Dan'l,' laying her head upon his
> shoulder, 'and you'll bear your sorrow better; for you know the
> promise, Dan'l, "As you have done it unto one of the least of these, you
> have done it unto me"; and that can never fail under this roof, that's
> been our shelter for so many, many year!' (ch. xxxi, p. 454)

It is left to Providence to drown Steerforth (but, tragically, Ham as well),
in the novel's great set-piece storm. The implication is the same as for
Anna Karenina: 'Vengeance is mine; I will repay, saith the Lord'
(Romans 12:19). Mrs Gummidge's appeal is to both memory and the
New Testament, reminding Mr Peggotty of his past mercies to the
outcasts, and adding Christ's sanction in the words of Matthew 25:40,
where it is promised that the blessed inheritors of the kingdom of God
shall be those who took in the stranger, fed and clothed him.

Dickens's concern for 'fallen women' here, as in *Oliver Twist* and
Dombey and Son before, is derived from what Tolstoy (who admired
David Copperfield immensely) would have recognised as a fundamentally
Christian position. This concern was reflected equally strongly in
Dickens's current (and increasing) involvement with Miss Burdett
Coutts's Urania Cottage, and it may be that Martha Endell and Emily do
not have to die (unlike Nancy and Alice Marwood) because of Dickens's
new faith in the practical possibilities of reformation and emigration
embodied in the Home for Fallen Women. (He was also aware of Mrs
Chisholm's 'Family Colonization Loan Society', many of whose female
emigrants were redeemed prostitutes, and in support of whom he wrote
'A bundle of emigrants letters' for *Household Words*, 30 March 1850.) On
the other hand, their fate is also intended to show the positive strength of
Mr Peggotty's carrying out of the 'social gospel', made quite explicit by
the hero himself after he and Mr Peggotty have followed Martha down to
the river where she contemplates suicide: 'In the name of the great
Judge', David says to the prostitute, 'before whom you and all of us must

stand at His dread time, dismiss that terrible idea! We can all do some good, if we will' (ch. xlvii, p. 686). Can we? Martha corroborates this hopeful exhortation by saving Emily from despair and suicide in her turn, after the girl has been helped by an anonymous Italian family (whose actions are, says Mr Peggotty, 'laid up wheer neither moth nor rust doth corrupt', in conscious echo of Matthew 6:20); and she helps unite the fallen woman with her foster-father again later (ch. li, pp. 728–9). Mr Peggotty, on accepting back his 'dear child' in compassionate forgiveness, is reminded of the dust in which 'our Saviour' wrote 'with his blessed hand' (ch. li, p. 725), as he carries out precisely the Christian demand implicit in John 8:3–11 (and see Illustration 12).

Evil in *David Copperfield* is represented essentially as that turning 'inward', to 'feed' on one's own heart, diagnosed in the Murdstones' religion (ch. lix, p. 834); while goodness involves admitting, as David comes to admit, that 'human interest' (ch. lviii, p. 816) which reflects our God-given, natural tendency to help others.

III

In *Bleak House* Dickens affirms his basic belief in a form of Christianity primarily concerned with relieving the condition of the poor and outcast by attacking every kind of contemporary religious activity not immediately helpful to them. With an indignant satiric thrust which has often led him to be criticised for exaggeration and unfairness, he suggests that whether 'by high church, or by low church, or by no church' (ch. xlvi, p. 627) the urban poor fail to be reclaimed; and that the Jellybys, Pardiggles and Chadbands of the world only make things worse by confounding charity with their own need to dominate and exploit. Despite the claims of offended special-interest bodies, and of the scholars who unearth their remarks, to the effect that these attacks concern identifiable groups or individuals such as the Puseyites (Mrs Pardiggle) or Mrs Chisholm (Mrs Jellyby), Dickens largely resists the temptation to lay the blame on any specific party, sect, or church, preferring the implication that nobody can escape responsibility.

His pessimistic analysis of the social effects of contemporary religion in *Bleak House* is, of course, part of a more general indictment of institutions and their failure to minister to the real needs of individuals, as has often been pointed out. This indictment is embodied in the corrupting influences of the Court of Chancery, which spread like a blight upon the lives of those, from the aristocratic Dedlocks to the miserable inhabitants of Tom-all-Alone's, who are brought into contact with it. But Dickens also hints at some larger, indefinite but all-pervasive

12 'Martha' (*David Copperfield*, ch. xxv, p. 365), by 'Phiz'. The print over the mantlepiece, echoing Martha's pose, reminds of Christ's compassion for Mary Magdalene.

spiritual malaise of Victorian civilisation, a malaise expressed not only in the overall futility of the lives of the characters (with the possible exception of Esther Summerson and Allan Woodcourt), but in the persistent imagery of darkness, disease and death which colours the narrative from the famous fog-bound introductory chapter onwards. At times, the Chancery case of Jarndyce and Jarndyce takes on the overtones of some primal curse upon mankind, as it stretches forth 'its unwholesome hand to spoil and corrupt' (ch. i, p. 5). Sin is not confined to any single individual.

In fact, Dickens was daring to suggest – at a time when the Great Exhibition had just made the gospel of material progress most triumphantly visible – that the whole social organism was in a precarious state, liable to slide back into a prehistoric chaos in which it 'would not be wonderful to meet the Megalosaurus, forty feet long or so, waddling like an elephantine lizard up Holborn Hill' (ch. i, p. 1). This grotesque vision sets a tone which, it is not surprising to learn, induced widespread disappointment among reviewers, accustomed as they were to the optimism of the earlier Dickens. Forster himself thought one of the 'many indications of the inferiority of *Bleak House* to its predecessors' was its lack of *David Copperfield*'s 'generally healthful and manly tone' (Forster, 1928, p. 552). When *Great Expectations* came out it was greeted as a happy exception to the darkening perspective of Dickens's vision. Modern criticism has, however, reversed this assessment, hailing *Bleak House*, in the language of Shakespeare criticism, as the first of Dickens's 'dark novels'. But this is equally misleading. Although it is generally true that in the 1850s and subsequently Dickens's novels reflect a gloomier view of human possibilities, partly, no doubt, because of the personal strains underlying is huge popular success, more importantly, because of the unprecedented depth of his analysis of society, it is also true to say that as early as *Oliver Twist* he expresses a profound despair with the affairs of this world, coupled with a deep yearning for some other, Platonic realm of ideality where things may be set right. Richard Carstone's desire to begin the world anew (ch. lxv, pp. 870–1) is a later version of Oliver's dreams of the heaven in which pauper orphans finally regain the happiness and security they have lost.

Nevertheless, in *Bleak House* Dickens does depict a state of isolation and alienation among his characters, from the 'legally non-existent' Gridley, to the suppressed and frigid Lady Dedlock, that is unique in his fiction. One of the most important characters in the plot exists only in memory and in his handwriting, which he has failed to disguise; appropriately, he is called Nemo, 'Latin for no one', as Mr Tulkinghorn explains (ch. x, p. 133); and, apart from having fathered the illegitimate Esther (who is thus also legally non-existent, the daughter of nobody, *filia nullius*), his main contribution to the story is his death. In a world of such insubstantialities, it is perhaps to be expected that a solidly delineated character such as Krook (a parody of the Lord Chancellor) can mysteriously transform himself into a heavy fall of soot. If Dickens here reaches for some metaphysical meaning, some point about the

atomisation of urban society, then it is also and more significantly true
that he has in mind the destruction of all things evil on the Day of
Judgement, the 'appointed time' when 'all authorities in all places under
all names soever, where false pretences are made, and where injustice is
done' shall come to an end (ch. xxxii, pp. 455-6). This is one of many
apocalyptic references, from the opening of the novel onwards.

The apocalyptic overtones of Krook's death (placed at the end of the
tenth number, structurally central) are a warning to all those who
participate in the reduction of human beings to nothing in this world.
Religion is presented as critically involved in this reductive process. The
'authorities' under 'all names soever', who create injustice under their
pretences, manifestly include the Church and the sects. The 'crowning
confusion of the great, confused city' is the summit of St Paul's
Cathedral, so far out of reach of the degraded crossing-sweeper, Jo (ch.
xix, p. 271; see Illustration 13). The Court of Chancery, located in a
converted church building, and supposedly dedicated to the ideals of equity
and justice, represents a false religion which distorts and confuses human
interconnections, with the result that the innocent cannot be recognised,
or even *seen*, in their suffering – the visual metaphor is central, whether in
the form of 'telescopic philanthropy' (ch. iv, p. 36), Esther's temporary
blindness (ch. xxxi, p. 442; ch. xxxv, pp. 488-9), or even, ironically, her
evangelical aunt's 'Watch ye therefore!' (ch. iii, p. 19: see Mark 13:35-6),
uttered as the woman collapses. We need to see, to pity.

For Dickens religion becomes meaningless unless it produces a direct,
practical effort to help the victims of society, a point made most
forcefully in the history of Jo, the most outcast and dispossessed of all his
characters. Based on an actual boy,[1] but also that ghastly, stunted being
which haunts his imagination as the visible product of society's failure to
aid and succour the poor, Jo is a triumph of pathos and plausibility. He
first appears at the 'Inkwich' for Nemo, where his evidence is rejected
because he 'Can't exactly say what'll be done to him arter he's dead if he
tells a lie', although he can say most exactly what Nemo did for him while
alive, giving him, a fellow outcast, the price of a supper and a night's
lodging (ch. xi, pp. 148-9). With obvious scorn for the prevailing
evangelical cant, Dickens sets the 'terrible depravity' of this 'graceless'
boy's inadequacy on a point of doctrine which, as was well known, not
even the most eminent theologians could settle, against the simple
human compassion of Nemo, the 'nobody'. (During the publication of
Bleak House F. D. Maurice was dismissed from King's College, London,
for the dangerously uncertain state of his views on future punishment.)
The point is clinched by the narrator's concluding apostrophe to Jo, as he
sweeps the step to Nemo's burial-ground:

Jo, is it thou? Well, well! Though a rejected witness, who 'can't exactly

13 'Ludgate Hill', by Gustave Doré, from G. Doré and B. Jerrold, *London* (1872). The 'crowning confusion of the great, confused city': St Paul's (*Bleak House*, ch. xix, p. 271).

say' what will be done to him in greater hands than men's, thou art not quite in outer darkness. There is something like a distant ray of light in thy muttered reason for this:

'He wos wery good to me, he wos!' (ch. xi, p. 152)

Robbed of his identity ('Name, Jo. Nothing else that he knows on'), brutalised to the level of the lower animals (he is compared to a drover's dog), Jo nevertheless exhibits some faint reflection of the divine in his response to a single remembered kindness. The Roman Catholic *Rambler* considered Dickens 'at once the creation and the prophet of an age which loves benevolence without religion' ([Stothert], 1854, p. 41). This misses the point: for Dickens, and for many who knew what festered in the dark jungles of the newly industrialised cities, benevolence may *be* a religion.

Jo is rejected as a witness by the law and respectable religion. Yet there is a sense in which he is always a witness, his presence testifying to the hollow sham of a professedly Christian society. In their reactions to him, both institution and individual reveal the extent to which they follow the gospel demand, powerfully expressed by Mr Jarndyce when he finds the orphan Charley Neckett, whose landlady has 'forgiven' the rent: 'the time will come' when we will find that forasmuch as it is done 'unto the least of these –!' (ch. xv, p. 211: Matthew 25:40). Ironically, Jo alone brings meaning to Nemo's funeral in that he recognises the humanity of 'our dear brother here departed', thus investing the words of the burial service with at least a shade of their original significance. Otherwise the ceremony is empty, worse than pagan. Dickens feels he is working in terms of a society not only unChristian, but *irreligious*. 'Our dear brother' – the repeated phrase underlines the notion of death as a sacrament to the brotherhood of all men – is placed in 'a beastly scrap of ground which a Turk would reject as a savage abomination, and a Caffre would shudder at', there to receive 'Christian burial' (ch. xi, p. 151). The blasphemy is a compound of practical incompetence and unconcern in a society which permits interment in an overstocked and disease-ridden graveyard, as well as outrage against the last and most important ceremony of a man's life.[2] The material and the spiritual cannot be separated, we 'sow him in corruption, to be raised in corruption' (loc. cit.), a further allusion to the burial service, suggesting the horror of replacing the hope of life after death with a resurrection of pestilence and disease, 'an avenging ghost at many a sick-bedside: a shameful testimony to future ages, how civilisation and barbarism walked this boastful island together' (loc. cit.). The avenging ghost is embodied in Jo, who carries the deadly retributory contagion (familiar from *Oliver Twist* and *Dombey and Son*) to all levels of society, finally to those who deny or are unaware of their connnection with the dead man – Lady Dedlock and Esther Summerson, Nemo's mistress and illegitimate daughter.

In this way Dickens enforces his belief in a social gospel, which involves recognising and admitting the essential ties binding mankind together, even if only in a community of suffering and death, which may be all that is possible in this corrupt society. The corruption is expressed variously and subtly: when Lady Dedlock (disguised as a servant) asks Jo to lead her to her secret lover Nemo's grave, 'I'm fly', he replies,

> 'But fen larks, you know! Stow hooking it!'
> 'What does the horrible creature mean?' exclaims the servant, recoiling from him.
> 'Stow cutting away, you know!' says Jo.
> 'I don't understand you. Go on before! I will give you more money than you ever had in your life!' (ch. xvi, p. 224)

Language itself can no longer offer meaning across class boundaries. Joe takes her to the graveyard:

> 'Is this place of abomination, consecrated ground?'
> 'I don't know nothing of consequential ground,' says Jo, still staring.
> 'Is it blessed?'
> 'WHICH?' says Jo, in the last degree amazed.
> 'Is it blessed?'
> 'I'm blest if I know,' says Jo, staring more than ever; 'but I shouldn't think it warn't. Blest?' repeats Jo, something troubled in his mind. 'It an't done it much good if it is. Blest? I should think it was t'othered myself. But I don't know nothink!' (ch. xvi, p. 225)

Here is no Gampian enjoyment of the surviving vitality of religious language. Dickens's humour is bitter, and pointed. Even the most familiar, traditional Christian words are become unfamiliar (Jo, like Oliver, has learnt, because he has been taught, 'nothink') and, by implication, ineffective. Jo's death-scene, in which a doctor (*not* a clergyman) takes him stumbling through the opening of the Lord's Prayer, and Dickens refuses to allow for mere pathos, stands as a further indictment:

> Dead, your Majesty. Dead, my lords and gentlemen. Dead, Right Reverends and Wrong Reverends of every order. Dead, men and women, born with Heavenly compassion in your hearts. And dying thus around us every day. (ch. xlvii, p. 649)

If there is sentimentality in Jo's death, it is not of Dickens's making: turning to his audience, turning *upon* his audience, he deflates any false consolatory hopes the preceding lines may have engendered. Critics continue to accept House's rash condemnation of this scene in *The Dickens World* without being aware of Dickens's irony, for which his own readers may have been all the more prepared by Elizabeth Barrett

Browning's widely familiar 'The Cry of the Children' (1st publ.
Blackwood's Magazine, August 1843), which includes the lines 'Two
words, indeed, of praying we remember,/And at midnight's hour of
harm,/"Our Father", looking upward in the chamber,/We say softly for
a charm . . .'. It is in any case an appalling comment on the clergy 'of every
order' that Jo can only be taken struggling through the words of the basic
Christian prayer on his deathbed, and then as a meaningless incantation
rather than a supplication to God. The only glimmer of hope is suggested
by the fact that people *could* help Jo, that there is an innate spark of divine
compassion in their hearts. If Dickens had not believed this it is difficult
to understand how he could have proceeded at all.

Perhaps the most powerful emblem of the ultimate brotherhood of
mankind in suffering and death is offered by Lady Dedlock's death on
the very step Jo has swept, her head in her illegitimate daughter's arms.
By a masterly stroke of structural irony, the dual narrative is manipulated
so that Esther arrives at her father's burial-ground knowing only that *a*
mother is there, a 'distressed, unsheltered creature' whom she believes to
be Jenny, the brickmaker's wife (ch. lix, pp. 811–12). Her pity for this
woman sanctions her pity for her own mother. 'Social' compassion
includes, and is even identified with, 'individual' compassion: they are
the same in the end, and any separation of them means the destruction of
both. Hence, the overall emphasis on doing what you can for those
immediately about you, and trying 'to let that circle of duty gradually and
naturally expand itself', as Esther tells Mrs Pardiggle (ch. viii, p. 104).
Like her dead father, Esther shows true Christian compassion towards
Jo: when the fever-ridden boy is delivered on to her doorstep at Bleak
House, she insists on taking him in, while her foster-parent Jarndyce
contemplates sending him to the workhouse, albeit with the best
intentions (ch. xxxi, pp. 432–5). The feckless Skimpole is simply callous:
'You had better turn him out', he says – although it should be added
that, for all his embodiment of everything Dickens despised in
impracticality and irresponsibility, Skimpole exerts an odd, intermittent
attraction, subverting the novelist's own urgent, evangelising aims.
Esther provides the ideal, by which we are to judge the behaviour of
others. Those about her make her more persuasive an image of good than
she manages to be on her own. When her orphan maid, Charley Neckett,
falls ill of Joe's disease, and is nursed by her, the girl speaks 'of what she
had read to her father, as well as she could, to comfort him; of that young
man carried out to be buried, who was the only son of his mother and she
was a widow; of the ruler's daughter raised up by the gracious hand upon
the bed of death' (ch. xxxi, p. 439: see Luke 7:12; Matthew 9:18). This
simple piety is endorsed, in effect, by her mistress's action; and Esther,
ironically but appropriately, has then to be nursed in her turn. The
Christian spirit of compassion which links these two orphans provides a

moving contrast to the activities of those irreligious philanthropists whom Dickens satirises with indignant scorn.

IV

At first, the product of an oppressively puritanical upbringing, Esther is too morally timid (a timidity akin to David Copperfield's, Arthur Clennam's and Pip's) to do more than observe the contradictions of those who pretend to help others while neglecting the needy. In the first number of the novel she is confronted with the 'telescopic philanthropy' of Mrs Jellyby, who seems always to 'look a long way off', as if there were nothing closer than Africa, where the cultivation of 'coffee, and natives', is her consuming passion (ch. iv, p. 36-7).[3] Mrs Jellyby neglects her daughter Caddy and her mournful husband, who once utters the memorable phrase: 'Never have a Mission, my dear child' (ch. xxx, p. 421). But under Esther's modest tutelage, Caddy Jellyby becomes a perfect wife and mother (in Victorian terms), reinforcing Dickens's fundamental point: charity begins at home, and sometimes ends there, too.

It is now familiar knowledge that Mrs Jellyby embodies several features of the woman whose Family Colonization Loan Society Dickens enthusiastically publicised in *Household Words*, Mrs Caroline Chisholm; and that the Jellyby project for settling families in Borrioboola-Gha, on the left bank of the Niger, is probably derived from Fowell Buxton's ill-fated Niger expedition of 1841-2, the folly of which Dickens rebuked in *The Examiner* in 1848. But it is significant that Dickens gives Mrs Jellyby no religion, although Mrs Chisholm was a Catholic, nor does he suggest any religious ambitions behind the Borrioboola-Gha plan, although the original expedition had strong, if diffuse, intentions to Christianise the pagan. Above all, it is important to notice that Mrs Jellyby is given no abolitionist notions, although these were central to the religious-moral aspect of Buxton's expedition. It was, in fact, the supposed anti-abolitionist message of the Jellyby episode which attracted the wrath of former Lord Chief Justice Denman. A friend of Dickens, and an abolitionist, he observed that the novelist was exerting his powers to 'obstruct the great cause of human improvement' by ridiculing Mrs Jellyby (quoted in Stone, 1957).

But, as Dickens pointed out in a letter to Denman's daughter, no reference to slavery is made, and, moreover, Mrs Jellyby's portrait was clearly intended as an attack on a general vice of the time - the neglect of 'private duties associated with no particular excitement, for lifeless and soulless public hullabaloo with a great deal of excitement', a vice damaging to any objects thus taken up by 'associating them with Cant and Humbug in the minds of those reflecting people whose sympathies it is most essential to enlist, before any good thing can be advanced' (Stone, 1957, pp. 194–5). Such people include, it has also to be said, though only on certain occasions, Dickens himself. Although he hammered 'the cant which is the worst and commonest of all, the cant about the cant of philanthropy' (Fielding *Speeches*, p. 132: toasting Lord Shaftesbury, 10 May 1851), he sometimes found the cant of philanthropy where a more discriminating judgement would have perceived traces of goodness – in Exeter Hall, for instance ('whatever Exeter Hall champions, is the thing by no means to be done', *MP*, p. 108), where the voices of men such as Shaftesbury, as well as the more extreme Thomas Binney, could be heard. As the *Eclectic Review* rightly remarked (new series, vol. 6, December 1853, p. 678), active concern for the heathen abroad was generated by the same class, and often the same individuals, who were most actively concerned for the heathen at home. Dickens ignores this – unless he means to refer to it in Mr Jarndyce's futile attempts to combine both kinds of philanthropy (ch. xv, p. 204)[4] – although he must have been aware that Shaftesbury and other leading evangelicals supported Ragged Schools and City missions with as much, if not more, vigour as they campaigned against slavery or in favour of the mission to China. When Dickens broadens his attack upon 'telescopic philanthropy' in *Bleak House* with the introduction of Mr Quale (with his 'Brotherhood of Humanity' cant), Mrs Pardiggle (whose eldest, Egbert, is persuaded to send his pocket-money to the Tockahoopo Indians), and the Society for the Propagation of the Gospel in Foreign Parts (whose doorstep Jo sweeps), there is no sign that anybody cares for more than 'everybody else's mission . . . the most popular mission of all' (ch. iv, p. 41; ch. viii, p. 101; ch. xvi, p. 221; ch. xv, p. 202).

But a novel is not an argument, and satire does not function by looking at every side of the question. Dickens firmly believed that the 'work at home must be completed thoroughly, or there is no hope abroad', as he put it in the *Examiner* article; adding, in unconscious anticipation of Esther's support for allowing one's circle of duty to expand naturally and gradually, that the 'stone that is dropped into the ocean of ignorance at Exeter Hall, must make its widening circles, one beyond another, until they reach the negro's country in their natural expansion' (*MP*, p. 123). He had no sympathy with missionaries, with one exception, Dr Livingstone, who perhaps seemed more of an explorer than a missionary (see Fielding *Speeches*, p. 290). One part of Christ's teaching with which Dickens did not agree was 'Go ye therefore, and teach all nations, baptising them in the name of the Father, and of the Son, and of the Holy Ghost' (Matthew 28:19).

Jo bears witness against false philanthropy, by being 'not a genuine foreign-grown savage', merely the 'ordinary home-made article', and so not qualifying for the attention of either Mrs Jellyby or the Society for the Propagation of the Gospel (ch. xvi, pp. 640-1). As for that august institution, he admires the size of their edifice, wondering 'what it's all about'; he has 'no idea, poor wretch, of the spiritual destitution of a coral reef in the Pacific, or what it costs to look up precious souls among the cocoa-nuts and bread-fruit' (ch. xvi, p. 221). Dickens's sarcastic, even facetious, emphasis may have been directed quite specifically at the SPG (as it was, and is still, known), the funds of which grew astonishingly during the first half of the nineteenth century, and one of whose missionary recipients was George Selwyn, a man of heroic mould who was particularly active among the Maoris (Carpenter, 1959 edn, pt 3, pp. 429, 435-42). But, as the novelist's reply to the angry Reverend Henry Christopherson (who called him 'irreligious' and 'antichristian' for his allusion to the SPG) indicates, the opposition of Jo and the Society was part of the broad point he persisted in making:

> If you think the balance between the home mission and the foreign mission justly held in the present time, I do not. I abstain from drawing the strange comparison that might be drawn between the sums even now expended in endeavours to remove the darkest ignorance and degradation from our very doors, because I have some respect for mistakes that may be founded in a sincere wish to do good. But I present a general suggestion of the still-existing anomaly (in such a paragraph as that which offends you), in the hope of inducing some people to reflect on this matter, and to adjust the balance more correctly. I am decidedly of opinion that the two works, the home and the foreign, are *not* conducted with an equal hand, and that the home claim is by far the stronger and more pressing of the two. (Dexter *Letters*, Vol. 2, p. 401)[5]

Unreasonable as this might seem from another religious standpoint, this is what Dickens believed, from the time of his depiction of the 'distribution society' ladies in 'Our parish' (*Sketches by Boz*, pp. 34-9), to the appearance of Mr Honeythunder in *Edwin Drood* (ch. vi, pp. 45-6); and it is in *Bleak House* that it emerges most strongly, most persuasively.

Despite Mr Honeythunder, it is striking that Dickens generally singles out women for censure as the most interfering. Benevolence is the province of men, it seems, from Mr Pickwick to Mr Boffin. In fact it was a new feature of the period for women to be conspicuously active in the promotion of good works since they generally lacked the power of a Pickwick or Cheeryble or Jarndyce to have money of their own (Miss Burdett Coutts was, of course, an exception). But Dickens's attitude towards female emancipation may be gathered from his depiction of Miss Wisk, who considers the notion of woman's 'mission' lying chiefly in the 'narrow sphere' of home 'to be an outrageous slander on the part of her Tyrant, Man' (ch. xxx, p. 423). That he may well have felt personally threatened, or at least aggrieved, by women's missions is suggested by the fact that at the time of *Bleak House* his wife was involved in the anti-slavery campaign, helping to draw up and sign 'An Affectionate and Christian Address of Many Thousands of Women' in Britain to their 'Sisters' in America, urgently pressing them to use their domestic influence in the abolitionist cause (quoted in Stone, 1957, p. 199). Dickens, who had been strongly abolitionist himself in *American Notes* and *Martin Chuzzlewit*, was less so by this time, although his views remained reasonable until the 1860s, when the Indian mutiny and the Governor Eyre controversy helped push him further towards Carlylean prejudice. The women's appeal was countered anonymously in *A Letter to those Ladies who met at Stafford House in Particular, and to the Women of England in General, on Slavery at Home* (1853, by Mrs Tyler, wife of the ex-president of the United States; see Hodder, 1892, p. 476) on the same radical grounds Dickens would have applied: that charity begins at home, where we have our own slaves – the poor. What was the point of petitioning America when there were so many here 'without the means of instruction in the religion we profess to believe . . . hordes of half-savage human beings' whom only the bravest clergyman dared visit? ([Tyler], 1853, p. 22).

In *Bleak House* Mrs Pardiggle exhibits this kind of bravery, but in her it becomes what Dickens memorably characterises as 'rapacious bene-volence' (ch. viii, p. 100). Critical attention has tended to focus on her supposed Puseyism: John Butt labelled her the principal Puseyite in the novel for naming her sons after the saints or heroes of the primitive church, and for pressing them to join her at matins, 'very prettily done' (ch. viii, p. 102). Other candidates for the Puseyite label Butt identified as the ladies who pester Mr Jarndyce for a subscription to establish a 'sisterhood of Mediaeval Marys' (ch. viii, p. 100), and those fashionable gentry at the Dedlock house who 'talk about the Vulgar wanting faith', a problem they would solve by making 'the Vulgar very picturesque and faithful, by putting back the hands upon the Clock of Time, and cancelling a few hundred years of history' (ch. xii, p. 160) (Butt and Tillotson, 1968, p. 180). But in his attack on Mrs Pardiggle Dickens rather wishes to show how she, and those she imitates, avoid or confuse the social issue by a distorted religion of outdated formalities, or 'Dandyism' (ch. xii, p. 160). To miss the novelist's emphasis here is to miss the main point. In their arrogant unconcern, the upper-class Anglicans of Chesney Wold are even further estranged from the 'Vulgar' than Mrs Pardiggle. It is entirely apt that the chapter introducing her to the reader should be called 'Covering a Multitude of Sins', in ironic allusion to the New Testament injunction – 'above all things have fervent charity among yourselves: for charity shall cover a multitude of sins' (1 Peter 4:8). A token interest is insufficient, especially when, as Mrs Pardiggle's speed of speech, hyperthyroid eyes and tendency to knock over furniture suggests, it involves an aggressive insensitivity to the real human needs of those taken into 'religious custody' (ch. viii, p. 107).

V

The depressing conclusion suggested by Dickens's account of the failure of charity to reach the poor is expressed by the thoughts of Esther Summerson and Ada Clare on their visit to the brickmaker's cottage with Mrs Pardiggle: 'between us and these people there was an iron barrier, which could not be removed by our new friend. By whom, or how, it could be removed, we did not know; but we knew that' (ch. viii, p. 108; see Illustration 14). But then the brickmaker's child dies suddenly, when Mrs Pardiggle's back is turned. Ada and Esther, reluctant as they had been to take part in the visit, experience a spontaneous outflow of compassionate fellow-feeling. Death, as so often in Victorian fiction at all levels, makes possible what was previously inconceivable. In Dickens the religious emphasis is clear if, by contemporary standards, discreet. The religion of the heart speaks in a whisper (in stark contrast to Mrs Pardiggle's hectoring boom), telling the bereaved mother 'what Our Saviour said of children'; and Ada's drooping hair, 'as her pity bent her head' over the dead infant, forms a halo, sanctifying the response (ch. viii, pp. 109-11). The static, purely pictorial quality of the scene may at first repel the sophisticated modern reader: but its primary appeal is to a widespread, popular area of basic Christian belief, an awareness of which prevents us from dismissing it. Nor is it as easy a moment as it seems, initially. As Esther says, 'What the poor are to the poor is little known, excepting to themselves and to GOD', and she and Ada are virtually alone in sharing at least momentarily in the 'grace of sympathy' which obtains among the poor (ch. viii, p. 109). Certainly no representative of organised religion comes any nearer to the destitute Jo than the cross of St Paul's, 'so golden, so high up, so far out of his reach' (ch. xix, p. 271), and a familiar, almost obsessive image for the novelist, from *The Old Curiosity Shop* (ch. xv, p. 116) to *Great Expectations* (ch. xx, p. 155), perhaps originating in a childhood experience of being lost in London, when St Paul's 'cross of gold' kept attracting his eye ('Gone astray', *Household Words*, 13 August 1853, repr. in *MP*, p. 397).

The type of independent, lay 'minister' originating in the class that most needs his help turns out to be the Reverend Chadband, unctuous, gormandising hypocrite in the Stiggins tradition, and a type of religious hypocrite labelled before Dickens began his writing career, for instance,

14 'The visit to the brickmaker's' (*Bleak House*, ch. viii, p. 105),
by 'Phiz'.

in 'The Reverend Mr Irving's orations', in *Blackwood's Magazine*
([Lockhart], 1823, p. 145), where Irving is a member of the
'Gormandizing School of Eloquence'. (He may, in fact, have been
Chadband's prototype, since he had the same affected manner, raising
his great hand before edifying an audience with elaborate, bombastic
speeches, according to Carlyle's *Reminiscences*, 1881, *passim*; see
Illustration 15.) Like his predecessors, Chadband battens on the poor
and ignorant, whom he exploits under cover of the fierce, evangelical
cant Dickens despises most, accurately identified by George Eliot as
'stringent on predestination, but latitudinarian on fasting' (Eliot, 1963
edn, p. 160). This time it is Mrs Snagsby, the law-writer's wife, weak-
minded like Mrs Nubbles and Mrs MacStinger before her, who 'likes to
have her religion rather sharp', and consequently is attracted to the
'vessel' Chadband when 'something flushed by the hot weather' (ch. xix,
p. 260). The hints of sexual frustration underlying her rigid piety (as with
Mrs Varden, Miggs and Miss Murdstone) are obvious.

But of course Chadband is more than the farcical object of Mrs
Snagsby's overheated religiosity. Addressing the starving Jo while
stuffed to the brim with sustenance, he discourses clumsily on the boy's
spiritual needs. Why is this 'human boy' unhappy? Because 'you are in a
state of darkness, because you are in a state of obscurity, because you are

15 'Mr Chadband "improving" a tough subject (*Bleak House*,
ch. xxv, p. 357), by 'Phiz'.

in a state of sinfulness, because you are in a state of bondage' (ch. xix,
pp. 269–70). Again, it is the doctrine of natural depravity that Dickens
shows being used to batter poor Jo. Just as Oliver Twist is accused of a
hellish origin to justify his treatment by authority, so too is Jo 'a limb of
the arch-fiend', as if to suggest that his suffering is deserved. This is the
final blasphemy (nicely reinforced by Phiz's illustration of Chadband
superimposed upon a print of John the Baptist) against the social gospel.
The 'true' religion presupposes the goodness even of bastards, as
Dickens's choice of the illegitimate Esther for the novel's idealised
heroine suggests. That contemporary attitudes continued unsympathetic
to this view may be gathered from the response of Mrs Gaskell's fellow
chapel-goers to *Ruth* (1853), in which an unmarried mother is
sympathetically described, and her illegitimate child exempt from
blame: they burnt the book (Gérin, 1980, p. 139). As in *Oliver Twist*,
Esther's illegitimacy, in opposition to the prevailing view embodied in
Miss Barbary and Mrs Rachael (Chadband's wife), is no barrier to her
being a good Christian, although the Mosaic, Old Testament
assumptions, according to which she should 'pray daily that the sins of
others be not visited upon your head, according to what is written' (see
Exodus 20:5), her sense of being 'set apart', even from those born 'in
common sinfulness and wrath' (ch. iii, pp. 17–18), contribute to her
timid, self-denying qualities. The crux comes when she anticipates her

final vindication: 'I knew I was as innocent of my birth as a queen of hers; and that before my Heavenly Father I should not be punished for birth, nor a queen rewarded for it' (ch. xxxvi, p. 516). To some extent her progress represents a search for the Father comparable to that of Oliver or David Copperfield: 'it was so gracious in that Father who had not forgotten me, to have made my orphan way so smooth and easy . . .' (ch. iii, p. 27). Mr Jarndyce is no substitute for the heavenly Father, nor, in the end, for her earthly husband (Allan Woodcourt). Her mother, Lady Dedlock, in effect condemns herself to the 'earthly punishment' inflicted by contemporary mores, and must die, insisting on being 'beyond all hope, and beyond all help', keeping her secret for the sake of Sir Leicester's honour, and not seeking help or forgiveness in her cold isolation (ch. xxxvi, pp. 510–11).

Contemporary critics, especially but not exclusively those viewing the novelist from an evangelical or Nonconformist standpoint, found Dickens's 'attempt to bring odium on the pastors of the *unprivileged* sects' highly offensive (*Eclectic Review*, n.s., vol. 6, December 1853, p. 676). Mrs Oliphant, in particular, railed against this further instance of what she called Dickens's 'oft-repeated libel upon the preachers of the poor', recounting in their defence her own experience of an uneducated dissenting minister whose odd appearance and errors of expression did not prevent him from reaching 'to the heart of his subject' (1855, pp. 463–4). But her defence is qualified by the admission that Dickens could indeed find a Chadband among the preachers of the poor, only he has 'at least an equal chance of finding an apostle instead' (p. 464). Such a chance is enough for the satirist, who works by selection and exaggeration, even when he knows the truth to be more inclusive.

Dickens's attack upon contemporary forms of Christianity for their failure to develop an adequate social gospel is undeniably justified. Of course religious men and women, many of whom represented a church, did much to relieve the poor; but there was a real problem facing the mid-Victorian believer who wished to bring the message of Christ to those necessary to the achievement of the new prosperity. The poor brickmaker makes the point as well as anybody when he growls, 'Don't I never mean for to go to church? No, I don't mean for to go to church. I shouldn't be expected there, if I did; the beadle's too gen-teel for me' (ch. vii, p. 107). It was the central conviction of labouring men that religion was for the middle and upper classes; how much more so of those on Jo's level of society, like the London scavenger who told Henry Mayhew:

> I never goes to any church or chapel. Sometimes I hasn't clothes as is fit, and I s'pose I couldn't be admitted into sich fine places in my working dress. I was once in a church, but felt queer, as one does in

them strange places, and never went again. They're fittest for rich people. (quoted in Quennell, n.d., p. 353)

In *Hard Times*, Dickens's next novel, the situation in the manufacturing towns is equally bad: the futile jangling of the bells of the 'eighteen religious persuasions' which have built their pious warehouses there hardly affects the listless loungers who gaze 'at all the church and chapel going, as at a thing with which they had no manner of concern' (bk 1, ch. v, pp. 22-3). In *Hard Times* only a visionary star reveals to Stephen Blackpool, the working man, 'where to find the God of the poor'. The hope of reconciliation is faint, and is denied him, as he goes 'through humility, and sorrow, and forgiveness . . . to his Redeemer's rest' (bk 3, ch. vi, p. 274).

Edward Miall, founder of the *Nonconformist* and ex-Congregational minister, wrote in his survey of British Christianity in 1849:

> But I am bound to say, that in watching the operations of our religious institutions, whenever I have endeavoured to put myself in the position of the humbler classes, and have asked myself, 'What is there here to interest such?' I have been at a loss for a reply. I do not arraign architectural magnificence – we cannot, indeed, boast much of it outside the Establishment – for in continental countries I am not aware that it discourages the humblest worshipper. But here, in Great Britain, we carry our class distinctions into the house of God, whether the edifice be a splendid monument of art, or whether it be nothing superior to a barn. The poor man is made to feel he is a poor man, the rich is reminded that he is rich, in the great majority of our churches and chapels. . . . Oh! for some revolution to break down for ever, and scatter to the four winds of heaven, our pulpit formulas and proprieties, and leave men at liberty to discourse on the sublime verities of the Christian faith, with the same freedom, variety and naturalness with which they would treat other subjects in other places! (Miall, 1849, pp. 210-13)

Sentiments – and an idiom – that Dickens shared. But to wish for a 'revolution' had implications which few could face; certainly not Dickens, for all his radicalism. To recognise an urgent need was (and is) not necessarily to be able to meet it. Dickens may have realised this, since he turned, after *Bleak House* and *Hard Times*, to a more private and inward, although none the less powerful, view.

7

Dickens and Religion: *Little Dorrit*

The spirit of Puritanism distinguished from that of the established
church was mainly this – the former drew its tenets and character
principally from the *Old* Testament, the latter from the New.
(Edward Lytton Bulwer, *England and the English*, 1833, bk 3, ch. 5)

I continue to find in all the English I have met a secret *principle of
unhappiness* . . . What is the reason for this? . . . Religion, perhaps.
(Stendhal, quoted in G. D. Klingopulos, 'The Literary Scene', in
From Dickens to Hardy, ed. B. Ford, 1964)

I

In *Little Dorrit* (1855–7) Dickens's work enters a new and final phase. No
longer satisfied with the 'social gospel' of *Bleak House* (or *Hard Times*),
although still indignantly calling in *Household Words* on 'people with a
respect for the spirit of the New Testament' to respond to the plight of
the urban poor ('A nightly scene in London', 26 January 1856, repr. *MP*,
p. 576), he now turns to a more subjective, indeed spiritual, concern.
That personal, ruminative, yearning note which runs through *The Old
Curiosity Shop, David Copperfield* and certain of the Christmas Books
reappears as a continuous strain in the meditations of his middle-aged
hero, Arthur Clennam, as well as elsewhere in his writings of this time.
This is not to say that the social or even simply topical dimension of
Dickens's fiction disappears. Clearly it does not. On one level *Little
Dorrit* gives us perhaps Dickens's greatest satire on contemporary social
and political ills, embodied in his depiction of the Circumlocution Office
and the rise and fall of Mr Merdle. But, as John Holloway puts it, 'in the
end the novel as a whole goes farther, and goes deeper, than any merely
social dimension of life' (Holloway, 1967, p. 14).

Holloway is uncertain how far or how deep *Little Dorrit* goes. He
rejects, for example, Lionel Trilling's familiar assertion, that the main
intention of the novel lies in its search for some ultimate religious truth,
'the non-personal will in which shall be our peace' (Trilling, 1953, p. xv);
and yet he cannot help expressing his own sense of its final purpose and
achievement in terms of what he goes on to call its 'more visionary

dimension of life's possibilities and potentialities' (p. 27). Holloway's difficulty exemplifies my main argument: if Dickens is not primarily a religious novelist, he none the less evidently expresses religious beliefs in what he writes. The problem of defining how far or how deep Dickens goes in *Little Dorrit*, or in any of his novels, is complicated by his independence of easily identifiable systems of worship, by his intuitive and shifting point of view, and, it should be added, by his discretion. These qualities have led to the common criticism that his religion is loose, vague, or unfounded; and a more theologically minded critic even claims that in *Little Dorrit* the religion which Dickens 'sincerely held, was the great absentee' (Cockshut, 1965, p. 154). But, as F. R. Leavis insists, Dickens's 'concern for the spirit' is such that the 'probing questions that theologically minded religious critics are moved to put', become 'beside the point, and unintelligent' (Leavis and Leavis, 1970, p. 274). This insistence is welcome, although Leavis's commentary on *Little Dorrit* in fact oddly fails to give the substantial, detailed evidence from the novel which this insistence demands.

In order to clarify this dimension, then, it is appropriate to begin once again with a central theme. The later novels are even more clearly dominated by single, obsessive themes than the earlier; and in *Little Dorrit* the obsessive centre would seem to lie in the contrasting views of Mrs Clennam's imprisoning Old Testament ethos and Little Dorrit's liberating New Testament spirit, a contrast which runs throughout the narrative, and which is brought to a climax in book II, chapter 31, with the heroine's offer of mercy and forgiveness to the older woman when she finally confesses her guilt. Dickens specified in his notes for this climactic scene his intention to set 'darkness and vengeance against the new Testament' (*Little Dorrit*, Appendix B, p. 827). The hero, Arthur Clennam, may be said to move from the one form of belief to the other, although perhaps 'form of belief' is the wrong phrase, for, as in his many earlier allusions to the 'gloomy theology' of the Old Testament by contrast with the love of the New, Dickens means rather the *ethos* or *spirit* of the Bible as it emerges in such contrasting passages as Exodus 21:23–5, which gives us the old law, the *lex talionis* of blood revenge, and Matthew 5:38–48, which overturns the earlier text by demanding a new law of love and forgiveness towards one's enemies. This view ignores the fact that, although often taken as the type of vindictiveness, the law of revenge was in origin a provision of mercy designed to preclude the worse evil of vendetta, just as it ignores the fact that Christ did not always teach mercy and forgiveness, and 'came not to send peace, but a sword' (Matthew 10:34). And yet, although the contrast between the two aspects of the biblical teaching receives in *Little Dorrit* a more intense and consistent realisation than before, Dickens reveals in pursuing Rigaud a sympathy for that Old Testament ethic of revenge he otherwise rejects.

Associated with his strong interest in contrasting the Old Testament ethic of Mrs Clennam with the New Testament spirit of Little Dorrit are the related themes of self-sacrifice and the change of heart. But specific themes such as these, while of great importance to the novel, are part of a wider and more profound search on Dickens's part for spiritual meaning in a world of darkness and uncertainty – a preoccupation suggested by the powerful, if intermittent, evocations of the unreality of this world in the perspective of the next, and by fierce attacks upon the total falsification of religion by the idolatry and materialism of contemporary society. In an important sense, religion is *itself* the central theme of *Little Dorrit*: it is the first, perhaps the only, novel of Dickens's in which plot, character and scene are all closely involved with religion. If, in the end, Dickens falls back upon a fundamentally, but not exclusively, humanist approach, it is not without the deepest struggle to reach a more 'ideal' and transcendent form of belief, a struggle which paradoxically links his inner life with his times even when he seems to be moving away from them.

II

At first the subjective concern of *Little Dorrit* seems, like that of *The Old Curiosity Shop* before it, to require a biographical perspective. Edmund Wilson noted more than thirty years ago that Dickens's personal difficulties make themselves felt 'like an ache at the back' of the novel, a view evidently based as much on Forster's account of the novelist's domestic upheavals before and during its writing as on the brooding melancholy of its middle-aged hero (E. Wilson, 1961 edn, p. 51). More recently, Lionel Trilling has made the further claim that what Dickens experienced during the mid-1850s was a 'crisis of will', most immediately represented in Arthur Clennam's purposelessness, sense of guilt and awareness of being unloved, all of which lead to his final 'sickness unto death' in the Marshalsea prison, and which, Trilling goes on to say, suggest 'the familiar elements of a religious crisis' (Trilling, 1953, p. iv).

But what was Dickens's state of mind at the time of writing *Little Dorrit*? It would be rash to assume that the kind of self-questioning which naturally accompanies the breakdown of a marriage as well as the onset of middle age should be predominantly, or even at all, religious; but, despite the vagueness of Forster's reports on the novelist's condition, there does seem to have been a deeper inner crisis which may be called religious. There is a new urgency with which spiritual consolation is yearned after, and a new realism with which it is grasped.

Forster is as reluctant as ever about giving us any 'other evidences' (as he put it in his account of the earlier crisis of the mid-1840s) of Dickens 'not having escaped those trying regions of reflection which most men of thought and all men of genius have at some time to pass through' (Forster, 1928, p. 350). At the same time he leaves little doubt that the 'unsettled feeling greatly in excess' of what was usual with Dickens, which gripped him as his home life collapsed, reinforced other symptoms of inner distress to create a new and profound despair. A brooding awareness of the possible drying-up of his creative powers, a deep unease over his position as a successful novelist in a class-bound society, as well as a growing fear of 'some possible break-down, of which the end might be at any moment beginning', all led to a desperate yearning for security and some guiding ideal in life which went far beyond the immediate discontent engendered by the dullness of Mrs Dickens, or the reappearance of Maria Beadnell as a stout, flirtatious matron. Early in 1855, after re-reading *David Copperfield*, perhaps in anticipation of the autobiographical turn he was to take in his new novel, Dickens exclaimed to Forster: 'Why is it, that as with poor David, a sense comes always crushing on me now, when I fall into low spirits, as of one happiness I have missed in life, and one friend and companion I have never made?' But, as with 'poor David', this yearning is for more than a friend could provide; it is for a 'rock' on which to base some deeper faith (Forster, 1928, pp. 635-9).

The increased burden of social and political disillusion pressing down upon the novelist at this time added to his need to adopt some individual, transcendent faith. 'I have no present political faith or hope', he told Macready while at work on the 'Whole Science of Government' for the third number of *Little Dorrit*; just over a year later, in a typical remark, he wrote to Bulwer Lytton that Parliament was 'just the dreariest failure and nuisance that ever bothered this much bothered world' (Dexter *Letters*, Vol. 2, pp. 695, 831-2: 4 October 1855, 28 January 1857). For the first and last time, he joined a public political agitation, the Administrative Reform Association, but despite his admiration for its leading light, Austen Henry Layard, and a stream of articles in *Household Words* during the first half of 1855 attacking government incompetence and implicitly supporting radical reform, he was soon disillusioned with the results. There seemed to be nowhere for him to turn except to his work, there to explore what Forster calls the 'unrealities' he sought (1928, p. 638).

Forster claims that in the end Dickens failed to 'get the infinite' out of the 'finite' in this way, that there was ultimately no 'city of the mind' for the novelist to turn to for relief from these various ills (ibid., p. 641). But these terms themselves imply the spiritual depths Dickens was plumbing, even if, in Forster's limited view, the novelist was unsuccessful in finding what he sought. Forster admits his limitations when he writes that 'the whole of the inner life which constituted the man' was to be found in Dickens's writings, rather than in the observable acts and remarks on which the biography was based (ibid., p. 816). Certainly the reserved, secretive being hidden from view in the philanthropist, public speaker, actor-manager and boon companion of the biography is more tellingly revealed in a work such as the semi-fictional Christmas Story, 'The Holly-Tree' (1855), than in anything that Forster is able to report of this period: in it Dickens reverts to his sensations some eighteen years before on the death of Mary Hogarth, the time when he was perhaps first driven into himself to contemplate the meaning of life and death, and the consolations which religion might offer. In his prologue to Wilkie Collins's *The Frozen Deep* (1856) Dickens suggested that 'the secrets of the vast Profound/Within us, an exploring hand may sound'. Comparing stories such as 'The Holly-Tree' or 'The Wreck of the Golden Mary' (1856) with earlier Christmas offerings such as *The Chimes*, one can discern a clear shift away from the intensely topical satire of the earlier period towards the personal and inward. In some ways Dickens's public life was as active as ever, but there is a falling off in his philanthropic work, for instance, with Miss Burdett Coutts (Coutts *Letters*, p. 310 and note 2), after the time of *Little Dorrit*; and his writings reveal an inner emphasis which remains until the end of his life. The crisis of the mid-1850s seems to have permanently shifted Dickens's attitude towards himself and the world.

Moreover, the extent to which he now begins to affirm that faith in the spirit of the New Testament, broadly interpreted, which in his earlier works is left to rather muted and indirect expression, is quite striking. This is true not only of *Little Dorrit* and the novels which follow it, but also of private and public utterances. In answer to the clergyman (Rev. R. H. Davies) who questioned him about the beliefs of 'The Wreck of the Golden Mary',[1] he exclaimed: 'There cannot be many men, I believe, who have a more humble veneration for the New Testament, or a more profound conviction of its self-sufficiency' (Dexter *Letters*, Vol. 2, p. 818: 24 December 1856). Two years later, in 1858, he retorted to Frank Stone: 'Half the misery and hypocrisy of the Christian world arises (as I take it) from a stubborn determination to refuse the New Testament as a sufficient guide in itself, and to force the Old Testament into alliance with it – whereof comes all manner of camel-swallowing and gnat-straining' (Dexter *Letters*, Vol. 3, p. 79). In a more public statement, uttered 'out of my personal heart', to the Institutional Association of Lancashire and Cheshire in 1858, he felt impelled to say that

The Divine Teacher was as gentle and considerate as He was powerful and wise. You all know He could still the raging of the sea, and could hush a little child. As the utmost results of the wisdom of men can only be at last to raise this earth to that condition to which His doctrine, untainted by the blindnesses and passions of men, would have exalted it long ago; so let us always remember that He set us the example of blending the understanding and the imagination, and that, following it ourselves, we tread in His steps, and help our race onto its better and best days. (Fielding *Speeches*, pp. 284–5)

The divine example is the core of what men should aspire towards.

This affirmation of the spirit of the New Testament represents a response to what Dickens understood was a contemporary tendency to taint or deny it. Indeed, Dickens was more aware of contemporary religious attitudes than he is often given credit for. His retort to Stone was part of a response to the receipt of some (unidentified) religious discourses, and there is other evidence of his not having missed at least those aspects of current religious debate which touched him most nearly. Perhaps his 'crisis' led to such interest. Certainly when he is put to the test he shows an active and intelligent understanding of the religious views of the time. When de Cerjat, his long-time Swiss friend and correspondent, questions him on the 'Colenso and Jowett matter' in 1863, at a time of intense wrangling over the liberal view on hell and the Old Testament, Dickens writes that

> The position of the writers of Essays and Reviews is, that certain parts of the Old Testament have done their intended function in the education of the world *as it was*; but that mankind, like the individual man, is designed by the Almighty to have an infancy and a maturity, and that as it advances, the machinery of its education must advance too . . . As I understand the importance of timely suggestions such as these, it is, that the Church should not gradually shock and lose the more thoughtful and logical of human minds; but should be so gently and considerately yielding as to retain them, and through them, hundreds of thousands. This seems to me, as I understand the temper and tendency of the time, whether for good or evil, to be a very wise and necessary position. And as I understand the danger, it is not chargeable on those who take this ground, but on those who in reply call names and argue nothing. What these bishops and such-like say about revelation, in assuming it to be finished and done with, I can't in the least understand. Nothing is discovered without God's intention and assistance, and I suppose every new knowledge of His works that is conceded to man to be distinctly a revelation by which men are to guide themselves. (Dexter *Letters*, Vol. 3, p. 352: 21 May 1863)

Dickens strongly supports the basic intention of the liberal Christian manifesto, *Essays and Reviews* (1860), to reconcile Christianity with the intellectual tendencies of the age and so save religion and the Church. He also enunciates his belief in the notion of 'progressive revelation' (that is, that God has progressively revealed his will in history) put forward by Colenso and Jowett, in terms which suggest how concerned he was about the appeal of Christian belief to intelligent and literate men such as himself, although he also wants this belief to spread to the 'hundreds of thousands'.

To supplement Forster's account of Dickens's 'crisis' at the time of *Little Dorrit* with evidence such as this is to alter the usual perspective in which that 'crisis' is seen. Not only did Dickens experience a deep longing for security and some ideal meaning in his disoriented life, he probably went some way towards finding a form of belief which could accommodate that longing, although not without doubt and struggle. Broad Church confidence in the New Testament as supreme moral guide and source of individual inspiration (anticipated years before by the Unitarians) may well have encouraged him in his own reinterpretation of Christian beliefs, his continuing urge to affirm the spirit and ethos of the gospels.

III

In a sense, it would be difficult to say whether Dickens was turning towards Broad Church ideas or whether they were turning towards him. His relationship with his age was always complex, and not easily unravelled. In one respect *Little Dorrit* evinces a very closely topical interest, though one familiar from his earliest writings. This is its attack upon Sabbatarianism in chapter iii, which opens with a gloomy sketch of a London Sunday as it strikes the returned traveller.

The passage needs to be read as a subjective reponse on the part of a character whose evangelical conditioning is central to the book; nevertheless, it seems probable it has its origin in a particular personal experience. On Dickens's return from a brief visit to Paris (one of his many restless dashes to the Continent at this time), he was met by a 'weeping' London in which, as he wrote to Sir Joseph Olliffe on Sunday 25 February 1855, 'the bells are making such an intolerable uproar that I can't hear myself think' (Dexter *Letters*, Vol. 2, p. 636). At the same time, the depiction of London's melancholy streets in their 'penitential garb of soot', steeping 'the souls of the people who were condemned to look at them out of windows, in dire despondency' (bk I, ch. iii, p. 29) is clearly an attack upon the contemporary worship of 'the Lord's Day'. Dickens begins with those tormenting bells:

> In every thoroughfare, up almost every alley, and down almost every turning, some doleful bell was throbbing, jerking, tolling, as if the

Plague were in the city and the dead-carts were going round. Everything was bolted and barred that could by possibility furnish relief to an overworked people. No pictures, no unfamiliar animals, no rare plants or flowers, no natural or artificial wonders of the ancient world – all *taboo* with that enlightened strictness, that the ugly South Sea gods in the British Museum might have supposed themselves at home again . . . Nothing for the spent toiler to do, but to compare the monotony of his seventh day with the monotony of his six days, think what a weary life he led, and make the best of it – or the worst, according to the probabilities. (bk I, ch. iii, p. 29)

Sabbatarianism is a kind of idolatry; but the basis of Dickens's opposition to the Sabbatarian view is primarily a moral and social one, and it is hardly surprising that many contemporary Christians took exception to it, especially as the Sunday issue had long since become one of the touchstones by which one could distinguish 'real' or evangelical faith from the merely 'nominal' brand purveyed by latitudinarians. Moreover, at the time when this appeared, many people were particularly conscious of the issue. It had been a matter of current debate and agitation from the previous summer of 1855, when Lord Robert Grosvenor attempted to introduce a Bill to legislate against (or 'regulate') Sunday trading. Dickens's campaign against gloomy Puritan Sundays was of course first launched in 1836, with *Sunday Under Three Heads*, and was waged again from time to time subsequently, for instance, in 'The Sunday screw' (1850) which appeared in *Household Words* in response to the stopping of Sunday post. But this represents a new and strongly felt outburst, and it is worth inquiring why. The best source, again, as with the New Poor Law, is probably *The Times*, from which he may well have derived, or at least strengthened, his views on the subject.

Lord Grosvenor introduced his Bill to Regulate Sunday Trading in the House of Commons in April 1855. Already on the second reading in May strong objections were being voiced by liberals and radicals such as W. J. Fox, who said that the Bill was class-biased, and that it should be altered so as to 'extend the means of rational enjoyment and instruction' to include 'the great mass of the people' (*The Times*, 3 May 1855, p. 7). Shortly after this public agitation began to make itself felt. On Sundays during June demonstrations against the Bill were held in Hyde Park, and aristocrats in coaches were loudly admonished to 'go to church' (*The Times*, 25 June 1855, p. 10). The meetings became increasingly large, until on 1 July nearly 150,000 people took part in a rally which ended in pitched battles between members of the crowd and the police. One man addressed the rally thus: 'His lordship wants to drive us to church and make us religious by act of Parliament; but it won't do, and we are determined to oppose the measure' (*The Times*, 2 July 1855, p. 12). The next day Grosvenor reluctantly withdrew his Bill, but the Sabbatarians, a powerful and influential group, were by no means defeated.

For, the following summer (1856), they returned to the fray and opposed the government's successful introduction of military bands to perform before the crowds in Kensington Gardens on Sundays. In the end Palmerston was forced to stop the bands, although not until after considerable public hue and cry was raised. *The Times* commented: 'So Exeter-hall has triumphed, and the working population of the metropolis is driven back to the public house' (14 May 1856, p. 8). Precisely Dickens's sentiments. He had attacked the restrictions which Grosvenor attempted to impose in an article entitled 'The great baby' in *Household Words* on 4 August 1855, not long after the Bill's failure, suggesting that the people were being treated like 'great babies' who were unable to look after their own affairs or to behave responsibly. Whatever the 'Monomaniacs' might do in trying to influence Parliament, he said, whether it is 'the Reverend Single Swallow' trying to recommend the closing of public houses on Sunday, or 'the Reverend Temple Pharisee' who supports him, or 'Mr Monomaniacal Patriarch' likewise, all of whom desire to restrict 'the rational wants and decent enjoyments of a whole toiling nation', the 'Great Baby' is growing up and will not have it (*MP*, pp. 552-9).[2]

That the sketch of the dreary London Sunday in *Little Dorrit* was both influenced by, and closely related to, contemporary agitation was immediately recognised by early reviewers. For instance, the Church of Scotland *Edinburgh Christian Magazine*, which adopted the tone one might expect of the stricter and more evangelical end of the religious spectrum, denounced Dickens for joining the advocates of a 'system of anticreeds' by his bold advocacy of 'Sabbath desecration' in *Little Dorrit* and *Household Words* (vol. 8, May 1856, p. 40). As the *Magazine* recognises, Dickens's attitude towards the Sabbath question is part of a system of belief, 'anticreeds' in its view. It was a system of belief which a writer in George Henry Lewes's *Leader* singled out for praise in reviewing *Little Dorrit*. Its author, he said, 'soars above all considerations of sect, above all narrow isolations of creed; and, though a more deeply religious writer is not to be found, in all those elements of religion which rise eternally from the natural emotions of love and reverence, he is never disputatiously theological or academically dogmatic' (quoted in Collins, 1971, p. 363).

Evangelical attitudes continued to survive and, indeed, to flourish. After the 'papal aggression' of 1850 the evangelicals entered a decade of new power and influence, evident in the rise of such popular preachers as Charles Haddon Spurgeon, the Baptist whose stern Calvinism, couched in lively but simple images, made him the most famous preacher of his time. (Dickens knew of Spurgeon, naturally, but was 'no friend' of his;

Meckier, 1975, p. 5.) Yet at the same time the vulnerability of the Old Testament was becoming increasingly apparent to thinking men, and Dickens, with his broad, humanist form of Christianity, crossing sectarian and class boundaries, and drawing on both liberal and Romantic sources, seems very much in line with progressive Christian thought of the 1850s and later, a development his earlier ties with radical and Unitarian thinkers would have enabled him to anticipate. The year 1855 saw the publication of Stanley's and Jowett's Pauline commentaries, and Rowland Williams's *Rational Godliness*. With their publication, the dismissal of Old Testament wrath and hellfire along with the encouragement of increasingly free interpretations of the New Testament became much more respectable. One could hold such views and remain almost happily within the Church, as, indeed, Dickens appears to have done. One reason for allowing his ties with Unitarianism to lapse after 1850 (and he seems to have performed what public acts of worship he did perform within Anglican walls from this time onwards) was that it was no longer necessary to look towards an unorthodox denomination for a religious framework.

IV

On one level *Little Dorrit* is a sustained attempt by Dickens to show that one can free oneself from the imprisoning forces associated with a narrow Old Testament faith of stern self-denial and wrathful vengeance by means of the broadly redemptive, loving spirit of the New. This contrast has both personal and social or historical implications. But it is expressed in terms which transcend the immediately personal or social, emphasising the more broadly spiritual nature of Dickens's concern.

As in *Bleak House*, but with this significantly different emphasis, the appearance of the main protagonists of the novel (the Clennams and the Dorrits) is anticipated by a crucial introductory chapter which both sets the prevailing tone of spiritual oppression and creates the narrative's basic metaphors, of imprisonment, darkness and, paradoxically but hopefully, light. In this chapter the contrast later made more explicit in the depiction of Amy Dorrit and Mrs Clennam is anticipated by fundamental contrasts to do with the nature of man. As the stunningly vivid sequence in Marseilles implies, man is typically housed in a gloomy prison shut off from the light which but dimly penetrates to him, but towards which he is instinctively drawn. It is a notion familiar from the long religious and literary tradition initiated by Plato's allegory of the cave in book 7 of the *Republic*, and it is only the first of several such Romantic, neo-Platonic hints scattered through the narrative to underline Dickens's sense of the human condition in an apparently fallen world seeking after spiritual fulfilment. The shift away from the 'social gospel' of the earlier novels should be clear. In *Bleak House*, the fog-bound opening sequence turns almost at once into an account of the institution which lies at the heart of its indictment of mid-Victorian society, the Court of Chancery, whereas in *Little Dorrit*, the 'villainous prison' with which we begin, far from being immediately related to any specific institution or individual, is left to define a state of spiritual imprisonment.

The story, of course, goes on later to tell of the young woman, 'Little Dorrit', born in the Marshalsea prison, the youngest daughter of the ruined William Dorrit, whose long imprisonment has led to moral and spiritual, as well as financial, bankruptcy. Like Nell's grandfather or Mr Dombey before him, he is no father to the child whose inspired devotion alleviates his lot. Amy's self-sacrifice continues even when Mr Dorrit changes from being pathetic to arrogant on the family's unexpected inheritance and release from prison. Meanwhile, this patient Griselda has conceived a deep love, at first unreturned, for the middle-aged hero Arthur Clennam, who befriends the Dorrits in his search for the hidden crime he suspects lies behind the self-imprisonment of his grimly puritanical mother. With impressive symmetry of plotting on Dickens's part, Clennam is finally in his turn brought to the Marshalsea a debtor; there he is found and consoled in his sickness and despair by the angelic Amy, who also helps partially redeem Mrs Clennam at the same time. After his release they marry in the neighbouring St George's Church (where Little Dorrit was made welcome in her lonely nights outside the prison), with 'the sun shining on them through the painted figure of Our Saviour', after which they go 'quietly down into the roaring streets, inseparable and blessed' (bk II, ch. xxxiv, pp. 801–2).

This concluding religious note, characteristically· drawing on a popular, visual metaphor to express the divine origin of the love and forgiveness which has brought about their modest consummation, is present from the start, if not throughout the narrative. It is Dickens's way of conveying his continuing if muted hope in the true faith which can bring light to man in his imprisoned state of irreligion and false belief, hatred and evil; a state which, as the end of the first chapter implies, is as deep as that deep hush upon the sea, which 'scarcely whispered of the time when it shall give up its dead' (bk I, ch. i, p. 14). Only at the apocalyptic end of time prophesied in the Book of Revelation (20:13) shall we see the light of that reality.

Dickens is quite clear about the spiritual condition of man as he conceives of it now. The prison in Marseilles contains, amidst the 'descendents from all the builders of Babel' (a phrase signalling the universality of the vision), two 'vermin', Cavelletto and Rigaud (bk I, ch. i, pp. 1–2). Their condition is one of deep degradation and isolation; they have the taint of the fallen:

A prison taint was on everything there. The imprisoned air, the imprisoned light, the imprisoned damps, the imprisoned men, were all deteriorated by confinement. As the captive men were faded and haggard, so the iron was rusty, the stone was slimy, the wood was rotten, the air was faint, the light was dim. Like a well, like a vault, like a tomb, the prison had no knowledge of the brightness outside, and would have kept its polluted atmosphere intact in one of the spice islands of the Indian ocean. (bk I, ch. i, pp. 4–5)

The impossibility of avoiding this primal stain is reinforced in the depiction of William Dorrit, and Dickens even suggests that Amy Dorrit is touched by the corrupting 'taint' when she asks Arthur if her father ought to have to pay his debts 'in life and money both': it is the first and last speck Clennam ever sees 'of the prison atmosphere upon Her' (bk I, ch. xxxv, p. 409). It may be more of a question than a complaint, yet there is a false note here, perhaps because Dickens, always eager, if not unrelenting, personally, about the repayment of debts, is too close to the middle-class morality of his hero to realise that Clennam's assumption of superiority compromises him.

Dickens retains, tenuously perhaps, but no less deeply in the end, a belief in the need to act here and now, which implies that this world is far from totally depraved. Arthur Clennam's desire to repair the wrong he dimly feels has been done by his family is expressed as 'Duty on Earth, restitution on earth, action on earth; these first, as the first steep steps upward' (bk I, ch. xxvii, p. 311). In context, this is intended in opposition to the falsely conceived other-worldliness of the 'fierce dark teaching of his childhood'. But it is also an expression of the broadly optimistic and practical view Dickens drew from the New Testament, and in particular the Gospel according to St Matthew. He tells of the difficulty facing Arthur in his attempt to act in this world by reworking several passages from Matthew, in particular (and ironically) that which is usually taken to show the exclusiveness of the Christian way and the certain destruction of those who do not follow it, Matthew 7:13–14. But Dickens omits these unwanted meanings by taking only the first words of each of the two key verses on which to base his exhortation: 'Strait was the gate and narrow was the way; far straiter and narrower than the broad high road paved with vain professions and vain repetitions, motes from other men's eyes and liberal delivery of others to judgement' (bk I, ch. xxvii, p. 311; see Matthew 6:7; 7:1–2, 13–14).

Hence an important distinction is drawn between the two prisoners in their cell in Marseilles: one is potentially good, while the other is downright evil. Rigaud represents the utterly depraved, he is a murderer beyond redemption. Dickens gives him the familiar, traditional diabolic attributes from morality play and melodrama: hook nose, hair shot with red (like Fagin), gentlemanly pretensions and a self-dramatising air. He also exhibits a sinister tendency to deny Providence by always claiming to be where he is by the mere shake of 'destiny's dice-box' (bk I, ch. i, p. 10); although, as one would expect of the devil, he also always appears just when the evil desires of others seem to require it – his arrival at the Clennam house nicely anticipated by Affery's fearful speculations during her mistress's 'ferocious devotional exercises' that 'some dark form' would turn up to 'make the party one too many' (bk I, ch. xv, p. 182). Rigaud is important in that he reminds us of Dickens's continuing belief in the possibility of absolute evil. Indeed, Dickens is so eager to enforce this view that he creates the little scene at the Break of Day Inn in which a Swiss pastor is made to affirm that very 'philosophical philanthropy' the novelist himself supports elsewhere against a very Carlylean French landlady. Ironically, the subject of the discussion, Rigaud, is present in one of his disguises as Lagnier. The pastor reasonably proposes a charitable attitude towards the unknown sinner who, as Dickens could have written in the full flush of his 'social gospel', 'may have been the child of circumstances. It is always possible that he had, and has, good in him if one did but know how to find it out.' But the landlady will have none of this: 'I know nothing of philosophical philanthropy,' she says,

> But I know what I have seen, and what I have looked in the face, in this world here, where I find myself. And I tell you this, my friend, that there are people (men and women both, unfortunately) who have no good in them – none. That there are people whom it is necessary to detest without compromise. That there are people who must be dealt with as enemies of the human race. That there are people who have no human heart, and who must be crushed like savage beasts and cleared out of the way. They are but few, I hope . . . (bk I, ch. xi, pp. 120–1)

And, appropriately, Rigaud is smashed to atoms by the collapse of the house of iniquity at the end of the story. This is no new note in Dickens, although, like Carlyle at this time (for instance, in *Latter-Day Pamphlets*), he was coming to sound it more vehemently. It is also a typical manifestation of that side of him which sympathised with those whose wrathful views he might otherwise disapprove of as part of what he felt was the stern Hebraic ethic.

If the fall of the Clennam house smashes Rigaud, its other inhabitants at the time escape retribution or are at least partially redeemed. Dickens allows for the more optimistic view of human potential, while avoiding what he felt was the cant of 'amiable whitewashers'. Thus we are presented with, alongside Rigaud in the prison cell, the more hopefully named John Baptist who, on seeing the 'divine compassion' which lights up the gaoler's child's face as it peeps into his cell, rises and moves towards it, 'as if it had a good attraction for him' (bk I, ch. i, p. 6). The child's reaction to him is similarly favourable; while her response to the offhand Rigaud, prefiguring that of Little Dorrit when she meets the murderer in that other 'prison' on the Great St Bernard Pass at the beginning of book II, is one of instinctive revulsion.

What this reflects is Dickens's deep sense of our instinctive awareness of the presence of both good and evil in human beings, an awareness that is beneath or beyond the rationalising intellect that creates the dogmas of formal religion, and that is so easily misused to create a religion which, as in Mrs Clennam, can reverse the truth and substitute evil for good. Powerful contrasts weave their way through *Little Dorrit,* suggesting both the darkly imprisoned state of man, and his search for the goodness and freedom of the light, culminating in that well-known passage in which the rising sun is visualised slanting its 'long bright rays' across the awakening city, 'bars of the prison of this lower world' (bk II, ch. xxx, p. 741). The hopeful context of this image is often forgotten; both Arthur Clennam and his mother are about to be redeemed by Little Dorrit, and when this happens the sharp distinction between light and dark is made to disappear in the twilight associated with the heroine's undying forgiveness and love: 'From a radiant centre, over the whole length and breadth of the tranquil firmament, great shoots of light streamed among the early stars, like signs of the blessed later covenant of peace and hope that changed the crown of thorns into a glory' (bk II, ch. xxxi, p. 771: see Mark 15:17; I Peter 5:4). Coming at the climax of the novel, when the spiritually imprisoned are released by the divine agency of Amy Dorrit's love and mercy, this coalescence of natural and Christian imagery has great power and conviction.

The nature of the technique adopted here, as well as the fundamental faith to which this climax alludes, indicate Dickens's intention of conveying a religious vision as such, rather than a particular set of beliefs. This intention is embodied in the more general, neo-Platonic intimations running through the text, including the Meagleses' morbid idea of Pet having a kind of ideal hovering about her in the form of her dead twin, living on in some other world as a reality towards which she aspires (bk I, ch. ii, p. 19). The stars come out at the conclusion of the day on which the novel opens, to be 'mimicked' in the 'lower air, as men may feebly imitate the goodness of a better order of things' (bk I, ch. i, p. 14). Life, it is suggested, is like a dream, as opposed to the reality 'far beyond the twilight judgements of this world; high above its mists and obscurities', to which Mr Dorrit and his brother approach as they go to be 'before their Father' (bk II, ch. xix, p. 632). This imagery, drawing on literary (Romantic) and religious sources, is also rooted in personal experience and memory. In particular, the opening image of the Marseilles prison is strongly reminiscent of a specific experience dating back to the summer of 1844, when a visit to the dimly lit dungeons of the Papal Palace at Avignon provided Dickens with a lasting impression which so dominated his consciousness that he could think of little else, 'then, or long afterwards'. It was an impression of the sun penetrating the 'Infernal Well' of the dungeons, an impression reinforced merely days later by the first sight of Marseilles, where a 'staring white' light darted 'fiercely aslant' into the cells of the mad-house ('Lyons . . .' and 'Avignon to Genoa', *Pictures from Italy*, pp. 278–82). The dominant image of *Little Dorrit*, in all its richly varied application from the opening sequence onwards, represents a controlled and complex re-creation by Dickens of an intuition into the condition of man which first came to him many years before.

V

Something similar might be said of the character and fate of Arthur Clennam, whose life gives a particular shape to the imprisoning evil which dominates human affairs, as well as to the hope for at least individual salvation. Clennam is ultimately based upon a personal intuition the novelist has come to in relation to his own past. As in *David Copperfield*, Dickens focuses on a hero who is an *alter ego*, sensitive, emotionally wounded, scrupulous to the point of being a prig, but redeemed by a generous and forgiving heart. Like David, he has to go through a critical change of heart, which brings a new and saving perception of the realities around him, in particular the nature and identity of the woman who offers him her love. Unlike David, he remains to the end self-aware and doubting and, instead of material success to seal his achievement, he loses everything and marries a woman as poor as himself. He is Dickens's most modern hero. He is also the character in Dickens's work who reveals the most convincing glimmer of a genuine religious sensibility, searching for a meaning in life on the profoundest level.

Like David before him – and Pip after – Arthur Clennam is the victim of the 'gloomy theology' derived from the Old Testament, here seen in all its repressive glory, the ungenerousness and materialism underlying its pious pretensions made most explicit:

> I am the only child of parents who weighed, measured, and priced everything; for whom what could not be weighed, measured and priced, had no existence. Strict people as the phrase is, professors of a stern religion, their very religion was a gloomy sacrifice of tastes and sympathies that were never their own, offered up as part of a bargain for the security of their possessions. Austere faces, inexorable

discipline, penance in this world and terror in the next – nothing graceful or gentle anywhere, and the void in my cowed heart everywhere – this was my childhood, if I may so misuse the word as to apply it to such a beginning of life. (bk I, ch. ii, p. 20)

This is the heart of the Victorian paradox imagined in personal terms: the paradox of an evangelical spirit which denied the world, the flesh and the devil, while compromising itself with a thoroughgoing, dutiful materialism. 'Thou shalt have one God only; who/Would be at the expense of two?' (A. H. Clough, 'The Latest Decalogue'). Mrs Clennam always balances her 'bargain with the Majesty of heaven' (bk I, ch. v, p. 48). This puritan, book-keeping conscience was evident long before: as Matthew Arnold observed in 1863, the English middle class had entered the 'prison of Puritanism', where the 'key' was 'turned on its spirit', some two hundred years ago (Arnold, 1964 edn, p. 123). But *Little Dorrit* may be said to witness the end result.

Little Dorrit appeared at a time when material prosperity was being widely celebrated, and yet the underlying tensions between worldliness and spiritual goals were becoming all the more sharply apparent. The 'Whole Duty of Man in a commercial country', according to Pancks the rent-collector, is keeping everybody 'at it' (bk I, ch. xiii, p. 154), a view Dickens does not completely oppose, even as he undermines it with that allusion to the famous devotional manual. In *Hard Times* it had been 'clearly ascertained by Philosophers' that the maximisation of profit comprised the 'whole duty of man' (bk II, ch. 1, p. 115); not long after (but before starting *Little Dorrit*) Dickens remarked that he objected to having the Crystal Palace 'crammed' down his throat, as if it were 'a new page in The Whole Duty of Man to go there' (Dexter *Letters*, Vol. 2, p. 602: 1 November 1854). Practical devotion to God has become devotion to material prosperity. Mrs Clennam's impact upon Arthur reveals the private side of this corrupt religion, but there is a public side too, as Pancks's remarks suggest. Later, both he and Clennam are infected (the metaphor returns from *Bleak House*) by the fever of speculation surrounding Mr Merdle, who is presented as a deity worshipped by society, Pecksniff's 'golden calf of Baal' writ large.

There is no sign that Merdle has any personal religion, much less that he shares Mrs Clennam's particular brand of hypocrisy, although it is perhaps significant that he also 'imprisons' himself in guilt by that tell-tale handcuffing gesture Dickens gives him. More important, he suggests what society as a whole has created to reflect its own mammonism and idolatry:

All people knew (or thought they knew) that he had made himself immensely rich; and, for that reason alone, prostrated themselves before him, more degradedly and less excusably than the darkest savage creeps out of his hole in the ground to propitiate, in some log or reptile, the Deity of his benighted soul.

Nay, the high priests of this worship had the man before them as a protest against their meanness. The multitude worshipped on trust – though always distinctly knowing why – but the officiators at the altar had the man habitually in their view. They sat at his feasts, and he sat at theirs. (bk II, ch. xii, p. 539)

This richly ironic and bitter passage hints at a wide variety of corruption and hypocrisy, all seen to have its source in the same basic denial of religious ideals. The allusion to pagan idolatry relates to a recurrent emphasis, revealed, as we have seen, in the idolatry of Sabbatarianism, but also in Mrs Clennam's impiety:

Verily, verily, travellers have seen many monstrous idols in many countries; but, no human eyes have ever seen more daring, gross, and shocking images of the Divine nature, than we creatures of the dust make in our own likenesses, of our own bad passions. (bk II, ch. xxx, p. 754)

The contemporary impact of such attacks should not be ignored. It is clearest in the depiction of Merdleism. The period 1855-6 saw several large bank failures, including that of the Royal British Bank referred to in Dickens's preface in support of his plea for recognition that 'a bad design will sometimes claim to be a good and an expressly religious design'; and it saw the suicide of John Sadleir, the acknowledged original for Merdle. As *The Examiner* pointed out, if 1856 'had any religion, it was the religion of the dirtiest of divinities, who had never before counted such a host of enthusiastic rogues in his services' (quoted in *The Times*, 5 January 1857, p. 9). Merdle is, in fact, a Dombey beyond redemption, a hollow man created by his time: 'The name of Merdle is the name of the age', the newly wealthy William Dorrit informs his entourage, Mrs General bowing her head 'as if she were doing homage to some visible graven image' (bk II, ch. v, pp. 468-9). Dickens alludes to Christian ideas in judging Mr Merdle: he is the rich man, 'who had in a manner revised the New Testament, and already entered into the kingdom of Heaven'; when he goes up the stairs in his house, 'people were already posted on the lower stairs, that his shadow might fall upon them when he came down. So were the sick brought out and laid in the track of the Apostle – who had *not* got into the good society, and had *not* made the money' (bk II, ch. xvi, p. 513; see Matthew 19:23-4; Acts 5:15). The allusion to St Peter also glances at the truckling of the Church to Merdle: 'Bishop', who attends at the 'innermost sanctuary' of the Merdle 'temple' (bk II, ch. xii, p. 542), unctuously supports the projected purchase of political influence, especially if it includes 'some half-dozen church presentations of considerable annual value'; and asks that a little largesse be shed in the direction of 'a mission or so to Africa', not to mention the 'Additional Endowed Dignitaries' (bk I, ch. xxi, pp. 245-6). Dickens adds a personal thrust by giving Bishop a High Church aura (bk II, ch. xii, p. 543).

Then, as with William Dorrit, it is death which brings reality into this world of fantastic yet dangerous corruption. With his suicide, Merdle's aura is 'the shining wonder, the new constellation to be followed by the wise men bringing gifts, until it stopped over certain carrion at the bottom of a bath and disappeared' (bk II, ch. xxv, p. 691). Merdle's death is classical, and starkly pagan, without hope of a hereafter. If the rest of his life has been some monstrous delusion, he has finally reached the truth, which is revealed as no more than 'the body of a heavily-made man, with an obtuse head, and coarse, mean, common features' (bk II, ch. xxv, p. 686). It is the kind of truth glimpsed by few, such as the Physician, who always brings 'something real' with him wherever he goes, and who alone officiates at Merdle's death, and who alone exhibits any personal emotion over it. There is an element of the spirit of the New Testament in what he is and what he does: 'his equality of compassion was no more disturbed than the Divine Master's of all healing was. He went, like the rain, among the just and unjust, doing all the good he could, and neither proclaiming it in the synagogues nor at the corner of streets' (bk II, ch. xxv, p. 683; see Acts 10:38; Matthew 5:45, 6:2).

VI

With Merdle, the worship of false gods as a public blasphemy corrupting society is made complete. But, even more important for Dickens, *Little Dorrit* traces the subtle psychological origins and effects of perverted religion; the fate of the individual spiritual life is central, even if it is inevitably tied to a more general concern as well. The Clennam house is described from the first in terms expressive of the irreligious nature of the woman in it: hidden away in the darkness beyond a 'Congregationless Church' (as ever, city churches, apart from St George's perhaps, have nothing to offer), it is a 'double house, with long, narrow, heavily-framed windows', in which Mrs. Clennam sits at her desk as if performing at a dumb church organ (bk I, ch. iii, pp. 31-4). She is the presiding genius of a kind of ungodly church. The atmosphere within is charged with the cruelty and vengeance breathed by the bloodier portions of the Old Testament. Typically, on the Sunday of Arthur's return, she prays that her 'enemies' might be 'put to the edge of the sword, consumed by fire, smitten by plagues and leprosy, that their bones might be ground to dust, and that they might be utterly exterminated' (bk I, ch. iii, p. 36). The grimly comic list of anathemata, reminiscent of Miss Murdstone's responses in Blunderstone Church (and similarly identified with no sect outside the Church), revives all the 'dark horrors' of Arthur's lost childhood.

Even Mrs Clennam's attendant, Jeremiah, seems named after one of the darker books of the Old Testament: one which may well have provided the pattern for her character, containing as it does a series of dirges on sitting in solitary bitterness, having 'become as a widow' in affliction and misery, beset by treacherous enemies, begging God to 'do unto them, as thou hast done unto me for all my transgressions' (Jeremiah 1:1-22). Mrs Clennam echoes this last plea when she opposes Arthur's request for understanding and forgiveness: 'Smite thou my debtors, Lord, wither them, crush them; do Thou as I would do, and Thou shalt have my worship' (bk I, ch. v, p. 45). But the true religion, as Little Dorrit will tell her, involves being generous and forgiving, if we in turn hope to be forgiven, being 'guided only by the healer of the sick, the raiser of the dead, the friend of all who were afflicted and forlorn, the patient Master who shed tears of compassion for our infirmities' (bk II, ch. xxxi, p. 770).

In fact Mrs Clennam's religion is evil even in terms of the Old Testament, for it reflects that pagan idolatry which was the basic sin of the peoples of the earlier dispensation, and for which they merited the misery and pain of alienation from God. The contrast is between a *false* view of the Old Testament and a true one of the New.

Significantly, Phiz's illustration of Mrs Clennam confronting Arthur reveals a print above her taken from Joshua 10:12-13, where the sun and moon stand still to enable the children of Israel to avenge themselves upon the Amorites (Illustration 16). Time itself is stopped to allow vengeance to take place, an idea evidently repeated in Mrs Clennam's self-imprisonment in an invalid chair, 'like Fate in a go-cart', as Flora Finching irreverently puts it (bk I, ch. xxiv, p. 276). She has immured herself from the outside world in what we learn is a desperate attempt to defeat change, trapping herself in a rigidly mechanistic conception of sin and guilt so as to 'pay' for withholding the codicil which would have released the Dorrits from servitude. In ironic parallel, Arthur Clennam must be imprisoned too, partly of his own will, to pay the true price of reparation in an act of 'real atonement' (bk II, ch. xxvi, p. 695). In doing so he becomes a scapegoat for the sins of society; but he is not Christ, his experience reflects Dickens's continuing belief in the idea that a profound crisis may precipitate a change of heart, bringing a new, redeemed vision. Amy Dorrit (like Florence Dombey) is his ministering angel.

Yes it is fundamentally a Christian paradox that Arthur Clennam's

16 'Mr Flintwinch mediates as a friend of the family' (*Little Dorrit*, bk I, ch. v, p. 51), by 'Phiz'. The print above Mrs Clennam's 'dumb organ' shows the sun standing still to enable the Israelites to avenge themselves.

deepest failures, his blindness to love as well as his involvement with the Merdle enterprise, bring him to the point where he can be saved. His uncertainty is the inevitable product of an oppressive and self-denying upbringing, more convincingly than ever before the root of character. The familiar charge is made against the tendency to 'hold the source of inconceivable mercy and goodness' before children as a vengeful God (Pilgrim *Letters*, Vol. 1, p. 568). The dreary Sunday bells remind Arthur Clennam on his return to London of a 'long train of miserable Sundays' beginning with

the dreary Sunday of his childhood, when he sat with his hands before him, scared out of his senses by a horrible tract which commenced business with the poor child by asking him in its title, why he was going to Perdition? – a piece of curiosity that he really in a frock and drawers was not in a condition to satisfy – and which, for the further attraction

of his infant mind, had a parenthesis in every other line with some such
hiccuping reference as 2 Ep. Thess. c. iii, v. 6 & 7. (bk I, ch. iii, p. 30)

The reference is apt, alluding to Paul's injunction not to walk
'disorderly', which has a literal meaning taken up by those who march him
to chapel later, 'morally handcuffed' to a companion.

Mrs Clennam, too, was 'brought up strictly and straitly', reminded
always of 'the corruption of our hearts' (bk II, ch. xxx, p. 753). Dickens
for once suggests the fearful continuity of that 'appalling system of
religious terrorism' (Lecky, 1892, Vol. 3, p. 77), which survived by
becoming an essential part of the inner lives of those it shaped. She sits
facing her young son 'behind a bible – bound like her own construction of
it in the hardest, barest, and straitest boards', and leaves him with no
more 'real knowledge of the beneficent history of the New Testament,
than if he had been bred among idolators' (bk I, ch. iii, p. 30) – which, of
course, he has been. Like Miss Havisham in that she has 'reversed the
order of the Creation' (bk II, ch. xxx, p. 754; see *Great Expectations*, ch.
xlix, p. 378) in her proud isolation, she has gone contrary to the divine
plan according to which we are essentially social beings. She has
substituted the views of men for the truth of the Bible, taking support
from a 'Commentary', in which 'pious men, beloved of the Lord'? have
cursed their sons, in order to threaten hers (bk I, ch. v, p. 48). As the
evangelical John Newton recognised, 'wiseheaded Calvinists', in their
consciousness of 'superior spiritual merits', could too easily forget that

> True Christians, through the remaining evil of their hearts, and the
> subtle temptations of the enemy, are liable, not only to the workings of
> that pride which is common to our fallen nature, but to a certain kind
> of pride, which, though the most absurd and intolerable of any, can
> only be found among those who make profession of the Gospel.
> (Quoted in Brown, 1961, p. 417)

This kind of pride is familiar in Dickens's writings, from Stiggins to
Chadband; but its inner workings are nowhere more effectively shown
than in Mrs Clennam.

It is possible to place too much emphasis upon Mrs Clennam. She is a
static figure until her release from self-imprisonment, and her ultimate
significance is determined more by what she is than by what she does.
When, finally, she reveals the manifold justifications for her behaviour as
well as the complex of interrelationships behind it all, little is added to
our understanding of what she represents. Dickens seems to have wanted
to get in everything he most detested about that distorted religion, from
its rationalisation of maltreating a 'love-child' such as Arthur according
to the dubious doctrine of double guilt enunciated earlier by Esther

Summerson's godmother, to Mrs Clennam's hypocrisy in blaming her hatred for Arthur's true mother (who was a singer) on 'those accursed snares which are called the Arts' (bk II, ch. xxx, p. 757). One may speculate that the exaggeration and repetitiveness here reflect the novelist's inability to be quite explicit about the underlying sexual repressiveness which has helped make Mrs Clennam what she is.

VII

In the end, it is Mrs Clennam's effect upon her son which is of prime importance. The heart of the novel lies in his slow regeneration as he frees himself from the negative, imprisoning forces she has exerted upon him, turning him into 'such a waif and a stray everywhere, that I am liable to be drifted where any current may set' (bk I, ch. ii, p. 19). This image of a drifting current seems to have been a potent one for Dickens, who noted six months before starting *Little Dorrit* a vision of the ferry-man 'on a peaceful river', who never leaves his post, growing old and dying while 'the same tune is always played by the rippling water against the prow' (Forster, 1928, p. 748); and three months before his death, the novelist enthralled the company at George Eliot's by telling them of Lincoln's remarkable premonitory dream of being in a boat on a great river all alone, ending with the words, 'I drift – I drift – I drift' (quoted in Cross, 1887, p. 460). The strange power of this idea may be felt in that moment of deep disillusion for Arthur Clennam when he contemplates the apparent ruin of his hopes for Pet Meagles's love drifting away with the Thames at Twickenham: at first he experiences a consoling Romantic vision of inner peace and divine calm mirrored in the merging of the landscape and its shadow in the water, a merging in effect of all the sharp contrasts between reality and ideality which run through the novel (bk I, ch. xxviii, pp. 326–7); then, as the trees darken and the light fails, he learns that he must give up his hopes and resign himself to the worst, imprisoning himself in a new delusion, as the roses from her breast, 'Pale and unreal in the moonlight', float away upon the flowing river; 'and thus do greater things that once were in our breasts, and near our hearts, flow from us to the eternal seas' (bk I, ch. xxviii, p. 330).

This dream-like, visionary element, familiar from Dickens's earlier attempts to suggest the participation of this world in the next, is present also in Arthur Clennam's own meditations, and suggests the saving apprehension of a truly religious view of life as opposed to the false, masculine religion of his de-sexed mother. Although he tends, in his isolation and disillusion, generated by his meeting with Flora Finching and then this experience with Pet Meagles, as well as by the whole nature of his upbringing, to meditate obsessively on his 'disappointed mind' (bk I, ch. xiii, p. 158), Arthur retains a sensitivity towards others and a belief in his obligations to them. He is rescued by what one might well call his religious sensibility, his vision of a true faith which will actually be embodied in the form of Amy Dorrit, the 'true' woman who serves as the at first unconscious but then eventually fully realised focus of his life. This is clarified for us, if not for Arthur, one night late as he sits before the dying fire in his lodgings, gazing at the blank vistas lying behind and, apparently, before him. His mind moves into a dreamy, prophetic vein of reflection which reveals how he has turned away from the deadly impulses of his childhood and youth:

> He was a dreamer in such wise, because he was a man who had deep-rooted in his nature, a belief in all the gentle and good things his life had been without. Bred in meanness and hard dealing, this had rescued him to be a man of honourable mind and open hand. Bred in coldness and severity, this had rescued him to have a warm and sympathetic heart. Bred in a creed too darkly audacious to pursue, through its process of reversing the making of man in the image of his Creator to the making of his Creator in the image of an erring man, this had rescued him to judge not, and in humility to be merciful, and have hope and charity. (bk I, ch. xiii, p. 158)

The concluding redemptive realisation, to be almost too opportunely underlined by Amy Dorrit's sudden entry, is expressed in terms derived from both the Old Testament (Genesis 1:27, on pride), *and* the New (Matthew 7:1 and I Corinthians 13:13, on mercy and forgiveness). Arthur's mind, we are told, is too 'firm and healthy' for such morbid introspection, but will leave him in the darkness of his disappointment, and rise 'into the light, seeing it shine on others and hailing it', a somewhat confusing allusion to Luke 11:34-6, suggesting, perhaps, some uncertainty about the value of this dreamy self-analysis. Of course, Arthur Clennam's diffidence and occasionally morbid but never really (as with Miss Wade, the placing contrast) self-tormenting or self-destructive introspection will issue in a strong desire to unravel the Dorrit mystery, even to the point of leading him to penetrate the corridors of the Circumlocution Office with that mildly persistent 'I want to know'. But, in the end, Arthur is unsuccessful in all except the true purpose of finding his only medium of salvation in this world, Little Dorrit; and in the process he is revealed as one of Dickens's most convincing good men, as well as, perhaps, the only one to evince persuasively an inner life of religious, even Christian, tendencies.

Beside Arthur Clennam, who is close (sometimes too close) to the central consciousness of *Little Dorrit*, there is the icon-like figure of the heroine. It is most interesting, in the light of Dickens's creation of Agnes

LITTLE DORRIT

BY

CHARLES DICKENS

LONDON

BRADBURY & EVANS. BOUVERIE STREET.

1857.

17 Title page vignette, *Little Dorrit*, by 'Phiz'.

before her, that he tries to make Clennam consciously reason himself out of turning Amy into another 'domesticated fairy'; but, despite a strong attempt to give her her own 'individuality', the Mary Hogarth ideal lives on in that 'youthful and ethereal appearance', that 'timid manner', the supposed 'charm of her sensitive voice and eyes' (bk I, ch. xxii, p. 252). There are moments when she lives: at their first meeting on the Iron Bridge, the 'little creature' glances at Arthur with 'parted lips', and he looks away so as not to (he thinks) embarrass her; and thus they emerge on to the quiet bridge, beyond the 'roaring streets' (bk I, ch. ix, pp. 91–2). The subtle hint of sexuality to which this repressed Clennam cannot respond is sharply felt; and yet, as the anticipatory echo of the end suggests, when the two of them go down into the roaring streets again, Dickens will not allow her to be violated by such a thought, and she remains an etherealised figure. As she begins, the bright light shining behind her as she steps from the dark prison door in the title page vignette (Illustration 17), so she will continue, a potent image, more potent in its way than any of Dickens's earlier, static, pictorial heroines, but therewith bringing difficulties which the simple, 'popular' figure of, say, Nell, did not. Perhaps the problem that Dickens fails to solve lies deeper than his personal impulses and contradictions: 'Goodness has only once found a perfect incarnation in a human body and never will again, but evil can always find a home there. Human nature is not black and white but black and grey' (Greene, 1970 edn, p. 17).

8

Conclusion: *A Tale of Two Cities,*
Great Expectations and
Our Mutual Friend

The only other news you know as well as I; to wit, that the country is
going to be ruined, and that the Church is going to be ruined, and that
both have become so used to being ruined, that they will go on
perfectly well.
(Letter to M. de Cerjat, 26 August 1868)

I now most solemnly impress upon you the truth and beauty of the
Christian religion, as it came from Christ Himself, and the
impossibility of your going far wrong if you humbly but heartily
respect it.
(Letter to Edward Bulwer Lytton Dickens, 26 September 1868)

I have always striven in my writings to express veneration for the life
and lessons of Our Saviour; because I feel it . . . But I have never
made proclamation of this from the house tops.
(Letter to John Makeham, 8 June 1870)

I

There is no more profound or original expression of the religious aspect
of Dickens's imagination than *Little Dorrit*, so I shall offer only brief
comment on its successors, important as these are from other points of
view. To do more than touch on a few points in the last complete novels,
indicating how one might proceed with them, would be to extend this
study intolerably. Moreover, my main aim has been not to give an
exhaustive account of Dickens's religion, but to establish an approach, a
way of reading and interpreting his books, which takes account of what is
essentially a religious dimension to them.

At the same time it has been my purpose to correct some of the easy
assumptions underlying what critics and readers in Dickens's time and
our own have found weak or objectionable in his beliefs. Even after *Little
Dorrit*, objections continued to be made to the novelist's 'gospel of
geniality', as it was characteristically – and condescendingly – called by
the learned clergyman George Stott (1869, pp. 224–5). Sir James

Fitzjames Stephen, better known as a campaigner against the 'soft' Dickens, seemed to relent on the publication of the first series of 'Uncommercial Traveller' essays from *All the Year Round*: 'pleasant, witty, shrewd and unhackneyed', they revealed 'an excellent popular critic of English institutions' (quoted in Collins, 1971, p. 409); for instance, in Dickens's account of Sunday preaching in 'Two views of a cheap theatre'. But, Stephen continued (ibid., p. 411), when the novelist

> comes to give his view of what preaching ought to be, he at once betrays that he does not care to reflect deeply on the matter. He is content to take up with the modern delusion that Christianity is a scheme for making things pleasant; and this notion runs throughout all his books. It is indeed a true notion within very narrow limits, and it is the only notion perhaps that can harmonize with the facetious view of life. We do not quarrel with it as a popular way of thinking. But that it should satisfy a man of vigorous mind shows that this mind is only concerned with the superficialities of things.

To attack Dickens's version of Christianity thus becomes an attack upon his vision and his art. These things are inextricably entwined, as Stephen, for all his antagonism towards the 'pleasant', 'facetious' and 'popular' view of life, accurately perceives; what he cannot see is that Dickens's popular, Romantic reinterpretation of traditional Christian belief, which does involve a very deep sense of the reality of evil, as well as a yearning awareness of transcendence, is as legitimate (if not as respectable) as, for example, Stephen's own combination of Calvinist Evangelicalism and rational utilitarianism. For Stephen, and many mid- and late Victorian intellectuals like him, religion was essentially a matter of dogma and theology, of miracles, original sin and eternal damnation; the liberal, Broad Christianity of men such as John Seeley, Benjamin Jowett, or even Matthew Arnold, had to be, and was, rigorously opposed.

From Stephen's standpoint, then, Dickens's reiterated belief that the commonest among us could work out our salvation by (as he put it in the offending article) 'simply, lovingly, and dutifully following Our Saviour' (*UT & RP*, p. 37) might well appear facile. But it is the sincere expression of a broad and humane faith, held to at a time when the novelist, like many of his contemporaries, felt despair for Church and society. Dickens's form of religion views every human being as of equal importance in the eyes of God, and this is what, he says, the truly Christian preacher should remember in trying to reach those who packed the Sunday theatres in order to hear his message:

> What is your changed philosopher to wretched me, peeping in at the door out of the mud of the streets and of my life, when you have the

widow's son to tell me about, the ruler's daughter, the other figure at the door when the brother of the two sisters was dead, and one of the two ran to the mourner, crying, 'The Master is come, and calleth for thee'? (*UT &RP*, p. 39)

It is this spirit which runs through all the writings of the last phase of Dickens's career, with varying degrees of conviction.

During this phase Dickens experienced a painful and exhausting series of reading tours, illnesses and separations (he broke finally from his wife in May 1858), and the deaths of relatives and friends, which was to end only on 9 June 1870. If, as Forster claims, his childhood sufferings had taught him 'the inexpressible value of a determined resolve to live down difficulties', the 'habit', in 'small as in great things, of renunciation and self-sacrifice, they did not teach' (Forster, 1928, p. 635). That he nevertheless yearned unceasingly to attain this 'habit' is implied by the pervasive, if not always convincing, presence of the themes of self-sacrifice and its concomitant, regeneration, in *A Tale of Two Cities* (1859), *Great Expectations* (1859–60), *Our Mutual Friend* (1864–5) and, as far as we can tell, *Edwin Drood* (1870), his last, incomplete novel. The religious dimension is more deliberately evoked than before, to the point of sounding contrived. Key-phrases from the Bible or the Book of Common Prayer play an increasingly important part: Sydney Carton goes to the guillotine to the repeated accompaniment of 'I am the Resurrection and the Life, saith the Lord', from the opening of the burial service (*A Tale of Two Cities*, bk III, ch.xv, p. 357); Pip reads the Bible to Magwitch during his final illness and, at the convict's death, exclaims 'O Lord be merciful to him a sinner!', rewording Luke 18:13 (*Great Expectations*, ch. lvi, p. 436); while in *Edwin Drood*, what Dickens's number-plans refer to as the 'key-note' is struck at the end of the first chapter, when Jasper hurriedly joins the cathedral choir, and the 'intoned words, "WHEN THE WICKED MAN –"' from the opening of evening prayer, rise among the roof-beams, 'awakening muttered thunder' (ch. i, p. 4). *Our Mutual Friend*, longer and more discursive, also reveals an insistent religious note, made most explicit by Lizzie Hexam's prayer to 'grant, O Blessed Lord God, that through poor me' Eugene Wrayburn may be (in common scriptural phrase) 'raised from death' (bk IV, ch. vi, p. 701).

Not surprisingly, in the light of these relatively clear expressions of Christian impulse, some at least of those contemporary periodicals formerly most antagonistic towards Dickens's religion, such as the evangelical *Eclectic Review*, now 'cheerfully' found his writings 'more free from objectionable material' than before, although offensively qualifying this by remarking that 'Mr Dickens knows as much of the ways and manners of religious people as a Hottentot' (n.s., vol. 1, October

1861, p. 459). Dickens was in fact no more orthodox than he had ever been; nor did he hesitate to continue anathematising the unctuous, bullying evangelical Christianity used to torment Pip (who recovers) and George Silverman (who does not). But, as the *Eclectic Review* observed, there *is* a toning down of the open dislike of evangelical hypocrisy, puritanism and Sabbatarianism; ludicrous religionists of the Stiggins and Chadband stamp disappear, to be replaced by favourable portraits of Anglican clergymen such as Frank Milvey and Septimus Crisparkle (although Mr Honeythunder, the sham philanthropist of *Edwin Drood*, continues the satiric line in a minor way).

On the other hand, no character in the later works embodies a religious attitude as persuasively as Arthur Clennam. It is a more desperate vision which offers only the dying or near-dead some form of affirmation: Sydney Carton's inspiration occurs on the scaffold, Magwitch is on his deathbed and Eugene Wrayburn is as near to his end as he could be, when he is attended by two female mediators of divine aid, the down-to-earth Lizzie, and the little cripple, Jenny Wren, who has her 'fancy' on his behalf. The last novels share the emphasis of *Little Dorrit* upon the redemptive potential of love in a world ineradicably blighted by evil; but this is hardly new ground, and at times Dickens manipulates the familiar themes with a self-conscious air which robs them of the force of their earlier, less explicit expression.

II

The more explicit, even systematic expression of Dickens's religious views in his last novels is most obvious – damagingly so – in *A Tale of Two Cities*, and least obvious in *Great Expectations*. This deserves some comment. The pious manner of Sydney Carton's final moments has led to *A Tale of Two Cities* being called one of Dickens's most patently Christian novels. But it is hard to know how far Dickens really holds the belief expressed at the end, or indeed, what it is, exactly, that he is trying to convey. The repetition of the famous refrain from the Gospel of St John in itself reveals little. Carton's death does not leave us unmoved, in so far as it concludes the otherwise self-centred, self-pitying, dissolute and purposeless life which has been transformed by his love for the golden-haired Lucie Manette, 'last dream' of Carton's degraded 'soul' (bk II, ch. xiii, p. 144). But his self-sacrifice is fundamentally as improbable as the resemblance between himself and the shadowy Darnay. More convincing is the moment of sympathetic identification with fellow humanity embodied in the anonymous seamstress who chances to go with him to the guillotine: 'But for you, dear stranger,' she tells Carton,

I should not be so composed, for I am naturally a poor little thing, faint of heart; nor should I have been able to raise my thoughts to Him who was put to death, that we might have hope and comfort here to-day. I think you were sent to me by Heaven.'

'Or you to me,' says Sydney Carton. 'Keep your eyes upon me, dear child, and mind no other object.' (bk III, ch. xv, p. 356)

The seamstress's expression of faith and hope is more persuasive than Carton's consciousness, projected by the narrator as 'I am the Resurrection and the Life'. Dickens cannot really go much further than the doctrine of subjective immortality reflected in his early work, which he here affirms in terms of Carton's memory continuing to live on in the hearts of generations of Darnays (bk III, ch. xv, p. 358). Again, it is nature, rather than Revelation, which encourages him, throwing a 'bridge of light' to span the air between his 'reverently' shaded eyes and the sun, as he emerges from the dark Paris night (bk III, ch. ix, p. 299). Lucie Manette, like Florence Dombey, inspires the 'better' feelings of the fallen man – a potential lover, rather than her father, which may reflect a personal element (in Dickens's relationship with Ellen Ternan) but, more important, which also suggests how much Dickens continues to envisage regeneration, as much as resurrection, in unorthodox terms.

Carton's 'prophetic' concluding vision, of 'a beautiful city and a brilliant people arising from this abyss' (bk III, ch. xv, p. 357), suggests that his act of renunciation is intended to reflect a deeper, divine justice at work in history. But the narrative fails to offer more than a sketchy outline of the connections between individuals and their time, leaving this vision somewhat empty. It is not enough to add only to the 'popular and picturesque' understanding of the French revolution, leaving it to Carlyle to provide the 'philosophy' (preface). Compared with *Barnaby Rudge*, Dickens's earlier attempt to show the inevitable social consequences of suffering, oppression and indifference, *A Tale of Two Cities* is thin, uncertain.[1] Even the characteristic humour is deficient, apparent only in Jerry Cruncher, the Quilpish 'Resurrection-Man' who enacts a lame parody of the main action through his conversion during the Terror (bk III, ch. ix, pp. 292–3), and who attacks his 'serious' spouse for 'flopping' in prayer (bk II, ch. i, pp. 52–3). Mrs Cruncher's zeal does not reflect any new sympathy on Dickens's part, if the depiction of Mrs Joe in *Great Expectations* is any guide: his sister and foster-mother was, Pip tells us, 'a very clean housekeeper', but she had 'an exquisite art of making her cleanliness more uncomfortable and unacceptable than dirt itself. Cleanliness is next to Godliness, and some people do the same by their religion' (ch. iv, p. 20).

Mrs Joe's self-denying hypocrisy is typified by her refusal to hear

Christmas carols on the grounds that she claims to be fond of them (ch. iv, p. 19). Her 'impregnable' bib (ch. ii, p. 6) and lack of children hint at a deeper resistance to the demands of nature; but the full effect of her evangelical rigidity may be seen in the results of Pip's 'bringing up by hand', a series of 'punishments, disgraces, fasts and vigils, and other penitential performances' which leave him 'morally timid and very sensitive' (ch. viii, p. 58). This has an autobiographical feel, enhanced, of course, by Dickens's use of the first-person form, which suggests, again, the memory of that powerful 'female hand' which dragged him as a young child to chapel, to be steamed by Boanerges Boiler. The autobiographical element in *Great Expectations* seems strong, a function of more than its setting in Kent of the 1820s: no wonder Dickens re-read *David Copperfield* during its creation, to ensure he fell into no 'unconscious repetitions' (Forster, 1928, p. 734). Paradoxically, he felt he was expressing an 'idea' which had taken 'complete possession' of him in writing the weaker *Tale of Two Cities* (preface), while the much more personal and persuasive story of Pip began quite casually, as a 'little piece' which happened to embody the 'very fine new, grotesque idea' of the boy's relation to the convict Magwitch, and which he subsequently expanded into a full-length narrative so as to boost *All the Year Round* (Forster, 1928, p. 733). Yet the result was a profound critique of Victorian achievement, in particular of the notion of self-advancement popularised so effectively by men whom Dickens otherwise doubtless respected, such as Samuel Smiles.

In religious terms *Great Expectations* does not seem to reveal any significant advance of the novelist's position, relying as it does on the familiar underlying pattern of sin, repentance and regeneration. But there is a new inwardness evident in Dickens's treatment of the pattern and, in addition, an emphasis upon forgiveness as, in Crisparkle's words, 'the highest attribute conceivable' (*Edwin Drood*, ch. x, p. 84). Forgiveness, in *Great Expectations*, seems to override all other aspects of Dickens's vision in a way which, one may speculate, is associated with his increasing preoccupation with death – a characteristic of his writings, both fictional and non-fictional, from about 1858 onwards. To deserve mercy, one must needs offer it to others: 'For if ye forgive men their trespasses, your heavenly Father will also forgive you' (Matthew 6:14).

Pip's necessarily indirect account, shot through with a remorseful, brooding irony, of his 'fall' through pride and desire, leading to a 'change of heart' through disillusionment and physical trial (by fire and water), gives new life to Dickens's familiar obsessions. In fact, an important part of the effect the novel has on us is derived from our sense of the self-conscious way in which the novelist seems to be reflecting upon many of his earlier interests and concerns, as it were casting an ironic light upon them. The character of Wemmick is perhaps the most obvious example: a man reduced by the pressures of his life as Jaggers's clerk and intermediary to mechanism and spiritual nullity, who, astonishingly, has both an 'Aged P' and a beloved fiancée in his secret suburban home, testifying to the survival, even in the cruelly materialist world, of the heart's affections. The ambivalence of this character reflects a deeper ambivalence in Dickens's attitude to money, more apparent in *Great Expectations* than in any other of his novels, except, perhaps, *Our Mutual Friend*: Pip may be able to resist Wemmick's call to secure 'portable property' at the last, yet this does not prevent him from subsequently becoming a partner in Herbert Pocket's commercial 'House', where 'We were not in a grand way of business, but we had a good name, and worked for our profits, and did very well' (ch. lviii, pp. 455–6).

This concluding note is not smug, any more than the conclusion to Pip's relationship with Estella which, held in that shadowy 'tranquil' light which hovers about them at the end (either version), may find its resolution in this life or the next, and is finally ambiguous. But this uncertainty is in strong contrast to the opening of the novel which, significantly, takes us back to that favourite festival of the Dickens religion, Christmas; only it is to a Christmas for the fallen, a bleak, inhospitable time, when smug, conventional piety within (Mr Wopsle saying grace with 'theatrical declamation', ch. iv, p. 22) serves to highlight the state of the desperate, hungry outcast without. Only Pip, in childish, unwilling opposition to the morality of his sister and her friends, Wopsle, the Hubbles and Mr Pumblechook, can bring these worlds together – although Joe, whom he later comes to recognise as 'this gentle Christian man' (ch. lvii, p. 439), also pities the poor convict out on the marshes. Those who, like Pip, are rejected or ignored, are supposed to be wicked and unregenerate – an association of social, moral and religious oppression very familiar by now. The fearful susceptibility engendered in Pip by being treated 'as if I had insisted on being born in opposition to the dictates of reason, religion, and morality, and against the dissuading arguments of my best friends' (ch. iv, p. 20) leads him to feel a terrible, pervasive guilt for the simple act of charity provoked by Magwitch – an act which, with a nice irony, involves stealing from his family and friends.

Dickens's strategy is quite clear: Pip's self-estrangement and guilt are the product of his knowledge that he has committed a sin in taking the 'wittles' and file for his convict; what Pip does not realise, but we do, is that on another level he is innocent. The exaggeration of Pip's perceptions of the world (including that black ox, which to his 'awakened conscience' has 'something of a clerical air', ch. iii, p. 14) alerts us to the presence of an alternative view of his guilty feelings, a view which Dickens has his older narrator suppress for the time being. According to this view, far from being the 'Naterally wicious' (ch. iv, p. 23) limb of the devil assumed by prevailing evangelical cant, Pip is the naturally innocent child of Dickens's Romantically inspired theology. What the boy does for the shivering outcast, for all that he may be (and in the end *is*, it seems, although Dickens cunningly leaves the truth ambiguous) a murderer, is what Christ enjoins us to do: offer him succour. Further, Pip has to be brought to recognise his kinship to the mysterious benefactor who tries to turn him into a 'gentleman', a kinship implied in Magwitch's tale of being 'brought up' to be 'A warmint' (ch. xl, p. 311). Magwitch's account begins by echoing the opening of the novel, when Pip first becomes aware of his identity:

> 'I've no more notion where I was born than you have – if so much. I first became aware of myself, down in Essex, a thieving turnips for my living . . .
>
> 'This is the way it was, that when I was a ragged little creetur as much to be pitied as ever I see . . . I got the name of being hardened. "This is a terrible hardened one," they says to prison wisitors, picking out me. "May be said to live in jails, this boy." Then they looked at me, and I looked at them, and they measured my head, some on 'em – they had better a measured my stomach – and others on 'em giv me tracts what I couldn't read, and made me speeches what I couldn't unnerstand. Thay always went on agen me about the Devil. But what the Devil was I to do? I must put something into my stomach, mustn't I?' (ch. xlii, p. 329)

Magwitch is a later version of Oliver Twist – as is Pip, who himself undergoes a version of the Parish Boy's Progress, a spiritual pilgrimage in which the metaphysical overtones of the earlier novel are psychologised, and more closely related to both individual and social reality. Yet, like Oliver, Pip recognises the existence of a higher reality, most notably at moments when death is near: trapped by Orlick in the sluice-house, when he 'humbly beseech[es] pardon . . . of Heaven' (ch. liii, p. 404); or at Magwitch's deathbed, when he prays God for mercy on the convict.

If there is a new religious phase in Dickens's works, then it is revealed in these movements towards mercy, forgiveness and reconciliation. Even the brutal, slouching Orlick, who bludgeons one person to death (Mrs Joe), and attempts to murder another (Pip), is permitted to escape the vengeful, retributory pursuit of evil-doers typical of Dickens's earlier fiction, and he simply disappears from the narrative (to a spell in prison for robbing Pumblechook, for which it is hard to blame him). When Orlick suggests to Pip that 'It was you as did for your shrew sister' (ch. liii, p. 404) he implies a complicity in guilt which, though distant, is true to the sense the novel conveys of nobody being immune from the contamination of evil. But this does not mean that Dickens accepts the doctrine of the depravity of human nature; rather, it means that he believes we share a universal potential for evil, just as we share a universal potential for good. This is the true religion, impressed upon us most strongly when Magwitch and thirty-one others are sentenced to death:

> The sun was striking in at the great windows of the court, through the glittering drops of rain upon the glass, and it made a broad shaft of light between the two-and-thirty and the Judge, linking both together, and perhaps reminding some among the audience, how both were passing on, with absolute equality, to the greater Judgement that knoweth all things and cannot err. (ch. lvi, p. 434)

Dickens characteristically manipulates both natural and Christian imagery to create a striking visual image which reinforces his point. 'My Lord, I have received my sentence of Death from the Almighty, but I bow to yours', says Magwitch, redeemed from the pagan, irreligious man who knew the Bible only as a 'charm' on which to swear Pip and Herbert to fidelity (ch. xl, pp. 311, 315).

Significantly, it is Pip who, very discreetly – since Dickens wants above all to avoid sounding like one of his own Chadbandian, evangelical religionists – has made it 'the first duty of my life to say to him, and read to him, what I knew he ought to hear', namely, the Bible (ch. lvi, p. 432). We are momentarily reminded of the death of the Chancery prisoner in *Pickwick Papers*, that 'what I knew he ought to hear' carrying an added emphasis. The chapter in which Magwitch dies concludes: 'Mindful, then, of what we had read together, I thought of the two men who went up into the Temple to pray, and I knew there were no better words that I could say beside his bed, than "O Lord, be merciful to him, a sinner!"' (ch. lvi, p. 436). It has been suggested by Julian Moynahan (1960, p. 61) and others that these last words constitute a pharisaical perversion of the publican's prayer in Luke 18: 'God be merciful to me a sinner.' But this is misreading Dickens, who knows precisely where he is going here, and who expects us to realise that the force of this new application of the Word lies in this very alteration to fit both the immediate situation and the whole process of sin, repentance and forgiveness which operates in the novel, in the lives of Pip and Magwitch, Estella and Miss Havisham. And, one might add, which operates even in the life of Mrs Joe, whose last words are 'Joe' and once 'Pardon' and once 'Pip' (ch. xxv, p. 269). Dickens surely also intended his readers to recall the rest of the parable, especially the words: 'for everyone that exalteth himself shall be abased; and he that humbleth himself shall be exalted' (Luke 18:14).

III

The compassionate hero of *Great Expectations* is perhaps the only male character in Dickens to act as a lay mediator of spiritual truths. In *Our Mutual Friend* Lizzie Hexam and Jenny Wren take on the familiar saving role. Lizzie is a more down-to-earth redeemer-figure than we have grown to expect from Agnes Wickfield, Florence Dombey, or Amy Dorrit, however, and literally saves her upper-class suitor from drowning by virtue of the strong arms developed in helping her father, Gaffer Hexam, in his trade of plucking corpses from the Thames for their money. But she prays, too, for aid from God, as her corrupt lover lies near death in the bottom of her boat, as so many dead lay in her father's before: 'And grant O Blessed Lord God, that through poor me he may be raised from death, and preserved to some one else to whom he may be dear one day, though never dearer than to me!' (bk IV, ch. vi, p. 701). Evidently her prayer is the purer for her concluding denial of any selfish urge to desire his return to life for her own sake; equally clearly, this means that Lizzie will get both what she has asked for and what she has not. When Eugene Wrayburn recovers consciousness, his first request is for Jenny Wren to have her 'fancy' on his behalf, before he relapses, and the crippled dolls' dressmaker understands: 'You mean my long bright slanting rows of children, who used to bring me ease and rest? You mean the children who used to take me up, and make me light?' (bk IV, ch. x, pp. 736–7). She, not Lizzie, is vouchsafed the visionary insight that has flickered intermittently throughout Dickens's work, though he cannot imagine it being available for any but the young, the dying, or, as here, the crippled.

Jenny's vision is a potent one for Dickens, revealed in the popular, visual idiom preferred by the novelist, and derived, perhaps, from a print of Jacob's dream (Genesis 28:12). He seems to refer to the same image as part of Nell's dreamy meditations in *The Old Curiosity Shop*, when the dying girl sees 'the roof opening, and a column of bright faces, rising far away into the sky, as she had seen in some old scriptural print once, and looking down on her, asleep' (ch. lii, p. 389: see Illustration 18). A means of escape from suffering, even death, is suggested. Indeed, Jenny, like Little Nell, has a vice-ridden old pack of sins to look after, too; and has her visions of transcendence appropriately high up above London's confused roar, on a rooftop where 'you feel as if you were dead' (bk II, ch. v, p. 281). The city, in *Our Mutual Friend*, is a sterile wasteland, across which hopeful pilgrims such as the patriarchal (and token) Jew, Riah,[2] wander, fortunate only if they can lead others in 'devotional ascent' to the roof of Pubsey and Co., in the heart of the corrupt, money-making town, the City itself (bk II, ch. v, p. 279). Even the (ironically) pagan moneylender, Fascination Fledgeby, characteristically accoutred in

18 'Behold, the angels of God ascending and descending' (Genesis 28), from *Dr Kitto's Illustrated Bible* (1871–6), based on Raphael. 'You mean my long bright slanting rows of children . . .?' (*Our Mutual Friend*, bk IV, ch. x, p. 737).

Turkish gear (bk III, ch. i, pp. 422–32), is permitted the sight of Jenny Wren 'looking down out of a Glory of her long bright radiant hair, and musically repeating to him, like a vision: "Come up and be dead! Come up and be dead!"' (bk II, ch. v, p. 282). But the peace and tranquillity she seems to offer are not for him; only those who have been brought near to death are finally allowed the earthly version of resurrection, a change of heart, and so can find their peace – Eugene, battered into the river so as to change from the wayward, careless tormentor of Lizzie and (more culpably, perhaps) of her schoolteacher admirer, Bradley Headstone; and John Harmon, the shadowy central figure who has, metaphorically at least, died and been reborn in the same river.

Unlike his obvious predecessor, Arthur Clennam, John Harmon fails to convince, either as the suppressed, repressed son of a money-grubbing old miser, or as the self-conscious searcher after a love purified of the desire for money. It is a measure of Dickens's uncertainty about his hero, and his own continuing ambivalence about money, that he should give the alienated Harmon a disastrously improbable inner soliloquy at the structural centre of the novel (bk II, ch. xiii, pp. 366–73, the end of the ninth number), to reveal his identity and hidden purpose. The object of Harmon's affections, the self-judging 'mercenary wretch', the delightful Bella Wilfer, is much more successful; and it may be significant that for all the fairytale qualities of the plot concerning her, she inhabits an entirely realistic mode, suggesting a Jamesian rather than a Dickensian heroine. Yet Dickens cannot relinquish the fantasy mode which permits characters such as Jenny Wren their transcendent visions, as the young James, in a notoriously severe review of *Our Mutual Friend* (1865, pp. 786–7), observed.

James found the novel laboured, lifeless and altogether a failure, as have many later critics. But the younger novelist was releasing himself from his former idol's influence, as well as marking out his own, more realistic territory; and it is not so much Dickens's 'fancy' which is at fault in *Our Mutual Friend*, the creation of Jenny Wren, little Johnny and the other familiar figures of his 'mixed' form of fiction, as the over-explicit, nervously insistent emphasis with which the newly affluent Veneerings are satirised, or the unreality of share-dealings made the opportunity for a page or so of rhetoric. Even the repeated invitation to contemplate the possibility of regeneration or resurrection through 'baptismal' immersion in the Thames (a possibility denied Bradley Headstone and Rogue Riderhood, who go struggling down together, of course), seems excessive, although the river-motif is at times finely touched. Perhaps we should be grateful that Betty Higden, who has doggedly wandered upriver to die out of the hands of the Poor Law authorities, finds Lizzie Hexam beside the water, to raise 'the weather-stained grey head', and lift her 'as high as Heaven' (bk III, ch. viii, p. 514).

More persuasive, because less promiscuously 'symbolic' than many such moments in the novel, is the response of the good clergyman of Holloway, the Reverend Frank Milvey, who reads 'in a not untroubled voice' those lines from the burial service which thank God for delivering 'this our sister', Betty Higden, 'out of the miseries of this sinful world' (bk III, ch. ix, p. 515). Milvey is characteristically 'troubled' in his role as vicar in the newly urbanised saharas of north London; yet he is a sympathetic, humble man, accepting 'the needless inequalities and inconsistencies of his life' (bk I, ch. ix, p. 103), and doing what he can to help his remarkably rich parishioners (we never see them in church, of course) the Boffins, to find a suitable orphan for adoption. He officiates in that modest, self-effacing manner Dickens always prefers in the clergy, at funerals and weddings, most notably little Johnny's funeral, and the wedding of Bella and John Harmon. Little Johnny dies in effect to prove to Mrs Boffin that even her charitable urge to 'rescue' the pauper orphan is tainted by her wish to replace the supposed dead John Harmon of blessed memory in her affections. Yet his death is brief, and moving, and when the Reverend Frank reads the burial service over the small grave he thinks of his own six children and reads 'with dimmed eyes'. Some of the clergyman's brethren, comments Dickens, 'had found themselves exceedingly uncomfortable in their minds, because they were required to bury the dead too hopefully. But the Reverend Frank, inclining to the belief that they were required to do one or two other things (say out of nine-and-thirty) calculated to trouble their consciences rather more if they would think as much about them, held his peace' (bk II, ch. x, p. 331). Charity, and the hope of resurrection, are more important than questions about eternal damnation.

Mrs Boffin (a more convincing creation than her 'pious fraud' of a husband) has to be brought to accept the harder task of adopting Sloppy, no 'boofer' baby like Johnny, but a dim-witted and physically unattractive adolescent 'love-child' brought up in a workhouse. Dickens is at his least sentimental, and most clear-eyed, in dealing with the Boffins in relation to the Milveys and the orphan 'market'. His long experience in philanthropic and educational enterprises for the poor certainly offered rich ground for the kind of understanding and perceptiveness which continues to be shown in his work. Yet there is a newly despairing note about even those possibilities which formerly seemed to have the potential, at least, of bringing the gospel to the poor. Charley Hexam's Ragged School is

> pervaded by a grimly ludicrous pretence that every pupil was childish and innocent. This pretence, much favoured by the lady-visitors, led to the ghastliest absurdities. Young women old in the vices of the commonest and worst life, were expected to profess themselves enthralled by the good child's book, the Adventures of Little Margery, who resided in the village cottage by the mill; severely reproved and morally squashed the miller when she was five and he was fifty; divided her porridge with singing birds; denied herself a new nankeen bonnet, on the ground that the turnips did not wear nankeen bonnets, neither did the sheep who ate them, who plaited straw and delivered the dreariest orations to all comers, at all sorts of unseasonable times. (bk II, ch. i, p. 214)

The adults, like the children (who seem to have a creature suspiciously like Little Nell with which to contend), are encouraged to stumble over the New Testament in a way designed to make the 'sublime history' unintelligible; and on Sunday nights the infants are handed over to the worst of well-intentioned teachers, typically drawling to 'My Dearerr Childerrenerr' about the 'beautiful coming to the Sepulchre', repeating the word 'Sepulchre (commonly used among infants) five hundred times, and never once hinting what it meant', the whole 'hot-bed of flushed and exhausted infants exchanging measles, rashes, hooping-cough, fever, and stomach disorders, as if they were assembled in High Market for the purpose' (bk II, ch. i, p. 215).

One cannot escape the feeling here of watching an enraged and despairing man discovering that the institutions he once thought might answer the extreme needs of his society are a disaster. *Our Mutual Friend* is Dickens's darkest novel, its central character barely alive, hopelessly divided, and most unconvincingly married off at the end, its typical landscape a 'grey dusty withered evening in London city', the closed warehouses and offices exuding 'an air of death', the 'towers and steeples of the many house-encompassed churches, dark and dingy as the sky that seems descending on them', offering 'no relief to the general gloom' (bk II, ch. xv, p. 393). Podsnap, the Veneerings, the Lammles, the whole social chorus, they all go into the dark, as Dickens contemplates what he has come to see as the decline and fall of a civilisation nearer at hand than the one Silas Wegg reads about to his patron.

If the ebullient creativity of the earlier works seems largely absent from *Our Mutual Friend*, this does not mean it is a failure, although it is evidently a seriously flawed novel. The circumstances revealed by Dickens's correspondence, by his Memorandum Book, and by the Postscript, suggest an explanation: the book was long and agonising in the making, and the novelist was involved in a near-fatal rail accident during its actual writing and publication (on his way back from Paris with Ellen Ternan). But it is at least equally probable that, struck evermore by the disconnection, even anarchy, of the corrupt, money-grubbing society in which he found himself (and on which he continued to depend), and yet unable to envisage a saving mediator of love and regeneration, he fell back upon an exhaustive, not to say exhausting, revision of old themes. The strength of *Our Mutual Friend* lies in Dickens's continued ability to allow, for example, Eugene Wrayburn to utter, in his extremity, 'Let the guilty man go unpunished!' (bk IV, ch. x, p. 739). Providence will not permit murderers to escape, and Bradley Headstone's inner life is delineated with the acute perception Dickens has always shown in dealing with the evil he understands as profoundly as he detests it (e.g. bk IV, ch. vii, pp. 708–9). But the most demanding thing for us, which we may only be able to do in extremity, is still 'to forgive those who have done us any harm', even if 'they do not come and say' they are sorry; for, we must, 'if we would hope that God will forgive us' (Dickens, 1934 edn, ch. v, p. 45).

IV

Dickens's religion was personal, and modest. If we are to believe what Blanchard Jerrold reported to the *Gentleman's Magazine* in July 1870 (pp. 231–2) – and there is no reason why we should not – Dickens told the dying Lady Lovelace that he prayed twice daily. He said the same to two sons departing from under the parental wing, reminding them that they had never been 'harassed about religious observances or mere formalities', but that they had been brought up to recognise the 'truth and beauty' of Christianity as expressed above all in the New Testament (Dexter *Letters*, Vol. 3, pp. 667–8, 673–4). His own knowledge of the Bible, especially the preferred New Testament (and in particular the Gospel of St Matthew), as well as the Book of Common Prayer, is testified to by frequent, accurate and often surprisingly relevant allusion throughout his works.

But if, as seems the case, he considered God and his only begotten Son essential to the scheme of things, the Church, much less the chapel, he did not. 'As to the Church, my friend', he wrote to de Cerjat on 5 October 1864,

> I am sick of it. The spectacle presented by the indecent squabbles of priests of most denominations, and the exemplary unfairness and rancour with which they conduct their differences, utterly repel me. And the idea of the Protestant establishment, in the face of its own history, seeking to trample out discussion and private judgement, is an enormity so cool, that I wonder the Right Reverends, Very Reverends, and all other Reverends, who commit it, can look in one another's face without laughing, as the old soothsayers did. Perhaps they can't and don't. How our sublime and so-different Christian religion is to be administered in the future I cannot pretend to say, but that the Church's hand is at its own throat I am fully convinced. Here, more Popery, there more Methodism – as many forms of consignment to eternal damnation as there are articles, and all in one forever quarrelling body – the Master of the New Testament put out of sight, and the rage and fury almost always turning on the letter of obscure parts of the Old Testament, which itself has been the subject of accommodation, adaptation, varying interpretation without end – these things cannot last. The Church that is to have its part in the coming time must be a more Christian one, with less arbitrary pretensions and a stronger hold upon the mantle of our Saviour, as He walked and talked upon this earth. (Dexter *Letters*, Vol. 3, p. 402)

Protestant to the core, Dickens allowed that there should be some ritual attending birth, marriage and death, but no more. With the exception of Frank Milvey, he did not draw a favourable picture of a clergyman officiating at one of the many deaths which occur in his fiction. It is given to laymen, such as the doctor, Allan Woodcourt, who tries to teach Jo the Lord's Prayer at the boy's demise, or Harriet Carker, who reads the 'blessed history' to the dying Alice Marwood, to suggest Christian hope.

Yet, despite his anti-clericalism, Dickens did not ever break entirely his connections with broadly Anglican faith and practice. Returning to the town of his childhood, Rochester, in the last work, he muses (in almost the last words he wrote) on the morning light shining gloriously in on the old city from gardens, woods and fields, to 'penetrate into the Cathedral, subdue its earthy odour, and preach the Resurrection and the Life' (*Edwin Drood*, ch. xxiii, p. 215). 'Natural' religion serves the Christian faith, and Dickens attended Church, taking the matter seriously enough to leave it for the more congenial, if less orthodox, Unitarians during the 1840s. Later he returned, at least nominally, to the fold: he probably found Anglicanism more amenable in any case as Broad Church views became widespread. Clergymen of whom he approved were either of the Sydney Smith stamp, worldly, urbane and cultured latitudinarians, who shared his dislike of evangelical theology and the puritan spirit (satirised almost throughout his works);[3] or modest, unpretentious men such as Steven Roose Hughes, who exerted themselves to aid all who came their way, in a spirit of humane fellow-feeling (Dickens recorded Hughes's compassionate attentions to the relatives of those drowned in a terrible shipwreck off the Welsh coast in an article reprinted in *UT & RP*, pp. 3–17). If he disapproved of any religious adherent inclined to dogma, ritual, or evangelical strictness, he always supported a man he knew to be doing good, such as Lord Shaftesbury, even while disagreeing with his doctrine. Shaftesbury himself thought him 'as much a servant of the Most High as the pagan Naaman', given by God 'a general retainer against all suffering and oppression' (quoted in Hodder, 1892, p. 658).

In Arras on his birthday in 1863, he observed a so-called *théâtre religieux* in preparation:

> one of the three wise men was up to his eyes in lamp oil, hanging the moderators. A woman in blue and fleshings (whether an angel or Joseph's wife I don't know) was addressing the crowd through an enormous speaking-trumpet; and a very small boy with a property lamb (I leave you to judge who *he* was) was standing on his head on a barrel-organ. (Dexter *Letters*, Vol. 3, pp. 341–2)

The vitality, as well as the absurdity, of popular belief at home and abroad always evoked a sympathetic response, even if the novelist feared and detested popular fanaticism, and what he saw as the aberrations of Roman Catholicism. But Dickens was too liberal-minded to be more than occasionally outspoken or aggressive about this.

In May 1868, two years before his death, and while recuperating from a much-publicised breakdown suffered during the penultimate series of public readings, Dickens received certain admonitory remarks from an unknown clergyman who had, as he put it, become 'vicariously religious' on his behalf. The clergyman's comments implied, Dickens noted with somewhat pained irony, that

> I had not, as I rather supposed I had, lived a life of some reading, contemplation, and inquiry; that I had not studied, as I rather supposed I had, to inculcate some Christian lessons in books; that I had never tried, as I rather supposed I had, to turn a child or two tenderly towards the knowledge and love of our Saviour; that I had never had, as I rather supposed I had had, departed friends, or stood beside open graves; but that I had lived a life of 'uninterrupted prosperity', and that I needed this 'check, overmuch', and that the way to turn it to account was to read these sermons and these poems, enclosed, and written and issued by my correspondent! ('A fly-leaf in a life', repr. in *UT & RP*, p. 355)

Dickens was characteristically undemonstrative and reticent about his religion, especially in so far as he expressed it in his writings. But he could be provoked into public confession, albeit of an indirect kind, by the presumptions of others. We may be far from assuming that, because he did not proclaim his feelings from the housetops, he had lived a life of 'uninterrupted prosperity', much less that we ourselves have answers to the problems he faced. But we could do worse than be warned by the presumption of this clerical correspondent.

Notes

Introduction

1 Only Humphry House's too short chapter on 'Religion' (House, 1942) may be described as indispensable, although fruitful advances have been made by, for example, Marcus, 1965, Collins, 1965, and Welsh, 1971. See also Further Reading.

2 Dickens's attitude to Jews has been thoroughly discussed by Harry Stone, 1959, pp. 223-53. On his attitude towards other races, see Simpson, 1970, and Oddie, 1972. On Dickens and Catholicism, see Chapter 4 below.

3 See Edgar Johnson, 1952, Vol. 1, pp. 16, 19-20, where it is assumed that the experience recorded in 'City of London churches' gave Dickens his 'lifelong hatred of Nonconformity and his revulsion from any formal activities'. Hibbert, 1968, pp. 30-3, speculates further, assuming Dickens's parents took him to their friend Mr Giles's nearby Baptist chapel, and so gave him his 'permanent distaste for Nonconformism'. Such speculations are unhelpful, and involve a very free idea about Nonconformity. By contrast, we *know* Thackeray's antagonism towards evangelicalism was rooted in his experience of his mother's gloomy persistence in that form of Christianity; see Ray, 1955, p. 110.

4 For an alternative interpretation, see Cunningham, 1975, p. 191.

5 See Pike, 1912, F. S. Johnson, 1925, and, for a full account of Dickens's relations with the Unitarians, my unpublished M.Litt. dissertation, 'Dickens and religion: a preliminary survey' (Edinburgh, 1969), pp. 104-63.

6 See Stonehouse, 1935, p. 63. A very informative account of Leigh Hunt's religious development may be found in Landré, 1936, pp. 11-58: Landré claims that *Christianism* was profoundly admired by Forster, G. H. Lewes and Carlyle, as well as 'sans doute des amis de Hunt entre 1825 et 1840, Novello, Bulwer, Dickens, peut-être les Tennyson' (p. 46).

Chapter 1

1 In 1850 the final phrases were altered to: 'than half the homilies that have ever been written, by half the Divines that have ever lived' (*Sketches by Boz*, p. 224). Dickens's sensitivity, presumably in response to that of his audience, on such points of possible profanity or indelicacy, is more fully dealt with in Butt and Tillotson, 1968, ch. 2.

2 The doctrine became 'obnoxious' to Wesley himself, one of the things which 'embarrassed him in his sober years', according to Southey, 1820, Vol. 2, p. 171.

Chapter 2

1 Almost any issue of either newspaper during January–February 1837 provides evidence of this. But see, for example, *The Times*, 27 January 1837, p. 6, for the direct response of a self-styled 'practising guardian' of St George's Parish, London, to a report in the *Morning Chronicle* (23 January, no page nos) on the money saved through the new law's provisions on bastardy. See Finer, 1952, bk 2, ch. 4, for a good overall account of the press response. It should be added that the severe winter of 1836-7 made the burden of the poor worse.

2 Blomfield is more favourably referred to later, in the preface to the Cheap Edition of *Oliver Twist* (1850). See also Fielding *Speeches*, pp. 104-10: 6 February 1850. Blomfield's subsequent career proved him to possess many of the virtues he seemed to lack earlier, and Dickens was at least partially reconciled to him through the efforts of Miss Burdett Coutts: see Coutts *Letters*, pp. 90, 98: 12 June, 28 October 1847.

3 The allusion is to II Samuel 12:7, where Nathan tells David (who has taken Bathsheba from Uriah) the tale of a poor man robbed by a rich, rousing David's anger, upon which it is revealed he is the 'rich' robber himself.

4 His name may have been derived from that of John Brownlow, a foundling who became treasurer's clerk in 1828, and then secretary in 1849, of the Foundling Hospital in Coram's Fields near Doughty Street, where Dickens lived while writing *Oliver Twist*. The novelist is said to have been a 'regular attendant' at the chapel in the Foundling Hospital; see Nichols and Wray, 1935, p. 285. On 26 February 1840 Dickens replied to a letter from Brownlow, regretting that he had forgotten to give notice at the Foundling, and that the chapel was now too far for him to attend (Pilgrim *Letters*, Vol. 2, pp. 33–4). He thought the preaching there unconventional, but sensible, eloquent and earnest; above all, free from 'any ism, not forgetting schism' ('Received, a blank child', *Household Words*, 19 March 1853, repr. Stone, *Uncollected Works*, Vol. 2, p. 456).

5 The novelist saw to it that the living room in 'The Home for Homeless Women' had 'two little inscriptions from the sermons of Jeremy Taylor and Barrow', also 'a little inscription of my own, referring to the advantages of order, punctuality, and good temper; and another setting forth the Saviour's exposition of our duty towards God, and our duty towards our neighbour' (presumably Matthew 22:37–40): see Coutts *Letters*, p. 106: 3 November 1847.

6 One can speculate on the origin of Dickens's interest in the Romantic notion of waking dreams. He wrote to G. H. Lewes, who asked him about such passages in his work, that they came 'ready made to the point of the pen' (Pilgrim *Letters*, Vol. 1, p. 403: ?9 June 1838). True? Perhaps, yet, according to Stonehouse (1935, p. 66), his library contained J. H. Jung-Stilling's *Theory of Pneumatology*, trans. S. Jackson, 1834, which offers an extensive account of such dream moments (pp. 224 ff.). The next chapter deals more fully with Dickens's links with popular Romanticism.

Chapter 3

1 *Master Humphrey's Clock*, 1840–1, Vol. 2, p. 94; the line is missing from the New Oxford Illustrated Edition, where it should appear in ch. liii, p. 397.

2 See Watson, 1912, p. 512. By an odd coincidence, the Reverend Maurice Davies, investigating *Unorthodox London: or Phases of Religious Life in the Metropolis* (2nd edn, 1874, pp. 227 ff.), attended a 'little chapel' in Goodman's Fields, which he found after great difficulty, and which reminded him, not of Little Bethel, but of the dream-like scenes through which the Trents wander and discover venerable clergymen.

3 A common way of disposing of suicides (which he is presumed to be), in order to render their restless spirits powerless; Ashton, 1886, Vol. 2, pp. 282–3.

4 Incorrectly referred to as 'ch. 72' in Pilgrim *Letters*, Vol. 2, p. 125, note 2, where the link is made.

5 See also Pilgrim *Letters*, Vol. 2, p. 269, note 1, for Irving's remarks on the sympathy of feeling between himself and Dickens. Master Humphrey could have been based on Irving, a mournful, ruminative figure, obsessed with the quaint and the weakly morbid; but he was more probably derived from 'Old Humphrey', that is, George Mogridge, author of *Old Humphrey's Observations*, a popular but dull piece published by the Religious Tract Society in 1839, which evinces enthusiasm for Gothic piles and old, grey-headed wanderers.

6 Edgar Taylor's translation of the Grimms' *German Popular Stories* (1823), illustrated by Cruikshank, was also familiar to Dickens; see 'Frauds on the fairies', *Household Words*, 1 October 1853, repr. in *MP*, pp. 406–12, in which the novelist deplores subsequent attempts by the 'serious' Cruikshank to edit moralised fairytales. Dickens's library included the 1826 edition of Roscoe as well as his eleven-volume *Spanish, Italian and German Novelists* (Stonehouse, 1935, pp. 98–9). Pilgrim *Letters*, Vol. 4, Appendix C,

p. 724, shows he owned *German Novelists* before 1844. His childhood reading evidently included the *Märchen* in *The Portfolio*; Thomas, 1972.
7 W. J. Carlton, 1951, has demonstrated that the witty allegory 'The story without a beginning', which appeared in the *Morning Chronicle* on 18 December 1834, was a parody by Dickens of F. W. Carové's fairy-romance, *The Story Without An End*, trans. Sarah Austin.

Chapter 4

1 Dickens's library contained an 1824 edition of Locke's *Essay Concerning Human Understanding* (Stonehouse, 1935, p. 73); and his Unitarian friend Edward Tagart was very enthusiastic about Locke on toleration in his book *Locke's Writings and Philosophy* (1855), pp. 426–7. On Locke's influence in general, see MacLean, 1936.
2 Interestingly, Dickens is drawn to much that was accepted as 'good' art at the time – Titian, Canova, Tintoretto and Salvator Rosa – while finding the works of Bernini and his followers 'detestable . . . intolerable abortions' ('Rome', p. 394). Compare George Eliot's experience in the Frauenkirche in Nürnberg in 1958: 'Nothing could be more wretched as art than the painted Saint Veronica opposite me . . . Yet it touched me deeply' (Haight, 1968, p. 256).
3 According to Harriet Martineau, Dickens and his sub-editor on *Household Words*, W. H. Wills, 'never would publish anything, fact or fiction, which gave a favourable view of any one under the influence of the Catholic faith'; Martineau, 1877, Vol. 2, p. 420.

Chapter 5

1 The allusion is to John 2:1–11, Jesus's first miracle, which Dickens interprets as a consecration of the natural human desire to celebrate a joyful occasion. Water of gall is given to sinners (e.g. Jeremiah 8:14). Dickens's view of the Mormons changed later: see 'Bound for the Great Salt Lake', *All the Year Round*, 4 July 1863, repr. *UT & RP*, pp. 220–32; also Dunn, 1968.
2 Paul's 'original' may well have been Henry, ailing son of Fanny (Dickens) Burnett, a 'singular child – meditative and quaint in a remarkable degree', who, lying on the beach at Brighton, used to utter 'thoughts quite as remarkable for a child as those which are put into the lips of Paul Dombey. But little Harry loved his Bible, and evidently loved Jesus. The child seemed never tired of reading his Bible and his hymns, and other good books suited to his age: and the bright little fellow was always happy' (Griffin, 1883, p. 209).
3 The 'lame demon' is Asmodeus, from Le Sage's *The Devil Upon Two Sticks* (1707). Dickens possessed a copy in French, dated 1840, and he frequently alludes to the work: see Stone, *Uncollected Works*, Vol. 2, p. 488. Le Sage may have derived the image from the Bible, from Christ being tempted by the devil (Matthew 4). The Destroying Angel of Revelation puts Dickens in mind of the seven plagues, apparently.

Chapter 6

1 George Ruby, whose evidence given in the Guildhall on 8 January 1850 was printed in Dickens's *Household Narrative* the same month; see Fielding and Brice, 1968, 1969, pp. 131–40, 35–41.
2 For a very full discussion, see K. J. Fielding and A. W. Brice, '*Bleak House* and the graveyard', in Partlow, 1970, pp. 115–39.
3 The idea of 'telescopic philanthropy' occurred to Dickens long before: in his 'Report of the second meeting of the Mudfog Association', *Bentley's Miscellany* (1838), repr. in

Sketches by Boz, p. 662, Mr Tickle invents a pair of spectacles enabling the wearer 'to discern, in very bright colours, objects at a great distance', but rendering him 'wholly blind to those immediately before him'; thus many could see the 'horrors' of the West Indian plantations, 'while they could discern nothing whatever in the interior of Manchester cotton mills'. The influence of Carlyle, often insisted upon in this connection, may be less than supposed.

4 Jarndyce may be based on 'my very particular friend' (Forster, 1928, pp. 674–5), George Moore; see Smiles, 1891, pp. 42–3, 63–4, *passim.*

5 For Christopherson's remarks, see *Letters of Charles Dickens* [ed. Mamie Dickens and Georgina Hogarth] (1893), pp. 263–4. Pope, 1978, p. 105, points out that in 1847 the Church Missionary Society, the British and Foreign Bible Society and the SPG all enjoyed annual incomes of over £100,000 while the London City Mission received just over £14,000.

Chapter 7

1 Of this Christmas Story, Dickens remarked: 'I never wrote anything more easily, or I think with greater interest and stronger belief' (Dexter *Letters*, Vol. 2, p. 811: 13 November 1856). This cannot apply to the Hymn so often mistakenly attributed to him, but it may well apply to sentiments such as those given to Captain Ravender, who, when he buries Lucy at sea, begins, 'I am the Resurrection and the Life, saith the Lord' (*Christmas Stories*, p. 151).

2 Many pieces in Dickens's journal testify to continuing anti-Sabbatarian interests, but the extent of his actual involvement in the anti-Sabbatarian movement is unclear. He is supposed to have been of assistance to R. M. Morrell, founder of the National Sunday League (see *The Dickensian*, vol. 8, November 1912, pp. 303–4), but otherwise, apart of course from his fictional and journalistic offerings, his 'protest' against 'the doleful way of keeping Sunday' is reported to have meant a friend in the garden of Tavistock House, a tray of bottled stout, 'churchwardens' and tobacco; see [Ley], 1919.

Chapter 8

1 Dickens again attacks popular superstition and incredulity as a feature of past and present, alluding to the pseudo-revelations of Mrs Southcott and the 'rapping' of the Cock-lane ghost on the first page of *A Tale of Two Cities*. On 'rapping' and other spiritualist activities during the years preceding this novel, and Dickens's scepticism towards the 'awful unseen world being available for evening parties at so much per night' (Dexter *Letters*, Vol. 2, p. 673), see also Peyrouton, 1959, pp. 19–30, 75–93. And compare Pip moving the table 'like a Medium of the present day, by the vigour of my unseen hold upon it' (*Great Expectations*, ch. iv, p. 25).

2 Riah was introduced to make amends for Fagin, whose character was taken by Eliza Davis at least (wife of the purchaser of Tavistock House, Dickens's home from 1851 to 1860) to be a libel on her race. But despite Dickens's good liberal intentions, Riah is much less convincing even than the Catholic Haredale. Frank Milvey's wife worries that the Jewish community which takes in Lizzie Hexam may try to 'convert' her; but Lizzie assures her that they leave 'us' to our religion (*Our Mutual Friend*, bk III, ch. ix, pp. 516–17).

3 Chauncy Hare Townshend (1798–1868), dedicatee of *Great Expectations*, was a clergyman of this type. He held to a loose, undogmatic faith, opposed to the doctrine of eternal punishment, and emphatic on the saving qualities of Christ, as his religious musings, edited by Dickens (1869), indicate. The work was not a particularly welcome chore (Dexter *Letters*, Vol. 2, p. 689).

References

The place of publication is London unless otherwise stated. As I have not included a separate bibliography those works which I consider particularly useful are marked with an asterisk. Anonymous articles in newspapers and periodicals of the day are cited in full in the text and also listed separately at the end of these references for the reader's convenience.

Arnold, Matthew (1881), 'The incompatibles', *Nineteenth Century*, vol. 9 (June), pp. 1034–42.

Arnold, Matthew (1964 edn), 'Heinrich Heine' [1863], repr. in *Essays in Criticism* (Dent/Everyman), pp. 110–35.

Ashton, John (1886), *The Dawn of the XIXth Century in England*, 2 vols (T. Fisher Unwin).

Aspinall, A., and Smith, E. A. (eds) (1959), *English Historical Documents 1783–1832* (Eyre & Spottiswoode).

*Auden, W. H. (1963), 'Dingley Dell & The Fleet', in *The Dyer's Hand and Other Essays* (Faber), pp. 407–28.

Bagehot, Walter (1911 edn), 'Charles Dickens' [1858], in *Literary Studies* (Dent/Everyman), Vol. 2, pp. 164–97.

[Barker, J.] (1880), *The Life of Joseph Barker, Written by Himself* (Hodder & Stoughton).

*Best, Geoffrey (1971), *Mid-Victorian Britain 1851-75* (Weidenfeld & Nicholson).

Blythe, R. (ed.) (1970), *William Hazlitt: Selected Writings* (Harmondsworth: Penguin).

Brand, C. P. (1957), *Italy and the English Romantics* (Cambridge: Cambridge University Press).

Briggs, Asa (1960), *The Age of Improvement 1783-1867* (Longman).

Briggs, Asa (1965), *Victorian People* (Harmondsworth: Penguin).

*[Broderip, F. F., and Hood, T.] (eds) (1869), *Memorials of Thomas Hood* (E. Moxon).

Brooke, Stopford (ed.) (1901 edn), *Life and Letters of F. W. Robertson, M.A.*, 2 vols [1891] (Kegan Paul, Trench, Trübner).

*Brown, Ford K. (1961), *Fathers of the Victorians* (Cambridge: Cambridge University Press).

Butt, John, and Tillotson, Kathleen (1968), *Dickens at Work* (Methuen).

Carlton, W. J. (1951), 'The story without a beginning', *The Dickensian*, vol. 47 (March), pp. 67-70.

*Carlyle, Thomas (1871-4), *Works*, People's Edition, 39 vols (Chapman & Hall).

Carlyle, Thomas (1881), *Reminiscences*, ed. J. A. Froude, 2 vols (Longman).

Carpenter, S. C. (1959 edn), *Church and People: 1789-1889* [1933], repr. in 3 pts (SPCK).

Carr, E. H. (1962), *Dostoevsky 1821-1881* (Allen & Unwin).

*Carrow, G. D. (1967), 'An informal call on Charles Dickens by a Philadelphia clergyman', *The Dickensian*, vol. 63 (May), pp. 112-19.

Cazamian, Louis (1904), *Le Roman Social en Angleterre (1830–1850)* (Paris: Bibliothèque de la Fondation Thiers).

*Chadwick, Owen (1970), *The Victorian Church*, 2 pts (A. & C. Black).

*Channing, William Ellery (1840), *Works* (Glasgow: Richard Griffin).

Chesterton, G. K. (1906), *Charles Dickens* (Methuen).

Child's Companion, The; or, Sunday Scholar's Reward (1838), 3rd series (Religious Tract Society).

Clark, G. Kitson (1966), *The Making of Victorian England* (Methuen).

Clayre, A. (ed.) (1977), *Nature and Industrialization* (Oxford University Press).

*[Cleghorn, T.?] (1845), 'Writings of Charles Dickens', *North British Review*, vol. 3 (May), pp. 65–87.

Cockshut, A. O. J. (1965), *The Imagination of Charles Dickens* (Methuen).

*Collins, Philip (1965), *Dickens and Education* (Macmillan).

*Collins, Phillip (ed.) (1971), *Dickens: The Critical Heritage* (Routledge & Kegan Paul).

Collins, Philip (1975), *Charles Dickens: The Public Readings* (Oxford: Clarendon Press).

Cooke, E. T., and Wedderburn, Alexander (eds) (1903–12), *The Works of John Ruskin*, 39 vols (George Allen).

Cross, J. W. (1887), *George Eliot's Life* (Edinburgh and London: Wm. Blackwood).

*Cunningham, Valentine (1975), *Everywhere Spoken Against: Dissent in the Victorian Novel* (Oxford: Clarendon Press).

de Castro, J. P. (1926) *The Gordon Riots* (London: Oxford University Press).

Dexter, Walter (ed.) (1935), *Mr. and Mrs. Charles Dickens: His Letters to Her* (London: Constable).

[Dickens, Charles] (1837), 'A board of guardians of the poor' [*Oliver Twist*], *The Times*, 31 January, p. 3.

Dickens, Charles (ed.) (1869), *Religious Opinions of the Late Chauncy Hare Townshend* (Chapman & Hall).

*Dickens, Charles (1934 edn), *The Life of Our Lord* [1846–9] (Associated Newspapers Ltd).

[Dickens, Henry] (1934), *The Recollections of Sir Henry Dickens, KC* (Heinemann).

[Dickens, Mamie, and Hogarth, Georgina, eds] (1893), *The Letters of Charles Dickens* (Macmillan).

Dolby, George (1885), *Charles Dickens As I Knew Him* (T. Fisher Unwin).

Dunn, Richard (1968), 'Dickens and the Mormons', *Brigham Young University Studies*, vol. 8 (Spring), pp. 325–34.

*Eliot, George (1963 edn), 'Evangelical teaching: Dr Cumming' [1855], repr. in *Essays of George Eliot*, ed. Thos Pinney (New York: Columbia University Press), pp. 158–89.

[Empson, William] (1831), 'Pretended miracles – Irving, Scott and Irskine', *Edinburgh Review*, vol. 53 (June), pp. 261–305.

Ewbank, Jane M. (1959), *The Life and Works of William-Carus Wilson 1791–1859* (Kendal: Titus Wilson).

Fielding, Henry (1753), *A Proposal for Making an Effectual Provision for the Poor* (A. Millar).

Fielding, K. J. (1963), 'Dickens criticism: a symposium', *The Dickensian*, vol. 59 (May), pp. 73–7.

Fielding, K. J., and Brice, A. W. (1968, 1969), 'Charles Dickens on "The exclusion of evidence"', *The Dickensian*, vols 64, 65 (September, January), pp. 131–40, 35–41.

Finer, S. E. (1952), *The Life and Times of Sir Edwin Chadwick* (Methuen).

Fitzgerald, Percy (1905), *The Life of Charles Dickens as Revealed in his Writings*, 2 vols (Chatto & Windus).

[Forster, John?] (1837), '*Oliver Twist*', *The Examiner*, 10 September, p. 581.

*[Forster, John] (1884), '*The Life and Correspondence of Thomas Arnold, DD*', *The Examiner*, 12 October, pp. 644–6.

*Forster, John (1928), *The Life of Charles Dickens*, ed. J. W. T. Ley (Cecil Palmer).

*Foster, John (1889 edn), 'On the aversion of men of taste to evangelical religion' [1830], in *Essays, in a Series of Letters* (George Bell), pp. 188–342.

*Gaskell, Elizabeth (1975 edn), *The Life of Charlotte Brontë* [1857], ed. A. Shelston (Harmondsworth: Penguin).

Gasquet, Abbot (ed.) (1906), *Lord Acton and his Circle* (London: George Allen; New York: Burns & Oates).

Gérin, W. (1980), *Elizabeth Gaskell* (Oxford University Press).

Gissing, George (1898), *Charles Dickens: A Critical Study* (Blackie).

Greene, Graham (1970 edn), 'The young Dickens' [1950], repr. in *Collected Essays* (Harmondsworth: Penguin), pp. 79–86.

*Griffin, Rev. J. G. (1883), *Memories of the Past* (Hamilton, Adams).

Haight, Gorden S. (1968), *George Eliot: A Biography* (Oxford: Clarendon Press).

[Haldane, E. S.] (n.d.), *Mary Elizabeth Haldane: A Record of a Hundred Years (1825–1925)* (Hodder & Stoughton).

*Halévy, Elie (1961), *A History of the English People in the Nineteenth Century, Vol. 3: The Triumph of Reform (1830–1841)*, trans. E. Watkin (Ernest Benn).

Harrison, Bernard (1975), *Henry Fielding's Tom Jones: The Novelist as Moral Philosopher* (Chatto & Windus for Sussex University Press).

*Harrison, J. F. C. (1971), *The Early Victorians 1832–1851* (Weidenfeld & Nicolson).

Hibbert, Christopher (1968), *The Making of Charles Dickens* (Book Club Associates).

*Hodder, Edwin (1892), *The Life and Work of the Seventh Earl of Shaftesbury, KG*, Popular Edition (Cassell).

*[Hoey, Mrs Frances C.?] (1871), 'Two English novelists: Dickens and Thackeray', *Dublin Review*, new series, vol. 16 (April), pp. 315–50.

Holloway, John (1967), Introduction, *Little Dorrit* (Harmondsworth: Penguin), pp. 13–29.

*[Hood, Thomas] (1840), '*Master Humphrey's Clock*', *The Athenaeum*, 7 November, pp. 887–8.

*[Hood, Thomas] (1842), '*Barnaby Rudge*', *The Athenaeum*, 22 January, pp. 77–9.

Horne, R. H. (1844), 'Charles Dickens', in *A New Spirit of the Age*, 2 vols (Smith, Elder).

*Houghton, Walter (1957), *The Victorian Frame of Mind, 1830–1870* (New Haven, Conn., and London: Yale University Press).

*House, Humphry (1942), *The Dickens World*, 2nd edn (Oxford University Press).

Houtchens, L. H., and Houtchens, C. W. (1962), *Leigh Hunt's Political and Occasional Essays* (New York and London: Columbia University Press).

*Hunt, Leigh (1853), *The Religion of the Heart. A Manual of Faith and Duty* (John Chapman).

Hutton, R. H. (1906 edn), 'The genius of Dickens' [1870], in *Brief Literary Criticisms*, ed. E. M. Roscoe, (Macmillan), pp. 48-58.

James, Henry (1865), review of *Our Mutual Friend*, *The Nation*, 21 December, pp. 786-7.

*James, William (1902), *The Varieties of Religious Experience* (Longmans).

Jarrett-Kerr, M. (1954), *Studies in Literature and Belief* (Rockcliff).

*Jay, Elizabeth (1979), *The Religion of the Heart* (Oxford: Clarendon Press).

Jerrold, Blanchard (1870), 'Charles Dickens. In memoriam', *Gentleman's Magazine*, new series, vol. 5 (July), pp. 228-41.

Johnson, Edgar (1952), *Charles Dickens: His Tragedy and Triumph*, 2 vols (New York: Simon & Schuster).

Johnson, F. S. (1925), letter, *The Dickensian*, vol. 21 (July), p. 158.

Keating, Peter (1976), *Into Unknown England: 1866-1913: Selections From the Social Explorers* (Fontana/Collins).

Keightley, T. (1839), *The History of England*, 3 vols (Whittaker).

[Kingsley, F. E.] (ed.) (1904), *Charles Kingsley: Letters and Memories of his Life* (Macmillan).

Kirkus, Rev. W. (1863), *Miscellaneous Essays* (Longman, Green, Longman, Roberts & Green).

Kitton, F. G. (ed.) (1903), *The Poems and Verses of Charles Dickens* (Chapman & Hall).

Landré, Louis (1936), *Leigh Hunt 1784-1859*, Vol. 2: *L'Oeuvre* (Paris: Société d'édition 'Les Belles-Lettres').

Leavis, F. R., and Leavis, Q. D. (1970), *Dickens the Novelist* (Chatto & Windus).

Lecky, W. E. H. (1892), *A History of England in the Eighteenth Century*, 7 vols (Longmans).

[Ley, J. W. T.] ('Old Fleet') (1919), 'Dickens, Mazzini, G. J. Holyoake and Sunday observance', *The Dickensian*, vol. 15 (October), pp. 208-9.

*[Lister, Thomas H.] (1838), 'Sketches (1st and 2nd series), *Pickwick*, *Nickleby*, and *Oliver Twist*', *Edinburgh Review*, vol. 68 (October), pp. 75-97.

[Lockhart, J. G.] (1823), 'The Reverend Mr Irving's orations', *Blackwood's Magazine*, vol. 14 (August), pp. 145-62.

Lucas, John (1970), *The Melancholy Man: A Study of Dickens's Novels* (Methuen).

*Lyles, Albert M. (1960), *Methodism Mocked: The Satiric Reaction to Methodism in the Eighteenth Century* (Epworth Press).

MacKenzie, Rev. C. H. (1884), *The Religious Sentiments of Charles Dickens* (Walter Scott).

MacLean, Kenneth (1936), *Locke and English Literature of the Eighteenth Century* (New Haven, Conn.: Yale University Press).

Macrae, David (1876), *Amongst the Darkies and Other Papers* (Glasgow: John S. Marr).

Madden, R. R. (1855), *The Literary Life and Correspondence of the Countess of Blessington*, 3 vols (T. C. Newby).

Maison, Margaret (1961), *Search Your Soul, Eustace: A Survey of the Religious

Novel in the Victorian Age (London and New York: Sheed & Ward).

*Marcus, Steven (1965), *Dickens: from Pickwick to Dombey* (Chatto & Windus).

Marcus, Steven (1966), *The Other Victorians* (Weidenfeld & Nicolson).

Martineau, Harriet (1877), *Autobiography*, 2 vols (Smith, Elder).

[Masson, David] (1851), '*Pendennis* and *Copperfield*: Thackeray and Dickens', *North British Review*, vol. 15 (May), pp. 57–89.

M[atz], B. W. (1914), 'Charles Dickens and the Italian refugees of 1849', *The Dickensian*, vol. 10 (December), pp. 319–22.

Maurois, André (1934), *Dickens*, trans. H. Miles (John Lane).

Meckier, Jerome (1975), 'Some household words', *The Dickensian*, vol. 71 (January), pp. 5–20.

*Miall, E. (1849), *The British Churches in Relation to the British People* (A. Hall, Virtue).

*Miller, J. Hillis (1968), *Charles Dickens: The World of His Novels* (Cambridge, Mass.: Harvard University Press).

Monod, Sylvère (1968), *Dickens the Novelist* (Norman, Okla: University of Oklahoma Press).

Morgan, B. Q., and Hohlfeld, A. R. (1949), *German Literature in British Magazines 1750–1860* (Madison, Wis.: University of Wisconsin Press).

Moynahan, J. (1960), 'The hero's guilt: the case of *Great Expectations*', *Essays in Criticism*, vol. 10 (January), pp. 60–79.

Nichols, R. H., and Wray, F. A. (1935), *The History of the Foundling Hospital* (London: Oxford University Press).

Nisbet, Ada (1952), *Dickens and Ellen Ternan* (Berkeley and Los Angeles, Calif.: University of California Press).

Oddie, W. (1972), 'Dickens and the Indian mutiny', *The Dickensian*, vol. 68 (January), pp. 3–15.

*[Oliphant, Mrs] (1855), 'Charles Dickens', *Blackwood's Magazine*, vol. 87 (April), pp. 451–66.

*[Oliphant, Mrs] (1871), 'Charles Dickens', *Blackwood's Magazine*, vol. 109 (June), pp. 673–95.

*Orwell, George (1965 edn), 'Charles Dickens' [1939], in *Decline of the English Murder and Other Essays* (Harmondsworth: Penguin), pp. 80–141.

Partlow, R. B., Jr (ed.) (1970), *Dickens the Craftsman: Strategies of Presentation* (Carbondale, Ill.: Southern Illinois University Press).

Patterson, Clara Burdett (1953), *Angela Burdett-Coutts and the Victorians* (John Murray).

Payne, Ernest E. (1965), *The Free Church Tradition in the Life of England* (Hodder & Stoughton).

Pearlman, E. (1972), 'Two notes on religion in *David Copperfield*', *Victorian Newsletter*, vol. 41 (Spring), pp. 18–20.

Pearson, Gabriel (1966), '*The Old Curiosity Shop*', in *Dickens and the Twentieth Century*, ed. John Gross and Gabriel Pearson (Routledge & Kegan Paul), pp. 77–90.

Perkin, Harold (1969), *The Origins of Modern English Society 1780–1880* (Routledge & Kegan Paul).

Peyrouton, N. C. (1959), 'Rapping the rappers: more grist for the biographers' mill', *The Dickensian*, vol. 55 (January–May), pp. 19–30, 75–93.

*Pike, C. E. (1912), 'Dickens and Unitarianism', *Unitarian Monthly*, vol. 9 (February), pp. 18–19.

[Poor Law Commissioners] (1836, 1839), *Second, Fifth Annual Report of the Poor Law Commissioners for England and Wales.*

*Pope, Norris (1978), *Dickens and Charity* (Macmillan).

Poynter, J. R. (1969), *Society and Pauperism: English Ideas on Poor Relief 1795-1834* (Routledge & Kegan Paul).

Proctor, Rev. W. C. (1930), *Christian Teaching in the Novels of Charles Dickens.*

Quennell, Peter (ed.) (n.d.), *Mayhew's London* (Spring Books).

Quiller-Couch, Sir Arthur (1925), *Charles Dickens and Other Victorians* (Cambridge: Cambridge University Press).

Quinlan, Maurice J. (1941), *Victorian Prelude: A History of English Manners 1700-1830*, Studies in English and Comparative Literature No. 155 (New York: Columbia University).

Ray, Gordon N. (1955), *Thackeray: The Uses of Adversity 1811-1846* (Oxford University Press).

Ray, Gordon N. (ed.) (1966), *William Makepeace Thackeray: Contributions to the Morning Chronicle* (Urbana, Ill.: University of Illinois Press).

*Richmond, Rev. Legh (n.d.), *The Dairyman's Daughter* [1814], in *Annals of the Poor* (Religious Tract Society), pp. 1-101.

Roberts, David (1936), 'How cruel was the Victorian Poor Law?', *The Historical Journal*, vol. 6, pp. 97-107.

Roscoe, Thomas (1826), *German Novelists*, 4 vols (Henry Colburn).

*Sherwood, Mrs [Mary M.] (1818-47), *The History of the Fairchild Family*, 3 pts.

Simpson, D. H. (1970), 'Charles Dickens and the Empire', *Royal Commonwealth Society Library Notes*, new series, nos 162-3 (June-July), pp. 1-28.

Smiles, Samuel (1888 edn), *Character* [1878] (John Murray).

Smiles, Samuel (1891), *George Moore: Merchant and Philanthropist* (George Routledge).

Smith, Goldwin (1861), *Lectures on Modern History* (Oxford and London: J. H. & J. Parker).

Smith, Sheila (1974), 'John Overs to Charles Dickens', *Victorian Studies*, vol. 18 (December), pp. 195-217.

*Smith, Sydney (1859 edn), 'Causes of the increase of Methodism and Dissension', 'Strictures on . . . the Subject of Methodism and Missions', *Edinburgh Review* [1808-9], in *The Works of the Rev. Sydney Smith*, 2 vols (Longman, Brown, Green, Longman & Roberts), Vol. 1, pp. 87-102, 138-45.

*Soloway, R. A. (1969), *Prelates and People: Ecclesiastical Social Thought in England 1783-1852* (Routledge & Kegan Paul).

Southey, Robert (1820), *The Life of Wesley*, 2nd edn, 2 vols.

*Stanley, Arthur Penrhyn (1845), *The Life and Correspondence of Thomas Arnold, DD*, 4th edn, 2 vols (B. Fellowes).

*Stanley, Arthur Penrhyn (1870), *Sermon [on] the Funeral of Charles Dickens* (Macmillan).

*Stone, Harry (1957), 'Charles Dickens and Harriet Beecher Stowe', *Nineteenth Century Fiction*, vol. 12 (December), pp. 188-202.

Stone, Harry (1959), 'Dickens and the Jews', *Victorian Studies*, vol. 2 (March), pp. 223-53.

Stone, Marcus (1910), 'Some recollections of Dickens', *The Dickensian*, vol. 6 (January), pp. 62-3.

*Stonehouse, J. (ed.) (1935), *Catalogue of the Libraries of Charles Dickens and W. M. Thackeray* (Piccadilly Fountain Press).

[Stothert, James] (1854), 'Living novelists', *The Rambler*, new series, vol. 1 (January), pp. 41-51.

[Stott, G.] (1869), 'Charles Dickens', *Contemporary Review*, vol. 10 (January), pp. 203-25.

Styles, A. (1909), letter, *The Dickensian*, vol. 5 (June), p. 163.

Tate, W. E. (1951), *The Parish Chest* (Cambridge: Cambridge University Press).

Temple, William (1958), 'Immortality in relation to religion and ethics', in *Religious Experience and Other Essays and Addresses* (James Clarke), pp. 112-23.

[Thackeray, W. M.] (1840), 'Going to see a man hanged', *Fraser's Magazine*, vol. 22 (August), pp. 154-5.

Thackeray, W. M. (1898-9), *Works*, Biographical Edition, 13 vols (Smith, Elder).

Thomas, C. (1972), 'Dickens and *The Portfolio*', *The Dickensian*, vol. 68 (September), pp. 170-1.

*Thompson, Flora (1976 edn), *Lark Rise to Candleford* [1939-43] (Harmondsworth: Penguin).

*[Tonna, Mrs C. E.] (1840), 'Charlotte Elizabeth', 'Illustrations: No. xii', *The Protestant Magazine*, vol. 2 (January), pp. 12-15.

*Trilling, Lionel (1953), Introduction, *Little Dorrit*, New Oxford Illustrated Dickens (Oxford University Press), pp. v-xviii.

[Tyler, Mrs J. G.](1853), *A Letter to those Ladies who met at Stafford House in Particular and to the Women of England in General, on Slavery at Home*.

Wagenknecht, E. (1965), *Harriet Beecher Stowe: The Known and the Unknown* (New York: Oxford University Press).

*Wagenknecht, E. (1966), *The Man Charles Dickens: A Victorian Portrait* (Norman, Okla: University of Oklahoma Press).

Watson, Lily B. (1912), 'Charles Dickens and Dissenters', *Notes and Queries*, 11th series, vol. 5 (29 June), pp. 511-12.

Welby, T. Earle (ed.) (1927-36), *The Complete Works of Walter Savage Landor*, 16 vols (New York and London: Chapman & Hall).

*Welsh, Alexander (1971), *The City of Dickens* (Oxford: Clarendon Press).

Westcott, B. F. (1888), *Social Aspects of Christianity* (Macmillan).

*Wilberforce, William (1834 edn), *A Practical View of the Prevailing Religious System* [1797] (John Davis).

* Willey, Basil (1964), *Nineteenth Century Studies* (Harmondsworth: Penguin).

Wilson, Angus (1969), Introduction, *Oliver Twist* (Harmondsworth: Penguin), pp. 11-27.

Wilson, Angus, and Dyson, A. E. (1976), 'Dickens', in *The English Novel: Questions in Literature*, ed. C. T. Watts (Sussex Books), pp. 53-75.

Wilson, Edmund (1961 edn), 'Dickens: the two Scrooges' [1941], in *The Wound and the Bow* (Methuen), pp. 1-93.

Wiseman, Nicholas (1839), *Four Lectures on the Offices and Ceremonies of Holy Week* (Charles Dolman).

Wolff, Robert Lee (1977), *Gains and Losses: Novels of Faith and Doubt in Victorian England* (John Murray).

Wright, D. (ed.) (1970), *Thomas de Quincey: Recollections of the Lakes and the Lake Poets* (Harmondsworth: Penguin).

Young, G. M., and Hancock, W. D. (eds), (1956), *English Historical Documents 1833-74* (Eyre & Spottiswoode).

References   223

Anonymous Articles in Newspapers and Periodicals

Christian Examiner (Boston), 'Dickens's *Oliver Twist*', vol. 27, November 1839, pp. 161-74.

★Christian Remembrancer, 'Modern novels', vol. 4, December 1842, pp. 585-96.

Christian Remembrancer, '*The Chimes*', vol. 9, January 1845, pp. 201-4.

Christian Spectator, '*Our Mutual Friend*', new series, vol. 6, December 1865, pp. 719-28.

★Dublin Review, '*Pictures from Italy*', vol. 21, September 1846, pp. 184-201.

Dublin Review, 'John Bull and the papists', vol. 21, September 1846, p. 261.

Ecclesiastic and Theologian, 'Charles Dickens', vol. 17, October 1855, pp. 467-77.

★Eclectic and Congregational Review, '*Posthumous Papers of the Pickwick Club*', new series, vol. 1, April 1837, pp. 339-55.

★Eclectic and Congregational Review, '*Bleak House*', new series, vol. 6, December 1853, pp. 665-79.

★Eclectic and Congregational Review, 'Charles Dickens' *Great Expectations*', new series, vol. 1, October 1861, pp. 458-71.

★Edinburgh Christian Magazine, 'A.W.', 'The "working classes" and their Literature. No. II, vol. 8, May 1856, pp. 37-41.

Literary Examiner, 'Bifrons', 'Country church-yards', no. 22, 29 November 1823, pp. 348-51.

Metropolitan Magazine, '*Master Humphrey's Clock*', vol. 30, March 1841, pp. 78-9.

Parker's London Magazine, 'Boz versus Dickens', vol. 1, February 1845, pp. 122-8.

The Protestant Magazine, 'The papal conspiracy', vol. 1, January 1839, pp. 23-5.

The Protestant Magazine, 'The papal Antichrist', vol. 2, June 1840, pp. 161-7.

The Times, 'Practising guardian', 27 January 1837, p. 6.

★The Times, leader, 2 February 1837, p. 4.

The Times, 'Formation of a new Protestant Association', 28 October 1839, p. 3.

The Times, 'The Protestant Operative Association', 17 June 1841, p. 5.

★The Times, leader, 6 November 1841, p. 4.

The Times, '*Pictures from Italy*', by Charles Dickens', 1 June 1846, p. 7.

★The Times, 'Sunday Trading Bill', 3 May 1855, p. 7.

The Times, 'Demonstration in Hyde Park', 25 June 1855, p. 10.

The Times, 'Demonstration in Hyde Park', 2 July 1855, p. 12.

★The Times, leader, 14 May 1856, p. 8.

The Times, 'The departed year', 5 January 1857, p. 9.

★The Times, 'A bishop on Charles Dickens', 14 June 1870, p. 12.

Further Reading

The list of references contains all articles and books referred to in the text, except for major works by standard authors or contemporary novelists. But I would like to mention here some additional items.

The usual bibliographical sources are omitted, but it should be said that *The Dickensian* (1905–present) contains invaluable material for researchers, Dickens enthusiasts and casual browsers alike, in the field covered by this book, as in many others (the several contributions of W. J. Carlton and N. C. Peyrouton in particular are worth following up). The unpublished sources I have found most useful are: Rev. C. E. V. Bowkett, 'The place of religion in some of the major novels of Charles Dickens', MA thesis (Durham, 1967), a brief survey from the Anglican viewpoint; and G. S. Larson, 'Religion in the novels of Charles Dickens', PhD thesis (Massachusetts, 1969), a brisk and uncritical run through the subject. Incidentally helpful, too, are William Kent, *Dickens and Religion* (London: Watts, 1930), Kathleen Tillotson, *Novels of the Eighteen-Forties* (London: Oxford University Press, 1961), Barbara Hardy, *The Moral Art of Dickens* (London: Athlone Press, 1970), Angus Wilson's delightful *The World of Charles Dickens* (London: Secker & Warburg, 1970), and William Oddie, *Dickens and Carlyle: The Question of Influence* (London: Centenary Press, 1972). On Dickens's religious satire, Arthur A. Adrian, 'Dickens and the brick-and-mortar sects', *Nineteenth Century Fiction*, vol. 10 (December 1955), pp. 188–201, and Trevor Blount, 'The Chadbands and Dickens' view of dissenters', *Modern Language Quarterly*, vol. 25 (September 1964), pp. 295–307, are worth consulting.

Among nineteenth-century surveys of religion, the following are helpful: J. Stephen, *Essays in Ecclesiastical Biography*, 2 vols (London: Longmans, Green Reader & Dyer, 1849); [W. J. Conybeare], *Essays Ecclesiastical and Social* (London: Longmans, Brown, Green & Longmans, 1855); and *Essays by the late Mark Pattison*, ed. Henry Nettleship, 2 vols (Oxford: Clarendon Press, 1889). More recently, L. E. Elliott-Binns, *Religion in the Victorian Era* (London: Lutterworth Press, 1936), offers a wider sweep than most. The most recent short account of evangelicalism may be found in Ian Bradley, *The Call to Seriousness: The Evangelical Impact on the Victorians* (London: Cape, 1976). Alan D. Gilbert, *Religion and Society in Industrial England: Church, Chapel and Social Change 1740–1914* (London: Longman, 1976), goes well beyond the emphasis on the *leaders* of evangelicalism current until very recently – a shift of viewpoint helped by E. P. Thompson's *The Making of the English Working Class* (Harmondsworth: Penguin, 1968). K. S. Inglis, *Churches and the Working Classes in Victorian England* (London: Routledge & Kegan Paul, 1963) and S. Meacham, 'The church in the Victorian city', *Victorian Studies*, vol. 11 (March, 1968), pp. 359–78, provide a sense of the hold (or lack of it) of religion upon the urban poor. Useful accounts of the liberal end of the religious spectrum may be found in C. R. Sanders, *Coleridge and the Broad Church Movement* (Durham, NC: Duke University Press, 1942); Bernard M. Reardon (ed.), *Liberal Protestantism* (London: A. & C. Black, 1968); M. A. Crowther, *Church Embattled: Religious Controversy in Mid-Victorian England* (Newton Abbot: David & Charles, 1970); and Geoffrey Rowell, *Hell and the Victorians* (Oxford: Clarendon Press, 1974).

Index